I CAN'T REMEMBER
IF I CRIED

I CAN'T REMEMBER IF I CRIED

ROCK WIDOWS
ON LIFE, LOVE, AND LEGACY

LORI TUCKER-SULLIVAN

Backbeat
Books

Essex, Connecticut

Backbeat
Books

An imprint of Globe Pequot, the trade division of
The Rowman & Littlefield Publishing Group, Inc.
4501 Forbes Blvd., Ste. 200
Lanham, MD 20706
www.rowman.com

Distributed by NATIONAL BOOK NETWORK

British Library Cataloguing in Publication Information available

Library of Congress Cataloging-in-Publication Data

Names: Tucker-Sullivan, Lori, author.
Title: I can't remember if I cried : rock widows on life, love, and legacy
   / Lori Tucker-Sullivan.
Description: Essex, Connecticut : Backbeat, 2024. | Includes
   bibliographical references and index.
Identifiers: LCCN 2023051667 (print) | LCCN 2023051668 (ebook) | ISBN
   9781493084142 (cloth) | ISBN 9781493084159 (epub)
Subjects: LCSH: Rock musicians' spouses. | Rock musicians'
   spouses--Interviews. | Rock musicians--Death. | Widows. | LCGFT:
   Interviews.
Classification: LCC ML406 .T83 2024 (print) | LCC ML406 (ebook) | DDC
   782.42166092/2--dc23/eng/20231201
LC record available at https://lccn.loc.gov/2023051667
LC ebook record available at https://lccn.loc.gov/2023051668

∞™ The paper used in this publication meets the minimum requirements of
American National Standard for Information Sciences—Permanence of Paper
for Printed Library Materials, ANSI/NISO Z39.48-1992

For Kevin. You believed in me from the start.
Your spirit will always guide me and
give me strength until the end.

And for Austin and Maddie. Of all the stories
I've written or will ever write, the story
of you two will always be the best. I love you.

CONTENTS

AUTHOR'S NOTE

Over the course of this project, people have asked me if my late husband Kevin was a musician. He wasn't. Not learning to play an instrument was actually something he came to regret, but our love of music was one of the greatest things we shared. We went to concerts together early in our relationship and told each other in detail about the concerts we had seen separately. Growing up in Detroit, music was inextricably part of our lives, from Motown to Bob Seger and Iggy Pop. We exchanged albums, and when eventually we moved in together and combined our record collections, we found several duplicates. I still had a place in my heart for 1970s stadium rockers like Queen and Elton John, while Kevin had moved on to The Clash and Elvis Costello. We both became fans of the other's favorites. Through our twenty-six years together, we developed a deep love for the music of John Hiatt, Warren Zevon, and Johnny Cash, among many others. Over the course of our marriage, we saw over a hundred live concerts, everyone from the Rolling Stones to David Bowie to the Platters and the Drifters.

It made perfect sense to both of us, then, that when Kevin was diagnosed with cancer, he would turn to music for comfort and strength. Hour after interminable hour spent with a chemotherapy drip, or minute after dangerous minute with a radiation beam inching along his spine, Kevin would tune in to his favorite songs. By the second cancer diagnosis, he had used his blog to ask for others' music suggestions, and he listened to them all. As I left his hospital room each night in the months before he died, the last thing I would do before kissing him was to put his earbuds in (by this point, he was quadriplegic) and tune his iPod to "Chemo Mix 1" or "Chemo Mix 2." An especially troubling day would cause him to request "Running Mix" to remind him of the time when he could take off from our farmhouse and run the nearby trails with nothing but wind and music. After his death, music was something that kept me connected to him.

It had once been a dream of mine to write for a music publication, although I never really developed the courage to do so. I interned for a few weeks at *Creem* magazine in Detroit and found it to be a difficult place for a sheltered, naïve young woman who was far more a fan than a critic. I interviewed a few local bands, wrote a couple of reviews that were never published, and mostly answered phones and returned empty aluminum cans to the nearby party store for the ten-cent deposit returns. After a few weeks, I left feeling disappointed in myself for not being more assertive. I had a deep love of music and musicians but didn't have the courage to seek out stories or demand to be let backstage. Like the high school athlete faced with a career-ending injury, I wondered what I could possibly do with myself if I didn't pursue the career I had wanted since the age of thirteen. Kevin was there for me, however, assuring me that there were many things I could do as a writer. So instead of rock music, I ended up in public relations, with dreams of marriage and children replacing those of interviews with musicians.

Through our marriage, I often felt something was missing in my life. It took years to realize it was writing, so I decided to return to a regular writing practice and to earn a Master of Fine Arts degree. Life was complete. Then cancer came along.

After Kevin died, I found myself again doing significant soul-searching. Within five years, I had lost my husband and both my parents, along with three close friends. I watched my children become self-sufficient young adults, no longer in daily need of my help. I sold the house we had built together and began to ask myself about my purpose, my identity; what I really wanted to do. I knew I would find my purpose in writing but wasn't exactly sure how.

In December of 2012, two years after Kevin's passing, I was listening to the radio on the anniversary of John Lennon's assassination. During the remembrance of Lennon's life, there was discussion of his widow, Yoko Ono. I quickly realized that I had a new perspective on what Yoko had accomplished in the years since her husband's death. There must be others like her, I thought. Other women married to musicians who died young. Other women left to figure out who they would become for the rest of their lives after the man to whom they were so connected passed away. It didn't take long for me to discover a remarkable list of twenty such women whose stories I wanted to know.

What follows are many of those stories, along with my own. Finding these women has allowed me to find myself. It has brought me full circle, back to writing about music, but also writing about those strong souls who carried on despite the loss of all that meant so much to them. Though they often see themselves as "keepers of the flame," they are so much more. The women on these pages have opened their homes and their hearts to me. From the very first phone call, from Gloria Jones in Sierra Leone, I've been thrilled at each contact, each woman's willingness to welcome me into their lives. They've shared the details of their relationships, and, even more difficult for them, they've shared what it was like in those first days and months after losing their spouse or partner. Those are not easy memories to discuss, and I appreciate their candor and generosity.

In looking back on the first interviews I conducted and profiles I wrote and comparing them to later entries, I see how I have changed, grown, come to a place of acceptance, and in my own way, moved on from my time of grief. The passage of time has something to do with it, but more importantly, meeting and learning from these strong, smart women has also given me a path forward, a path that I didn't realize I badly needed and one that has delivered me to an amazing place. This experience has taught me about love, legacy, and telling your own story. The women whose stories follow have shown me how to celebrate, grow, and live again as a widow and a woman. I am forever indebted to them all.

Lori Tucker-Sullivan
Detroit, 2024

"I can't remember if I cried,
When I read about his widowed bride."

Don McLean, from *American Pie*, referring to
Maria Elena Holly, the first rock widow

LIFE

1

GLORIA JONES

I first spoke with Gloria Jones from her home in Makeni, Sierra Leone. When she called, I immediately recognized her voice—rough and gravelly as the dust and grit of her adopted home. It wasn't the desert that made Gloria's voice sound as it did, of course. That was caused by the accident. We spoke for several minutes and made loose plans to meet in Los Angeles if our travels coincided. She was headed to the United States to see a colleague from her Motown days who was dying of cancer and to also spend time visiting her two sons, Rolan and Walter. Gloria gave me her email address, and I sent her my itinerary. After not hearing from her for two weeks, I became nervous and tried other methods to reach her: a "contact us" form on the website for the Marc Bolan School of Music and Film, which Gloria runs, and a message on her Facebook page. Checking her Facebook page a few days later, I saw that someone had created a one-word post to the page. "Murderer," it said.

After a few more attempts, we finally reconnected and made plans to meet at a hotel on Sunset Boulevard in LA.

"Are you up for a walk?" she asked as I greeted her in the hotel lobby. Her black hair was cropped short and dyed a bright yellow-blonde. She was comfortable in black sweats and a t-shirt, a far cry from her days with boyfriend Marc Bolan and T-Rex.

Marc Bolan and Gloria Jones, 1976, at a party thrown by fellow pop star Rod Stewart, in London. PA Images / Alamy Stock Photo

"Let's go down to the Roxy and the Rainbow Room," she said.

Although we had met face-to-face just moments before, Gloria took my hand and led me out of the hotel to the famous bar just down Sunset. We walked into the darkened room, past an abandoned Pac-Man machine and a hostess in heavy makeup and tattoos.

"Oh Lori, this was *the* place in the early 70s."

Walking from one red, half-round booth to another, Gloria regaled me with stories of her time at the nightclub with Marc and their friends.

"We used to hang out here with Harry Nilsson. We'd sit in that booth over there with Danny Hutton and the guys from

Three Dog Night. I remember a night sitting over there with David Bowie. Oh, all the stars would hang out in this room. It was amazing. This was *the* place to be. Here and the Troubadour. I'm talking about 1973, '74. Such wild days."

"You were living in LA at the time?" I asked.

"We lived in the sky, really. Some of my friends called it 'the big party in the sky' because we were always flying around, traveling. It was easier for tax reasons not to stay too long in one place. We had a condo in Monaco, a house in London, and a home here, in Benedict Canyon. Beverly Hills proper wasn't really happening during that time. Marc and I were the only rockers on Beverly Drive. We would drive down here in Marc's gold Cadillac. I loved it here. That's why I wanted to bring you."

Unlike the woman I was standing next to, 1970s Gloria was flashy, dressed in satin pantsuits and platform shoes. She alternately wore a huge afro or had big-hair curls draped across her shoulders. Never to be outdone by her glam-rock boyfriend, the two were often photographed in full eyeliner-feather-boa-regalia. Though still stunning, her face no longer appears as it did in those photographs. Age has changed her somewhat, but the auto accident that killed Marc Bolan—when Gloria was driving—also broke her jaw and altered the structure of her face. And because she was driving, many, like the poster I encountered on her Facebook page, still accuse Gloria of some responsibility for the accident, despite an inquest that exonerated her long ago. Though their many travels may have been exciting, it cost Gloria dearly in the end.

Having conducted her tour of the Rainbow Room, Gloria settled into our booth and began to tell me her story.

Before she ever met Marc, Gloria Jones was a successful singer, songwriter, producer and backup singer. She called herself the only Ike-ette who never went on the road because she sang on all of Ike and Tina Turner's hits, including "Proud Mary," "Nutbush City Limits," and "Higher," but she never toured with them. Gloria regularly took Ike's calls to come into the studio at 2:00 a.m. and she speaks about this work in the 2011 documentary *Twenty Feet from Stardom*, in which she is featured. She recorded several songs for Motown and hit the charts in 1964 with the original version of "Tainted Love" (later a #1 hit for Soft Cell). So successful was her version of "Tainted Love" in England that she became known as the Queen of Northern Soul. She spent several months touring with Wayne Newton and in 1970 returned to the studio to cowrite and produce "If I Was Your Woman" for Gladys Knight. The song brought Gloria her first Grammy Award nomination. She also did session work during this time for VanDyke Parks and Ry Cooder.

Simultaneously, Marc Bolan's career was exploding in the UK. Starting first as a member of a folk band named John's Children, Bolan then formed his own group, Tyrannosaurus Rex. They, too, were initially a folk-rock band, although electrified and with a hint of the psychedelic. Heavily influenced by the peace/hippie movement in the United States and the writings of JRR Tolkien, the original Tyrannosaurus Rex was made up of Bolan and bandmate Steve Peregrine-Took. The band released three albums and four singles, but Peregrine-Took was fired from the band after their unsuccessful American tour in 1969.

"The first time Marc came to America was with Tyrannosaurus Rex," Gloria says. "They opened for Jimi Hendrix in LA. He was signed to A&M at the time. That was his first taste of America, but not much happened for him here then. I think he was very discouraged when he got back to England."

His career in the UK was another story. Marc scored several top-ten singles from 1970 to 1972. His first, "Ride a White Swan," began his partnership with producer Tony Visconti, and went to #2. He then released "Hot Love" and appeared on Top of the Pops in the UK, solidifying his place as a teen idol and, with glitter on his face, introduced the world to glam rock. Around that same time, he changed the band's lineup to include Steve Curry, Mickey Finn, and Bill Legend and shortened their name to simply T. Rex. Their next hit, "Get It On," brought T. Rex international fame, and Marc was once again touring in the United States. In America, the song was renamed "Bang a Gong" so as not to be confused with another hit at the time also called "Get It On." Marc was also married during this time to June Child, who he credited as his songwriting muse. The couple separated after Marc became involved with Gloria, but they never divorced.

"The success in the UK with 'Get It On,'" she continued, "opened the door for him to come back to America. There were times when he opened for bands, for example, when he opened a few shows for ZZ Top, but there were also some places where bands like Blue Oyster Cult opened for Marc.

"Around that time was when *Don Kirschner's Rock Concert* was on. They fell in love with Marc and gave him a lot of television exposure. He had one gig to perform that would have broken things open for him in the United States, but he had laryngitis and couldn't go on. That was the Long Beach Arena in 1972. And he packed the place out. Can you imagine when they told these people that T. Rex wouldn't be performing?"

Gloria became introspective at this point, with a refrain she returned to several times during our conversation.

"Once again, this is fate, this is life. How do you make all those pieces fit? You're so close to having everything and just. . ." She snaps her fingers.

"But Marc understood his destiny. He understood. His mother bought him his first guitar when he was nine years old. He would watch the TV shows, like Cliff Richard and the different stars. He knew he wanted to be a star. Not just a performer, but a star. I never had the chance to do that, to plan, to know exactly what I wanted to do and what I would be. I always thought that was so special about him."

She credits this same destiny for bringing the two of them together. Marc and Gloria crossed paths multiple times before starting a relationship. Gloria first encountered Marc at a party in the Hollywood Hills.

"I was performing at the Aquarius Theater on Sunset in *Hair*. Joe Bryant invited me to come to Mercy's for a party. Mercy was one of the GTOs, Frank Zappa's girls. Joe said you have to come and meet Marc Bolan of Tyrannosaurus Rex. This guy's just incredible. He's from England. I had no idea what he was talking about. I never went to any of those parties, but that night I decided to go."

Gloria recalled that she was playing the piano when Marc arrived in platform shoes and a shirt with long, flowing sleeves that looked like wings and an air of cockiness as he walked through the door.

"He saw me at the piano and gave me a look as if to say, 'Well, you might as well get up because the star has arrived. So, whatever you think you're doing isn't happening.' And that was our instant connection.

"For the rest of the night I just stayed with him. Wherever he went, I followed, and he never said don't come or why don't you go somewhere else. We just connected that night. But then he left the country, and I didn't see him again for three years.

"Those three years, from 1969 to 1972, were when I was trying to decide if I was going to be a mother and raise my oldest son, Walter, or if I was going to continue as a backup singer or stay in the studio writing and producing. Even after the Grammy nomination I still wasn't happy. I was missing the stage. I tried to get onto Broadway in *Hair*, but that didn't work, it wasn't my time. So, in 1972, I thought maybe I should just go home for a while and not worry about all this music stuff and just be with my son.

"But then I spent the summer of 1972 on tour with Joe Cocker. We were performing at the Crystal Palace Bowl with The Beach Boys, Melanie, and several other big acts. That next night after the show, Joe took us all to the Speakeasy. Marc's white Rolls was out in front of the club, but we didn't know whose car it was. He was there with Elton John, and Marc was coming out, and he said to Joe, 'Joe, you'd better be careful with those girls!' And Joe said, 'Who, these? These are my backup singers.' And Marc said, 'Well, I'd still make sure they don't rob you!'" After touring with Joe Cocker, Gloria again began to wonder about the next phase of her career and contemplate the possibility of taking time off.

"Then I got a call from Tony Howard, who was Marc's manager, and he said I had been referred by Bob Regere [a Warner Bros. record executive] because he knew of my session work. So, I went to the meeting. My nephew William was with me. William told me that the minute I walked in, when

Marc saw me, he said Marc was so happy. William said he had never seen a man so happy to see someone. I think he knew me from my songs in the 60s and the popularity of 'Tainted Love.' I had done TV shows like *Where the Action Is*, so he knew who I was. And we had had our chance encounters."

After that, Gloria became a back-up singer for a newly reconstituted T. Rex at a time when Marc had gone from a poetry-writing flower child to a full-fledged teen idol. The two quickly became friends, commiserating over their shared concerns about the next steps in their musical careers.

"A lot of people didn't understand it, because once again, this is what happens with life. We cannot control fate and destiny. For some reason, man thinks we can do this. We cannot change and we cannot stop: we have to try to understand all these experiences. You could never have told me that I would not be with this man. He and I visualized being old together. And I was always concerned about whether Marc would still love me if we grew old. He always told me, 'Don't worry about that, I'm with you, I'm always with you.'"

The two took full advantage of the rock lifestyle. According to Gloria, the timing of their relationship was fortunate. They were young and creative at a time when boundaries were being pushed all over rock music. Bands were experimenting with instruments, vocals, appearance, and the length of songs. Sexuality was much more overt. Watch any T. Rex video of that time and Marc will be seen flaunting his long curly hair, kohl-lined eyes, and pouty lips. I asked Gloria if it was difficult to share him with millions of young girls.

"At first, no. He always let me know when he came home that he loved me. But then, when they got older, it was hard because they moved into my space. They grew up and became women and were still after him. Sometimes it was almost like I didn't even matter. They thought they knew him as well as I did, but of course, they didn't. We loved each other. I was never afraid of having that emotion, of letting people know how in love we were. This was also a time of women's liberation. I watch women now in third-world countries who've not gone through a movement like that, and they are timid and soft. We

American women have to feel strong and carry so much responsibility, but it's not wrong to bring out the emotion. Don't shy away from that. I'll never be afraid to say how very much I loved him. I had a chance to love someone, to give him all my heart and have it returned."

They were also an interracial couple, a fact that Gloria feels never fazed either of them.

"We never thought about that," Gloria says emphatically. "Looking back, I know it wasn't accepted at the time, but we really never thought about it. I remember my father telling me 'Be careful when you're down South with Marc,' and I asked him why? We were in Atlanta, walking through the airport. Marc had on backless high heel shoes and the glitter and the boa and the satin. I had all the big hair. Someone pointed at us and said 'looky there,' and his companion said 'don't worry about them, that's just some freaks.' They probably thought we were two women! But we really never thought about that. It didn't dawn on Marc about race. He was a huge rock star and we were always in the public. We had a ball and never thought twice."

The couple visited their home in Benedict Canyon at Christmas in 1974. Shortly after, Gloria knew she was pregnant. I asked her if she worried about how Marc would receive the news.

"Marc came from the world of fantasy. He knew that his rock-and-roll career was also fantasy, a persona. He said in several interviews that he had accomplished everything he wanted to do in life, but the thing that brought him the most joy was having his child. It was really an awakening for him and a beautiful thing. He was a giver, a generous man. He felt that he gave his art to the fans, and that's why they loved him so much. But with a child, he was able to go outside himself. He once told Tony Visconte, 'You can produce me if you can get inside my head.' And what he meant was that he lived in his head, in this fantasy world. But he also realized he was getting older and that it was a blessing for him to have this child."

It was 1975, and Gloria and Marc had returned to London from their travels in LA and Monaco. Marc undertook a small tour that year, with Gloria on backing vocals and keyboards. He was set to appear on the television show *Supersonic*, and the couple was in the studio when Gloria went into labor (at nine months pregnant, Gloria was still performing with T. Rex on backing vocals and clavinet). She took a car to the hospital while Marc completed production, instructing her not to have the baby until he could get there. In a move that was quite unusual for the times, Marc made it to the hospital, suited up in scrubs and ran into the delivery room just in time to see his son being born. For Gloria, she now sees having Rolan as another twist of fate, a way to "weave" their lives together since Marc's would be so short.

Once Marc's music career began to stall, he attempted a new direction for his music, with significant influence from Gloria. Marc brought several well-known Motown session artists in to play on a new album, including Ray Parker Junior, Sylvester Rivers, Wah Wah Watson, Bobby Hull, Stevie Wonder, Ed Green, Ali Brown, and Billy Preston.

"All these people respected and would tell people that they played with Marc Bolan."

After the album failed to achieve the same success as past efforts, Marc struggled to understand how his fortunes could change. Many have credited Gloria with getting him through this time. In 1977, he was contracted by the British Granada Television channel to host six episodes of his own afternoon music television program called *Marc*. The family settled into a rather domestic life. He used the show to introduce many new punk bands to UK audiences, and the last episode of the show featured old friend David Bowie in a raucous ending number.

A few weeks later, Marc and Gloria went to dinner at Morton's restaurant. Marc had never learned to drive as he thought he would kill himself by driving. That evening, his Rolls Royce had been loaned to a friend, so Gloria drove Marc's Mini. Several friends stopped by to say hello that night, which Gloria now feels was a sort of harbinger of what was about to happen. As the two drove home, with Gloria's brother driving in a separate car just behind them, the car spun out of control, struck a fence, and hit a tree. Marc was killed instantly, and Gloria suffered a broken arm, broken jaw, lacerations to her chin and damage to her vocal cords. Marc's body was found several feet from the vehicle, while Gloria lay unconscious across the car's hood.

Nearly thirty-five years later, tears still well in Gloria's bright brown eyes as she talks about the weeks after the crash. After a coma that lasted three days, she woke to the news of Marc's death.

"Tony Howard came to me and said 'I have very bad news. Marc is gone.'"

Marc's funeral had taken place that day, attended by David Bowie, Rod Stewart, Les Paul, Tony Visconti, and Eric Clapton, along with many hundreds of fans and onlookers.

Gloria's brother Richard stayed by her side during this time.

"My brother was with me, and he didn't allow any mirrors in the room, so I didn't know how bad I looked. I waited until everyone left one night and I went into the bathroom. I saw my face. My head was as large as a basketball."

A few minutes pass as Gloria composes herself, still shaken remembering that time. U2 was playing on the bar's sound system. Gloria took a sip of beer and a deep breath.

"You know, Lori, I remember looking in that mirror and saying 'Who is that?' I made it back to the bed, sobbing, and a nurse came in and took my hand and said, 'You can make it.' But I just didn't know how. I didn't have any desire to ever leave that bed.

"I was shocked by my appearance, and my brother was concerned about that. He was worried because I had cuts and stitches. But the worst part, aside from Marc, was my voice. No one ever knew, but the power in my voice in the 60s and 70s was all from one vocal cord. One! A doctor once said he thought I might have had an injury when I had my tonsils out in the 1950s, but the power I had as a singer came from one vocal cord. That cord was injured in the accident. So, my entire life was lost with that accident: my love, my career. If I had my voice, I could have gone to Mick or Elton and asked for work. Out of all the injuries I could have had, it was my voice."

Rolan also helped Gloria to keep going. During her recuperation, some of Marc's musician friends brought Rolan, along with their own children, to visit Gloria in the hospital. She was in a ward with others who had been in accidents and had noticeable injuries or had undergone plastic surgery. She was concerned about the children's reactions, but Rolan's reaction, or lack of reaction, to Gloria's appearance helped her to keep going.

"Rolan came and took my hand and gave me a teacup he had been playing with. I asked 'Is this for me,' and he said 'Yes.' And he was so proud and so glad to see me. He told me I was going to be alright, and then he left and ran around with the other children as though nothing was wrong. That kept me going, the acceptance of that child. I don't know how they knew to bring him there, but it was the right thing to do. It was a very deep moment for me."

After Gloria was sufficiently recuperated, she left the hospital and returned home to a house that had been completely looted. Marc's brother had been to the house on the morning of the accident. Returning that afternoon, he found the place nearly empty, cleaned out of everything, including Marc's guitars, original tapes of his music, clothing, and other memorabilia. The crime remains a mystery, but for Gloria, it was an act of extreme violation.

"Everything was gone. Our personal garments, our jewelry, even towels, bedsheets, all of Marc's things. Our whole life, my whole life with Marc was gone. I kept asking myself, what are people going to do with it? What could they do? Why would they do this?

"In the end, they wanted a piece of him. I had lived through it before. There was a time when women came at Marc with scissors to cut a lock of his hair. There was a concert where he was trampled and his eyes blackened.

"When he died, fans that had turned their backs on him all came back. The fans all loved him again and wanted something of him. But I had nothing. Everything was up in the air. Financially, nothing was settled. I wanted to do something simple like put Rolan in nursery school when he was two, but I couldn't. I didn't have the funds. We didn't have anything. Marc and I never thought about that day. We never prepared. And I was never with Marc for his riches, so I never encouraged that conversation. I just stayed out of that."

Gloria tried to live in London. Marc's parents helped to care for Rolan, but no one was quite sure what to do with Gloria. A few weeks after the accident, Gloria insisted on going to see fans and conducting interviews. She expected that they would be glad to see that she was okay, that they would have sympathy for her injuries and her loss. She was still on crutches, and her face was swollen and twisted. She remembers trying to wear a hat.

"Some of the people were nice, but not many. I remember we went to someone's house. There was a Christmas celebration. One of the women came up to me and told me to leave. I was shocked. I thought to myself, so now on top of everything else, I was dealing with hate. Blame and hate."

Shortly after, she was visited by a record executive who suggested that she go home to the United States.

"He said 'Stop. Just stop this. Go home, rest, stop this.'"

Many people turned on Gloria and blamed her for Marc's death. There were accusations of drunkenness, which Gloria dismisses.

"There were so many people around us that night, so many people who saw us that cared about Marc. If someone was concerned about our condition, don't you think they would have said something? Don't you think someone would have called a cab or insisted on driving us home?"

No one ever came forward to say that Gloria was incapacitated from alcohol, and the case was reviewed and closed. Gloria decided to take the recommendation and return to the States. Both the record company and her brother were unsure of what to do with her, but they felt it would be best if she left London. No one knew how to respond to her grief. She felt on the verge of insanity.

"They wouldn't take me out. They kept me inside in isolation because they didn't know how people were going to react. They wanted me to leave, but that would mean taking me from the place where I could have been with Marc. I still don't know how I did it. I don't know how I got through that time. I just figure it was the love of Marc that kept me holding on." Gloria finally took Rolan to the United States and lived for a time with her family in Los Angeles. She remained in touch with Marc's parents and eventually returned to London, where Rolan attended school and received financial support from Marc's friend, David

Bowie. Marc's fortune was tied up in a trust established in the Bahamas to avoid British taxes. It is only recently that Rolan has been able to access a portion of these funds, after years of legal battles. Gloria was listed in Marc's outdated will as his secretary and was left a mere £10,000.

Gloria speaks philosophically about having no control over one's destiny, about being unable to prevent a person's leaving when it's time. This strong belief in fate or destiny has obviously gotten Gloria through the difficulty of coming to terms with the accident that killed Marc and severely injured her. She lived with overwhelming grief for fourteen years, telling herself that he was still alive.

"In order to survive, I had to keep him alive. I could not go into mourning or listening to music for the memories. I had to keep him alive in my mind."

Gloria stops and places her hand on the journal in which I'm taking notes.

"It will come to you, too. You're waiting for that peace. You're dealing with things, but the peace, it will come, you don't know when, but it will come."

When I asked what she wants people to remember about Marc, her answer is surprising.

"There was the rock and roll side of Marc, but the person I knew was a quiet, humble, beautiful Jewish boy. He was proud of his music; he believed in it, but he loved me, he loved his mother and his family. He was generous with his music and his wealth. He just knew what he wanted and that was to be a star. People only see that part of him and not the person I knew."

In 1995, Gloria traveled to Sierra Leone, West Africa. Gloria's father was a Pentecostal preacher, and with a desire to honor her father, Gloria traveled to Africa to become a preacher and missionary. She settled in the township of Makeni and soon began noticing that the children were always dancing. Whether or not they had adequate food or clothing, they still danced. Several people approached her and asked her to help the children of Sierra Leone, who had been brutalized by war and exploited for years in the diamond mines.

"I invited Rolan to come and didn't say anything to him about my love of the place or desire to help in some way. But he felt it; he felt the connection. We traveled throuhout Sierra Leone, all the way to the Liberian border. I asked him what part he liked best, and he said Makeni. Rolan met these kids, these teenagers, and they told him their stories, more so than they told me. Several had been child soldiers. Rolan went back to America, and I stayed. I later came to visit Rolan, and he asked me if I ever saw those children. Many of them didn't want to be a part of society. They survive by picking mangoes or getting bottles of water and selling them along the highway."

With Rolan's encouragement, Gloria began helping the children by collecting expired foods from the local grocery and taking them to those in need. In this way, Gloria met many families with HIV-positive babies, many of whom would die between visits. She found one young girl who was born with several bones missing in her feet. This prevented her from being of use to her family, so she was hidden away. Gloria helped get the girl tested, and she was found to be smart enough to attend school. After speaking with Rolan, Gloria knew the best way to help would be to build a school, so she began looking for teachers.

"Many of the teachers I spoke with had been educated in Great Britain. Many of the older teachers lived in England and Germany in the 1970s, and they knew Marc's music. They fell in love with Marc's music there. They say that Marc's music helped them to heal from the wars and helped them being so far from home. They were these people that were studying in England away from home and enjoying Marc's music. If you come to visit Sierra Leone, you will feel the love and appreciation for Marc's music and their gratefulness that we are thinking of them and their future."

The school began with two teachers, one teaching guitar and the other keyboards. The theory of the school was that it was important for children to learn how to read music and receive training in music theory so that they have a skill to make a living. The school began with seven students and now has fifty.

"Because the people know Marc's music and are proud to be a part of that, they've embraced us and this idea. You know, this is Africa. I'm proud. I'm an American—my skin may be black, but I'm still American, an outsider. But because it's about music, and Marc's music, a bridge was already there. I want something that will be there for generations. I would love to see these schools all over the world, in the American south, in London, in Detroit. My dream is that Marc Bolan is known all over the world. We want to honor his music in all parts of the universe because that's who he was. He was a universal man and a cosmic force who had no boundaries when it came to sharing."

Plans are now in the works for a larger school building and community center that will house community resources, including an amphitheater so the children can learn staging and production.

"When I first considered this idea, I sat in the yard of my home and said, 'Marc, the family wants to do this, but I don't know; we don't have to. If you don't want this, don't worry, I'll let it go.' Within a few minutes, a black and white butterfly came to me. And I said, okay. That's not the first time I've seen a butterfly. Many times when I've been despondent over something, a butterfly comes."

Gloria speaks of other "visitations" from Marc as well. When he comes to her, she can feel his presence, sometimes even a physical feeling of someone sitting next to her. Through the years, his appearances have had a purpose—encouraging her to keep going, to move on.

"The last vision of him I had about ten years ago. He came to me so clearly: an older Marc with beautiful gray hair. He came to me as a mature man. We didn't say anything, we just sat silently."

Recently, Marc has begun receiving the level of acclaim Gloria feels he always deserved, with many calling his music revolutionary. In 2020, Marc and T. Rex were inducted into the Rock and Roll Hall of Fame. In his induction speech, Ringo Starr noted that Marc most considered himself a poet and wanted to be remembered that way. Rolan was on hand to receive the induction on his father's behalf. In 2023, a documentary of Marc's life, *Angel Headed Hipster*, which includes interviews with Gloria, was released to critical acclaim. Gloria is thrilled that Marc is finally getting his due, but she is also thoughtful of the entire history. "So did I get along with everyone? To that, I say, 'love.' They proclaimed to love him, but they didn't follow through, because when he decided to change [his music], they said, 'We don't want change.' That broke his heart more than anything else. You say you're not going to believe the hype about you, that you're stronger than that. But then you do, and it's great until it ends. If you go along with the hype, you also have to go along with the disappointments. They say now his work was genius, that it was ahead of its time. He always tried to believe that, but when I saw him heartbroken because his music wasn't accepted, it was so hard.

"I had to keep that man alive. I couldn't go into mourning or sit and listen to his music. I had to keep him alive in my mind. And when I came out of the shock of Marc's death, it was four-teen years later.

"I remember getting into my car, sitting behind the steering wheel getting ready to go to the market and it all came back. It was like 'boom!' through my whole body. I said Marc is gone. It was almost like a heart attack, though I knew it wasn't that. I just felt like I was back in the world, and I hadn't really been here since he died. When I think about hearing Marc's music and how it affected me, I have to realize that for so long I just never accepted that he was dead. That's not to say I didn't deal with things. You're dealing with things, but you're still devastated that your man isn't here. I think that's more acceptable now, we know that we all have to take our time grieving. But in the 70s, we had pretty primitive ideas about dealing with grief."

After talking with Gloria, I wonder how well I am function-ing. Am I just getting by, doing what needs to be done but still in shock and grief and mourning? I have come to the realization of loss, but there are still flashes of time when I ask myself if it hap-pened and continue to ask why and how. Will there be a time or day when the colors suddenly seem brighter, or the world seems happier? Am I discouraged by the thought that it might be fourteen years? Gloria and Marc's love affair lasted only four years but flamed with a bright intensity.

As I listened back on my conversation with Gloria—our voices and laughter mixing with the rock and roll sounds of the Rainbow Room and the voices of tourists at the next table—I am also struck by the ways in which she described him. I research other interviews Gloria has participated in and find a pattern. In her 2007 story on the thirtieth anniversary of Marc's death, Rachel Porter, with the British paper *The Express*, noted that friends remembered him as "an extraordinary talent who, through a fog of brandy and cocaine, became an addled egotist, with a furious temper, fatalistic outlook and unfulfilled potential."[1] To Gloria, however, he was someone else: a lover, a giver, a humanitarian. How can people have two such opposing appraisals of the same person, Porter wonders. So do I.

I read this and wonder if it is the propensity of the widow to romanticize the partner who has died. Did I do that in remembering my husband? Thirty-seven years later, is that what Gloria Jones is still doing? Or was Marc someone who knew how to be two different people—the performer, the rock and roll star, and, away from that stage, with the people he most loved, the husband and doting father?

Gloria Jones has rebuilt her life from one of the most complete and absolute losses I've ever heard of, losing her lover, her lifestyle, her ability to do what she did best, and even all of the physical manifestations of her former life. Yet she has made her new life into something that she feels is worthwhile and has purpose. For that, I have great respect. She has built it through hard work and yes, some amount of illusion, denial, and removal from all that reminded her of Marc Bolan. Perhaps that is not the worst prescription one can choose for going on.

2

PEGGY SUE HONEYMAN-SCOTT

A warm California breeze comes off the ocean and through the palm trees as I knock on Peggy Sue's door. She welcomes me in, and we settle across from each other on sofas decorated with Union Jack pillows—stuffed versions of the British flag and a guitar case in the corner are the only indications of Peggy Sue's past connection to her late husband, Pretenders guitarist James Honeyman-Scott, who died in London at the age of twenty-five.

Peggy Sue was twenty-two when she met James, backstage at a Pretenders concert. At that time, I was still in high school, only dreaming of walking backstage at a show, having the guitarist fall madly in love, and begging me to go on the road with him. That would never be my story, but it was Peggy Sue's.

"We met at the Armadillo World Headquarters, a music hall in Austin that's no longer there," she tells me. "I had just moved back from LA maybe one or two days before. My sister called and told me the Pretenders were playing in town. She asked me if I wanted to go and I was like, 'Are you kidding?' I loved them, I thought Chrissie Hynde was cool."

Though she went to the show to see Chrissie, she left with James. As the concert ended, she and her sister ran into a friend from LA, Stan Tippins, who was road managing the Pretenders tour. He invited them backstage and introduced them to James and bass player Pete Farndon.

James and Peggy Sue Honeyman-Scott on their wedding day in London. Courtesy of Peggy Sue Honeyman-Scott

"I'm sitting there thinking oh my God, and the backstage area is literally smaller than this living room. There were all these people huddled around Chrissie, and I'm thinking I just want to meet that girl. A journalist came over and squatted down in front of us and asked if he could ask Jimmy some questions. Jimmy said 'Sure, fire away,' and the first question the guy asked was, 'Is this your wife?' Well Jimmy doesn't skip a beat, he says, 'No, but she's going to be.' At that moment, the journalist started taking pictures, and I'm just thinking 'umm, what's going on?' I really had no interest." Forty years later, Peggy Sue discovered the journalist through social media and found the photos of that night.

Growing up in Herefordshire, England, James began playing guitar at age seven, forming his first band at age fourteen, and teaching himself to play along the way. He played with various friends until getting together with future Pretenders bandmates

Pete Farndon and Martin Chambers. In 1978, while Peggy Sue was working on a modeling career in Los Angeles, Pete called James to play at a series of rehearsals in London with Chrissie Hynde, a US expat who was hoping to put together a band. Of that time, Hynde has said, "As soon as I heard Jimmy Scott, I knew I was getting close. Jimmy and I turned out to have a genuine musical affinity."[1] Honeyman-Scott's playing had an energetic, melodic sound that worked well with Hynde's more angsty punk playing. In order to get Jimmy into the band, Chrissie recruited her friend Nick Lowe to produce their first album. Jimmy was a huge fan of Lowe's and Hynde knew that his commitment to produce the album would sway Jimmy into joining. Much has been written about the musical combination of Hynde and Honeyman-Scott—how each played off the other's musical style to create a new sound that, in a very short time, became recognized as one of the most distinctive in the new wave genre.

The band recorded their first album in 1979. Hit singles like "Stop Your Sobbin" and "Brass in Pocket" quickly allowed the album to shoot to #1 on the British charts. They soon began a US tour that took them to Austin, where Peggy Sue had just returned home.

After meeting James after that show in Austin, Peggy Sue and her sister went along with the band to their hotel, where they "sat in the bar drinking and telling stories and laughing so much." What was it that so quickly connected her to James?

"The guy was just the funniest person I've ever met in my life. Still. We had the best time. And then the next day, they were gone. I thought, well that's that, and went back to getting myself settled in Austin."

A few days later, Jimmy called Peggy Sue and asked her to come to California. Without a second thought, she jumped on a plane and met him in Los Angeles. She would spend two weeks with him while he toured around the West Coast before returning to Austin. He called her intermittently over the next few months from the UK.

One time, Jimmy called Peggy Sue from London. "We're coming back," he said. "Meet me in Chicago."

Peggy shakes her head thinking of this time.

"I left my friends, my clothes, my house, I left everything. I went to Chicago, and that was it. We were rarely apart from that day on.

"We were on tour for a month. Then we went to England for seven months. We married in April 1981. We spent little time at our flat. We spent seven months traveling around England and settling in. We really had no time to do anything there. In July, we left for a world tour. Really, we were on tour for eight months.

"I got really fried from all the traveling. I met a woman who was the girlfriend of the band's agent, and she offered to let me stay with her in Japan while the band did their Australian tour. She thought I could do some modeling there. So, I was like, okay, I'm going to stay put for a while, try to adjust. I was just dizzy from the past year. It was such a whirlwind. I stayed in Hong Kong. I got my visa for Japan and lived with her for two months while the band did the Australia and New Zealand leg of the tour.

"Jimmy came to visit me in Japan. He met me in April for our first anniversary and then went on to LA. I had to finish my modeling contract, so we planned to meet in LA after that."

After meeting up in Los Angeles, the two went to Austin to spend some quiet time together. Jimmy went into the studio and did some recording with local Austin musicians. Peggy realizes now that Jimmy wasn't well, that all the touring had taken its toll on his health.

"As soon as I saw him in LA, I knew that something was wrong. He was yellow. His skin was yellow; the whites of his eyes were yellow. And I knew that that meant jaundice, liver problems. I had a friend whose baby had died of jaundice, so I knew the symptoms. I was more health conscious. I was jogging and eating healthy, drinking smoothies, the whole Southern California thing. Jimmy, of course, was never like that. They were into drinking beer, having a pint with friends, eating fried food. But I knew something wasn't right with him. I couldn't tell exactly what it was, so I just thought, we'll get some rest, spend some time eating better, and getting healthy, recovering from the past two years on the road.

"Jimmy had been told not to drink at all when I met him. The doctor told him not to drink any alcohol. I don't know exactly how or why the doctor gave him that information. I just remember Jimmy telling me more than once, 'You know, the doctor says I'm not supposed to drink, or I could die.' To me, that sounded serious. But he was twenty-five, and part of this wild experience, recording an album one day and finding it wildly popular almost the day it was released. Then going on this never-ending tour. You just don't think about being healthy. He kept telling me he felt fine. But he did have headaches. He had awful migraines. Once we got back to Austin, I started feeding him better. He didn't drink and he took vitamins. I think he went several months, almost a year without a headache. I think it was all part of him not being well. I think he had problems for many years that went undetected or ignored."

For almost a month, the couple lived blissfully in Austin. Jimmy recorded music and made plans to produce a local Austin band. Peggy Sue set up a sewing machine on the kitchen counter and began designing and making clothes. The two rested, got healthy, and spent quiet time together. They talked about buying a house in Austin, about Jimmy producing music, about starting a family and what they would name their kids. But then Jimmy got a call from Chrissie summoning him back to London.

Bass player Pete Farndon had become increasingly unstable due to heroin use. Chrissie decided to fire Farndon and called for a band meeting. Peggy Sue last saw Jimmy when he left their place for the trip to London.

"He said, 'See you next week,' kissed me and left. He called me from London and told me about the meeting. Then he said he was going out with friends. The next day, he was found dead at a friend's flat."

Most sources now list Jimmy's cause of death as "heart failure due to cocaine intolerance." Peggy Sue can live with that. What breaks her heart are the stories that list Jimmy's cause of death as a drug overdose.

"He had been out that night and had been drinking. He had brandy. He did a little coke. That was it. When I went to London, I was like a detective. I spoke to people. I found out exactly what happened. It wasn't an overdose. It was all a part of him not being well. He had liver problems and heart problems that we never really understood. But I've heard it all. They say oh, he died of a drug overdose, he died of a speedball, he was a heroin addict, just like Pete. I actually got into a debate at a bar in the Valley about fifteen years ago. Two guys were arguing about whether Jimmy died of a drug overdose. I couldn't stay quiet. I told them he didn't, and of course they asked me how I would know. I told them I'm his wife. They challenged me, said 'No you're not, show us your license.' So, I did. Then they're like, 'Oh, I guess you *would* know. Sorry.'

"I wanted to fight the misinformation at first. Absolutely I did. I've talked to lawyers about how much I can do. There's so much now, websites, books, everything. And the truth is that, you know, even members of the band never really asked for clarification. They just said, oh another drug overdose. It kept being repeated, and I don't know why they would do that, except it sounds more 'rock and roll.' I've never understood it."

She shrugs and says, "There's only so much I can do. At a certain point, I just realized, it won't change anything for me. It won't bring him back. I would rather the truth be out there everywhere, but it's hard to think that I could do it myself. I just can't.

"He was such a bright star. He was very shy. I was always pushing him to go out and meet with his fans. He was uncomfortable with all that. I always let him know that I was cool with that, that I understood it was part of his job. I tried to never be jealous. He was bright and intelligent, probably more than he got credit for being. And his musical impact was great, even in the short time he played. Jimmy was completely self-taught and pretty much a genius in the way he knew music. He never tried to show off or get anything because of who he was. Others would do that around him, and he would be embarrassed for them. He had no ego at all. He just loved playing the guitar."

I ask Peggy Sue about the days after Jimmy's death. I'm not surprised when, even thirty years later, she becomes emotional. She shifts in her seat and pulls one of the pillows onto her lap.

Her head shakes slightly as if still trying to understand that it happened as it did.

"I got a call from the band's manager, Dave Hill. I collapsed on the floor, and the only thing I knew to do was to call my mom. She came as quickly as she could. Then my sister and a friend came to help care for me. All I really remember is that they shot me full of Demerol because I couldn't function. I couldn't stop crying. I was howling, actually. Did you do that?"

We sit quietly for a few minutes, and I acknowledge to her that yes, I cried uncontrollably for hours. Sitting with Peggy in her quiet, sunny apartment, I am reminded of the line from Sylvia Plath's poem "The Elm": "A wind of such violence / Will tolerate no bystanding: I must shriek."

I think of Kevin and my own experience. I remember seeing him in our living room, the color leaving his face: panic, fear, and disbelief filling my lungs and then escaping in the only way I felt it could, through long, deep howls; keening. I understood what I was doing, and it felt like the most primal yet essential human sound. Even after the realization of how loudly I was crying and how it must seem, I couldn't stop. Continuing was the only tiny thing that felt right in a world where everything else was horribly wrong.

"I couldn't stop howling, couldn't stop wailing," Peggy Sue says. "I had to get on an airplane, so they wrapped me in a blanket and strapped me into the seat, and I just cried through the whole ten-hour flight. I couldn't not do it; I just couldn't stop myself." She pauses and pulls a tissue from a nearby box.

"Isn't it odd? I remember that time as clear as day, as though it happened yesterday. I can't believe it's been so long. It's weird how it's just right there, even after all these years.

"I remember when my mom arrived at my place. She lived an hour away and got there in thirty minutes. She lay with me on the bed, and I asked her 'When is this pain going to stop?' and she said, 'It won't,' and I just cried. 'Don't tell me that,' I told her. It was a harsh reality, but she was right. She lost her husband, my dad, when she was forty-five. I'm sure, thinking about it now, that it was hard for her to see her daughter go through that."

Peggy Sue stayed in England for eight months. She barely remembers Jimmy's funeral. She agreed to have him buried in his hometown of Herefordshire but has had second thoughts about that decision because Jimmy had talked to her once about being buried in Highgate Cemetery in London. "It's not like he talked about it often, but he did tell me once when we were walking through Highgate that he'd want to be buried with the artists and poets there. But it was important to his family that he be back in his hometown, so I honored their wishes.

"It was all such a nightmare. Someone even implied that I would just return to the United States and forget him, anyway. Which broke my heart. We were just starting out. It wasn't like he was a huge celebrity, but he was beginning to become one. And he was admired in his little part of the world. Dealing with any spouse's death is a lot to wade through, but add the public aspect of things, together with the business stuff, it was just awful. I remember being curled up on the couch and someone telling me that I had to make decisions and sign papers. I couldn't even think.

"I remember ordering his headstone. The one guitar he really wanted was a Firebird 7. It was the last guitar he was looking for to add to his collection, and he could never find it. So, I gave it to him by having it engraved on his headstone. It was my last gift to him.

"My sister and a friend stayed for a month. Then I told them to leave because I just wanted to be alone. Every night, I just went to bed and cried and cried and talked to Jimmy. I just tried to deal with it even though I had no idea how.

"I didn't do very well. I was twenty-four and completely alone. I thought about suicide a couple times. I'm sure it was strange for people to see me out, but I didn't know what else to do. I hated being alone. I recently found a photo of myself out at a Mexican restaurant with the guys from Spandau Ballet. I must have weighed ninety pounds, a shell. I couldn't even recognize myself. I felt like I really wasn't even there. I kept feeling like I was out of my body.

"I had some friends that visited. But it seemed as though they didn't want to acknowledge what I was feeling. They'd ask how I was doing and if I said I wasn't well or that I really missed him, they'd basically say, 'Oh, here you go, have a cup of tea. It'll be alright.' Probably the worst place I could have been was England because they have this whole thing, this stiff upper lip idea. It's almost as though grieving is treated as taboo, like something is really wrong with you if you are grieving.

"I used to run five miles a day, and I just stopped that. One day, I went into my kitchen and saw all these empty liquor bottles and said, 'Okay, I have to stop this.' So, I just stopped. I started running again. I just told myself that I have to shake this off. I have to start my life again. Some girls asked me to be in a band, so I did that. It was a distraction for a while." That band was called Girls Can't Help It, and they released a single that had a bit of success on the British dance charts. But her heart wasn't in the music so she left after the first single. She returned to the United States and settled in Dallas, where she opened a boutique selling clothing that she designed as well as items she imported from England.

"I knew one person in Dallas. I opened the shop, called Dressed to Kill, in order to keep myself busy. I felt like I was going to lose my mind if I didn't. I had been through other tragedies and knew I had to force myself to snap out of it. I faced that either I was going to get out of how I was feeling, or I was going to curl up and die."

Peggy Sue wasn't a stranger to tragedy. Though Jimmy's death was the worst she had ever faced, she had also lost her father, grandfather, a favorite uncle, two boyfriends, and a best friend by the time Jimmy died. It has made her truly value every day, yet she struggles sometimes to feel that she's moving forward.

"It hits me at the weirdest times. Of course, I've moved on in thirty years, but sometimes I feel that I just kept living: just getting on with the day-to-day of life. When I moved to Dallas, I felt as though I was making a conscious decision to move somewhere where I didn't know anyone just to not have people giving me that look with those sad eyes anymore.

"I've moved around a lot since my time in Dallas. After three years, I moved back to England and began work on a cookbook called *Rock and Roll Cuisine* with my friend Robin. That was fun. I finally began grief therapy during that time, and it helped me. I knew I needed help. I had a lot of rage about how unfair it all was. So unfair. The musician Mike Oldfield, who made *Tubular Bells*, had donated money to an organization to set up low-cost grief therapy. At that time, I didn't have a lot of money, and it really helped me to be able to get this counseling for four pounds a session.

"The thing I remember about that time was that I look back now and think, you just don't know what's going to happen in twenty-four hours. You might feel suicidal one day, and if you just wait long enough, something good will happen."

She has continued through the years to deal with issues around James's estate, especially regarding his equipment and guitar collection. "Because these items are connected to someone who has had fame, they have value, so people want them. I've carried around so many of James's guitars for years. I still have several. He had an extensive collection. And yes, some of them I sold. When I asked him once about how many guitars he was buying, he said, if we ever needed the money, we could sell them. So, when I needed to, over time, I did. I had to take care of myself, and that was one way to do it. I worked closely with the auction house and have a pretty good idea of who has them. I'm certain they're in good hands and even being played and enjoyed rather than being locked away somewhere. But all of it was so hard for a twenty-four-year-old who was alone and in the midst of significant trauma. And of course, I would trade them all just to have him back.

"And the terrible thing is, the trauma continues today with certain people who want to know where the guitars are, and am I just selling them off to the highest bidder to make money. They are my connection to James, and I care about them. Whether I have them in my possession or not, I care about them." This idea that the possessions of the husband belong to anyone but his wife is something unique to this group of women.

During the time of working through her grief and compiling the cookbook, Peggy Sue was in a relationship and became pregnant with her daughter. After her birth, Peggy Sue remained in England for ten years to raise her. She began studying the healing arts and considered becoming a homeopath. Having her daughter helped Peggy to begin moving beyond her grief. "Focusing on someone else is really the key. Being responsible for someone else that needs your attention, it brings you out of yourself. You can't just feel sorry for yourself. I think I was maybe drawn to the healing work I do because it helps me."

Moving on, forgiveness, happiness, gratitude: these emotions are all part of the grieving process, and their presence ebbs and flows over time, disappearing for long periods and then returning when we least expect them. How do we move past anger and disbelief into a place where we can be grateful for what we had? Just writing that word "had" brings about the realization that my happiness is, for the most part, now in the past tense. I see this in Peggy Sue—a longing for the fairy-tale happiness that she had for just a brief time. There's still a feeling of anger because her happiness was so fleeting. When I tell her of my own envy of how she and Jimmy met and fell in love, her response is quick and definite.

"How long did you have together?" she asks me.

"We were married a little over twenty-six years."

"I had two. You may envy my experience, but I envy your twenty-six years. I, on the other hand, have nothing but fantasies of what might have been. What I wouldn't give to have your experience rather than mine."

"Fair enough," I respond. We sit in silence for a moment, each of us weighing what we had and what we lost.

"The whole gratitude thing has been very hard for me," she says, finally. "I've struggled with it a lot. I've seen situations where people are forgiving and thankful despite terrible experiences or loss, and I really don't get it. I really still teeter back and forth. Sometimes, it's hard to not live in the world of 'if only.' People think that because we were only together for such a short time, I should get over it quickly. It doesn't always work that way."

And what about my experience, I wonder. As I leave Peggy Sue, I drive out to the ocean. The sky above is perfectly blue, the salty air warm on my face. As I walk and think of Peggy Sue and Jimmy's short but intense life together, I must admit that there were times when I wondered why I settled for a life so ordinary. Why did I marry so young and forego a career in writing? Where was my rock star? I pick up a small shell on the beach, its outer edges flat and smooth, worn soft by time and tides. I think about what we have, and what we lose, either in a few years' time, or over the course of twenty years. I know with either, the pain can be great. I know, too, that when I realized what I had would be lost, I made every possible bargain for that quiet, normal life returned to me.

3

CRYSTAL ZEVON

I was thinking quite a bit about loss and letting go in the weeks before my conversation with Crystal Zevon. The fifth anniversary of Kevin's passing was approaching while I was planning to take my youngest child to college. As if I needed any additional stress during this transition in my life, I was also packing up to move to a new house. Grief was quite prevalent in those days, both for all I had lost with Kevin's passing and for this new loss of my youngest child who would be moving on and making her own way without me at a college three hundred miles away.

They are different kinds of grief but bereavement nonetheless. One is filled with sadness, anger, and the always-unanswered question of why. Another brings with it feelings of pride and accomplishment, of excitement for all that lies ahead, but also a realization that it's time to let go. Sometimes we choose to let go, as when one decides that a relationship is no longer working. But even that has its own feelings of fear, loss, and, yes, grief.

Loss came to Crystal twice. The first was as much an act of letting go as of losing when she decided to leave her husband, singer, songwriter, and musician Warren Zevon, and walk away from their marriage. Though she left—divorcing Warren and creating a new life for herself and their daughter Ariel in Paris—there were always connections back to Warren, resilient

Crystal and Warren with their daughter Ariel. Courtesy of Crystal Zevon

threads of love and understanding that survived even the worst moments of their tumultuous relationship. The second time loss visited Crystal, it was the permanent, grievous loss of death, when Warren, at age fifty-three, succumbed to lung cancer. She was one of the first to know about Warren's diagnosis. He called her immediately upon receiving the news from his doctor.

"You're going to come out, right?" he asked from Los Angeles as Crystal sat across the continent in Vermont trying to understand. It had been years since they lived together, months since they had even spoken. "You're the wife," he said. "You need to come take care of me."

It had all begun for Crystal and Warren in LA; it was fitting it would end there as well. Arriving at LAX in 1968 to pick up her then-boyfriend, session musician Waddy Wachtel, from a tour he had recently completed with the Everly Brothers, Crystal was introduced to Warren, a fellow musician who had gotten Waddy the gig. Waddy and Crystal had come to California at the behest of the Cowsills, the 1960s family group who inspired the television show *The Partridge Family*. Waddy worked for father Bud Cowsill while Crystal ran the group's fan club in Beverly Hills. Warren had been working for a few years with the Everlys and offered Waddy a spot on the tour.

"Waddy would call me from the road and tell me about Warren, how he was a crazy guy, but he wrote great music and had already written these amazing songs. He would sing me bits of 'Carmalita' and 'Frank and Jesse James,' the two songs Warren had written. He loved Warren.

"When I got to the airport, I was driving this huge Chevy Supersport van. I had two foster kids that I'd taken in, so I had a van that I drove around like a mom. I was maybe twenty or twenty-one at the time. Warren got in and Waddy asked if I could give Warren a ride to the Tropicana Hotel. He had recently broken up with his girlfriend Tule and was staying at the Tropicana. It was a very rock and roll hotel. I said sure."

Crystal remembers an immediate connection, a sudden electricity she felt looking at Warren through the rearview mirror. "I couldn't even fathom that something so significant was happening at that moment, but I felt it. It was so electric. We passed a joint back and forth, and Warren would hold my finger for a few seconds each time we passed it to each other."

It was fall in Los Angeles, and Crystal remembers the two of them encountering each other at odd places through the city. "Los Angeles is a big city, yet we kept bumping into each other. At the dentist, I'm sitting in the chair, and I hear Warren's voice in the waiting room. As I left, we started talking and finally the dentist had to tell us he had a schedule to keep. Then a few days later, we saw each other again at Hugh's Market shopping for Thanksgiving dinner. Warren was there with Tule and their son, Jordan. I didn't know if they were back together or what was going on, but they were shopping. We said hello and exchanged a few words. Apparently when they left, they had a huge argument where she said we were obviously having an affair. At that point, other than a few chance meetings, nothing had happened. We had barely seen each other.

"There was a recording session that Waddy was producing that had a clap track on it. He invited a bunch of people to come help with the clap track. We all needed headphones, but they were short a few pairs. Warren and I both arrived a few minutes late, and people were sharing headphones. There were two pairs left, but Warren quickly gave the second pair to someone else and said that we could share a headset. And of course, Waddy's in the control booth watching.

"Finally, there was a bar called Benny K's on Santa Monica Boulevard. It was a little dive bar that Waddy played on Friday nights for $10. They got to play whatever they wanted, and they could play loud, so they made it a regular Friday night thing. I was always there with them. One Friday night, I was sitting in the booth; it was circular, and I was in the middle with people on either side. Warren came in and managed to maneuver things around so that he was sitting next to me. It was like we had barely had a conversation at this point, but there was something going on. We ended up on the dance floor during a slow song, and Waddy's on stage and Warren kissed me, and that was it. That was just *it*! He came home with me that night—we had to drive Waddy home, but Warren was with me, and we couldn't imagine it being any other way. I had a piano. Warren had just started writing 'Desperados Under the Eaves' about his time at the Tropicana, and he played me bits and pieces of it. He finished that song within three or four days of moving in.

"He didn't stay for good after that night. He ended up going back to Tule because he said they shared a car, and she needed the car. He had told me that they were completely finished, that he had gone back there because of the car, and Jordan, and finances. He said he was looking for a place that he could afford because he couldn't afford to stay at the Tropicana. That's what he told me, and I suppose I chose to believe it. Whether I really believed it or not, is questionable.

"The next couple days were agony. We would call each other, but it was very clear quickly that he wasn't as free as he had indicated, but we couldn't stop talking to each other or being in touch. He would do things like volunteer to do the laundry and go to the laundromat so we could meet. Or I would get a friend to call his house then give the phone to me. It was kind of absurd, really. I look back on it and think, it was shameful, really. But it was like a freight train. We couldn't stop it.

"The next time he came over, he still had the car. I think they had just fought it out about whether he was going to stay or go. I don't know for sure, but he showed up. We made love. Afterwards, he looked at me and said, 'I could live here.' So, we did it. We went back to his place and got the rest of his things. It was very awkward. I played with Jordon while Warren got his things and fixed something he had broken. I later learned that it was something he had broken in a fight between them, but I didn't know that then. It was December. We stopped on the way back to my place and got a Christmas tree and decorated it with the foster kids. It was instant family."

Much of Warren's career was a struggle. Though meeting with critical acclaim and praise from fellow musicians, commercial success almost always eluded Warren. Except for the hit "Werewolves of London," much of his career was spent trying to secure a recording contract, or publishing deal. This external struggle was added to internal identity struggles and other mental health issues like obsessive-compulsive disorder. Warren grappled for many years with alcohol and drug dependency issues with Crystal there with him, often on the receiving end of the abuse.

"Warren started out with an interest in classical music. It's fairly well known he spent time as a teenager with Igor Stravinsky. He was always writing his symphony, always. He had this fantasy that when he got signed to Asylum Records and their classical label was Nonesuch Records, he would be able to do his symphony. He wrote the string parts and got to conduct the orchestra on 'Frank and Jessie James.' He knew music, he read music, he visualized music in a way that most rock musicians don't. That set him apart. But despite being looked up to by most of his musician friends, he never got the public acclaim that they received. Of course, he was grateful that he got to do what he loved. Within our marriage, that was something we dealt with. There were moments when he was angry, and other moments when he was just grateful. The level of how much we were drinking sort of dictated how the conversation went."

Over the course of his career, Warren recorded thirteen albums; several of his songs were also covered by other artists like Linda Ronstadt ("Poor Poor Pitiful Me" and "Hasten Down the Wind") and others. He began writing music in the mid-1960s and continued prolifically for nearly forty years. But each success was accompanied by a struggle and usually involved bouts of severe alcoholism. Unable to stay sober, Zevon moved from record label to record label, never quite finding a recording home-base. After the failure of his first album and unable to complete the second, Warren and Crystal headed for Spain, where they hoped a simpler life of playing music in bars for expats would make them happy.

"Spain was a magical time for Warren and me. After he was diagnosed with cancer, we went through a lot of time talking and remembering things. He told me, 'You know, when you get sad, we always had Spain.'"

It was a time filled with friendships, with making music for music's sake, with creativity and writing. But the success of his friends like Jackson Browne and Lindsey Buckingham back in the United States motivated Warren to return and try again. Shortly after returning to Los Angeles, Crystal became pregnant with their daughter, Ariel. Warren made attempts at both recording and staying sober, but it wasn't easy.

"I was his caretaker for much of our marriage. I remember mornings when he was shaking so badly he couldn't tie his shoes, and I would do it. I didn't have the understanding at that time—really until he entered treatment—that I was enabling; I was helping it to continue."

It took a few more years for Crystal to realize she couldn't stay with Warren. The abuse became more frequent and violent. Many times, he didn't remember what had happened.

"When I did leave, yes it was because of his drinking. He'd been sober for quite a while, and then he started drinking again. We had a house in Santa Barbara, and I was living there with Ariel and a Dutch *au pair*. Warren was spending time in LA recording and coming up to Santa Barbara on the weekends.

During the week, we rented a house near the studio for him, and that's where he stayed. Sometimes, I would go down on the weekends, maybe with Ariel, maybe not. I went down this one weekend, and we shopped for curtain fabric and a new stereo system. For some reason, he had the whole weekend off from the studio. We spent the day shopping and then went to our favorite French restaurant, Robert's, on La Brea. We had this fabulous dinner. Don Henley was there, and he joined us for a while. We left really happy. We came home, and the house had this red whirlpool tub. We took a bath. We were watching TV and laughing and laughing. He was writing a song, and we were batting back and forth lyric ideas. We made love. At one point, he said, 'we're always going to love each other.' It was like a grand pronouncement that, no matter what happened, we'd always love one another. And this statement was from him. Like, why don't we just decide that no matter what happens, let's not ever let the idea of coming apart enter the picture. And that's how we went to sleep. So in love.

"I woke up first, as usual, and I went to wash the car and go to get a few more swatches of curtain fabric. I went home and was standing there with these fabric swatches in my hand, and he's standing in the dining room. We were renting the house from Karla Bonoff, and she had left some things in the house that she thought we might use. One of the things she left was cooking sherry. Warren had drunk it. And he looks at me walking in, and I'm smiling and holding fabric swatches while he's on the phone. He's holding a coffee cup and talking on the phone. I stopped because I realized what he was doing: he was refilling a prescription for Darvon, which he was very addicted to. He had not been taking it since he had been sober. He hung up the phone, and I said, 'Really? Darvon?'

"He looked at me and just started yelling and screaming. He threw the coffee cup at me and started yelling, 'I'll never be like your father. You should leave.' Then he said, 'See that cup, my coffee was spiked with sherry.' He threw his coffee cup at me; it hit the wall and shattered, and he's yelling at me to get out, that he didn't need me or want me and that I was trying to turn him into my father. I had these very *Leave It to Beaver* parents. But I had felt so much like things were coming together for us and we were going to work things out. We had already been through one intervention. He stayed sober for a while, then started drinking again, then he had been sober for quite a while. And he was sober the night before, and I believed it was going to last, that we were going to last. But it was clear he was ordering Darvon and was drinking anything he could find."

Crystal was devastated. Her belief in Warren and their future together, which seemed so certain just the night before, was now destroyed. In retrospect, she believes he once again was battling the identity demons.

"I think the commitment we made the night before terrified him. Even though we'd done that before, we were married, we'd made a commitment, we'd made those promises, but I think he was trying to figure out who he was. I also think he was being set up with someone else."

Shortly after their break-up, before they were divorced, Warren began dating Kim Langford, an actress on the television series *Knott's Landing*. Crystal now believes the relationship had already begun, and Warren was finding a way to end his marriage in the only way he knew how.

"He had been set-up in that relationship by mutual friends. I don't know for certain, but I suspect that set-up had been happening while we were married and living apart. Warren struggled with who he was supposed to be. People were always telling him, you know, it's rock and roll, you gotta be a rock star, do certain things, be with certain people. As his wife, I didn't necessarily fit with that. Warren didn't know how to be a rock star and be a husband and father. He was never Paul McCartney.

"It was something we fought about often. He would tell me, 'I'll be faithful to you, but you have to be with me all the time,' which was impossible."

So Crystal left, heading back to Santa Barbara. As she drove, she realized she hadn't eaten all day. She stopped for a burger, and while eating, she overheard two women sitting at a nearby table talking about Al-Anon. They were doing the fourth step wherein the person who has been affected by a loved one's addiction takes a thoughtful moral inventory of their life. Crystal listened to the conversation, then approached them.

"I went over to their table and just said, 'I need help.' The sponsor said, 'You need to go back and tell him, you know he's drinking and because of that, you can't give any credence to what he's saying, but you know it's not your fault and you're not responsible. Tell him when he sobers up you may be there, or you may not because you're getting on with your life.'"

Crystal heard similar words from her therapist, who told her it was time to move on. She had left previously, but always with the thought that she'd return once he sobered up, or if he agreed to stay sober. But this time was different. She knew it was for good.

"He didn't see me or acknowledge me or that I had left. He didn't come to Santa Barbara at all. He didn't see Ariel for a month. It was even more devastating for her because he had been around so much. He may not have been fatherly, but there was always a physical presence."

Crystal spent time going back to school and completing her degree in psychology. Studying counseling and substance abuse issues helped her process what she had experienced with Warren.

"Everything I was doing those first couple years was wrapped around my life with Warren and trying to understand what was going on. There was hope for a long time that we would get back together, but also a fear that we would get back together and it would just be more of the same."

The two remained married for three years even though Warren dated a series of women during that time. Crystal wanted Warren to be the one to file, hoping that the action would create a sense of realization for him. Finally, he did. The divorce decree, however, disallowed Crystal from having any rights to royalties, both current and future. She was advised not to sign the agreement by her attorney, by the judge, and even the couple's mutual friend, Jackson Browne.

"I had lots of lines in songs that I've never been given credit for. But I didn't feel I necessarily deserved credit because I made a comment or a remark and it ended up being in a song. I didn't write the songs, so I was okay with it. Everyone was advising me against it. They kept telling me it was my only security. Warren was still an alcoholic, and it really was all we had. Even the judge asked me if I really understood what it meant.

"What I knew was I couldn't move on if I was going to be held hostage by Warren's resentment over money and who deserves what. My lawyer told me women do this all the time, but men never do. And the women regret it later, and, of course, I did. But I did it for my reasons. It was a way for me to establish myself on my own, apart from him. I had to do it."

Crystal remained in southern California for another year but realized building a new identity would be nearly impossible there, where she was known as "Warren Zevon's ex." Instead, she moved to Paris, traveling there first on her own to make certain it was the right move, and then bringing Ariel with her. She lost all contact with Warren for most of the time she was there, though he would call her from time-to-time, especially if he had broken up with a girlfriend.

"That, of course, is the big difference between divorce and death. He was still there, and we maintained a relationship. He came to Paris, and we came back and visited. During that time, I think we realized that we still loved each other. We still had something between us that was real; it didn't go away, we knew that. Over time, we were able to become friends."

In the years after their divorce, Crystal worked hard to become her own person and develop her own identity. She became a political activist, something Warren hated. She raised Ariel and established her life back in her home state of Vermont.

Until the call came from Warren in 2002.

"Through the years, we had connected many times, making decisions about Ariel, or he would call me when he had a break-up. Sometimes, he would even call me to ask directions if he was lost. We just always had that connection. But after he got sick, there was that spiritual connection, that one-heart connectivity. We used that time to go back through our lives and reflect. We laughed and cried and talked about everything. The last time I saw him was when I was in LA when our grandsons were born, and he said, 'I'm so sorry I started drinking again and we didn't get to do what we were supposed to do.' He wanted me to come take care of him after he was diagnosed, but it was shortly after he started drinking again, so though I came to California, I didn't stay."

Crystal and Warren had made arrangements to meet while Crystal was in Los Angeles for Ariel's engagement party. She recollects that they had talked about her going to Warren's place after the party, but he expected her to come directly from the airport. The two connected the day after she arrived, and Warren was outraged.

"I'd gone to stay at a friend's house, and I called him the next afternoon. He was livid. 'Where are you? I've been waiting for you. You were supposed to come here. I've been waiting.' As though I had broken some solemn promise. He told me he was going to bring a girlfriend to the party, and I said fine. I asked if I could visit the next day, and he said I could if I wanted to. At the party, he was very cold. At one point, I helped him into the bathroom, and he looked into my eyes. I think he forgave me, but the damage was done. He and his girlfriend went out that night, and he ordered wine at dinner. He was drinking heavily very soon after that.

"I've asked myself over and over again: did I really misunderstand the plans we'd made? Did I just not want to see him? Did I not want to get involved in caring for him? I really didn't think in my mind that I was supposed to go from the airport to his place. But now it's one of those things; he's gone, and we can't resolve it. He said it was just miscommunication, but he never quite let it go. He let me know it hurt him."

I ask Crystal about maintaining the role of caretaker. It changes the relationship; throws it off balance. The fact that one person has a need that the other fills makes things unequal. So much of their relationship involved those roles, with Crystal taking care of Warren through his bouts of drunkenness and drug use. Could it be that she didn't want to return to that role during the end of his life?

"Absolutely. It was a huge part of our marriage. When he called me after his diagnosis, part of what he was calling me about was that he kept saying, they're [doctors] giving me those

'Elvis drugs.' He definitely wanted me to talk him out of taking the pain killers the doctors were prescribing. I didn't feel that was my role. I felt as though he had to make that call. I would say, 'Is that how you want to go out?' We would talk about what he wanted to do. He was very concerned about his legacy and his last days and how he was going to die. He decided to make the album, and that's what he did."

In the months after his diagnosis, Warren recorded his last album, *The Wind*, assisted by many of his musical friends and with what many consider some of his very best songwriting. He would win a posthumous Grammy for the album.

"But then, he began drinking, and I realized that was it. I wasn't going to go back into that role. Just after his diagnosis, we were talking on the phone five to ten times a day. Once he started drinking, the calls weren't as frequent. We were still talking, but it was different."

Despite his original prognosis of three to four months, Warren lived for eleven months, long enough to see Ariel give birth to his twin grandsons. He willed himself to live, Crystal believes, so that he could experience that birth. After he completed work on *The Wind*, he told her he was done with music; that was it. But he wanted to be present for this event.

"Our last conversation was after the twins were born, when he asked me to promise to write the book. He made me promise to tell the whole truth, even the awful, ugly parts. Warren began calling me 'old girl' around that time, saying that he had written a song with that name. He referenced that song often in his last days whenever we talked. When we were married, and even for a time after, there was always this kind of unspoken feeling that, when we got old, we would wind up together. I don't think I really believed it, but I think he did."

Warren and Crystal shared an intense, once-in-a-lifetime sort of love, and it doesn't surprise Crystal that neither of them moved on into permanent relationships after they divorced.

"I think I moved on in my life in certain ways after the divorce, but I never had another relationship that could equal that kind of love, *that* love. I don't think it's necessarily healthy love. I got into other relationships that weren't healthy, and that's been a part of my struggle. Warren and I led separate lives, and yet, he would call me, and it was as if I was still his wife. He would call me after every break-up. He referred to me as 'wifey,' always."

What happens to the grieving process in that kind of relationship, I wonder? The grief Crystal felt after Warren died cannot be discounted because of their divorce. If anything, there's a realization that she grieved twice, once for the loss of their marriage and again upon his death.

"After he died, I did go through a grieving process. That was when I had to separate from him even more than previously, in a much more final way. It took much longer for me to get over missing his presence when he died than when we separated. You know, I never remarried, he never remarried. We both came close a couple times, but then we didn't. He remains for me, the husband, the father of our child, the grandfather of our grandchildren."

Crystal kept her promise and told Warren's story in her *New York Times*–bestseller *I'll Sleep When I'm Dead: The Dirty Life and Times of Warren Zevon*. Through interviews with friends, musicians, family members, and even girlfriends, Crystal pieced together the story of Warren's life, even the awful, ugly parts, just as he requested. Much of the book is based on detailed journals that Warren kept for much of his adult life. He wrote about the minutia of his day, including things like a new type of mustard he tried on a sandwich. But he also wrote about his relationships, his sexual exploits, and his feelings about Crystal and their marriage.

"Reading his journals was hell. There were parts where he said wonderful things about me and the kids. But there were also many difficult parts. He also had this microscopic handwriting. I had to get a large map-reading magnifying glass to read them. I started trying to read them in my house, but then I had to quit, it was just too hard, too traumatic. I would get through the stuff about the sandwich and who called to collect bills, and then there would be these moments of brilliance or anger or narcissism, or just this really beautiful writing." And the subject matter was often challenging.

"All the girlfriends were there, too. He was always very sexual, but after our divorce, he was a sex addict. He replaced the alcohol with women. And he detailed all of it. Reading it was really hard. I had to go through stuff I didn't know about or hadn't had to live through the first time around. It took me a long time. Warren had a distinctive voice. I'd be driving in my car after reading the journals, and that voice would come into my head and I'd find myself having conversations with him. Then I'd have to remind myself all over again that he was gone. It was a very difficult process."

So where does forgiveness fit into Crystal and Warren's story? Was she able to forgive the abusive husband after their divorce, or at least by the time that he died?

"I've forgiven him several times, in fact," she responds. "I think the fact that, after we separated, I dove into studies, looking at it from an intellectual perspective was something that I needed to do so I could come to an understanding and try to forgive. And then, when I had to deal with my own problems with alcohol, the forgiveness became even more complete. Then I got it. Because I had my own issues and shameful behavior, most of it happening when Warren and I were no longer together and I was trying to be a good mom. I had to go through it again. When I got sober, my acceptance of Warren became more complete.

"I remember one time after we divorced and Warren and I were together, and I was trying to get some resolution for anger I still had for his behavior. I said something about his physical abuse of me. He got this blank look on his face. There was one time when he gave me a black eye. I left the house, but I went back the next day so he could see it, so he knew about that. But all the other times, I realized then, he didn't know what he had done. He was too drunk to remember. The day after a fight, we would walk on eggshells trying to make sure the fight didn't happen again, and he knew there had been a fight, but he had no recollection of the details.

"So that was a huge revelation for me. It was a powerful moment for me to realize about forgiveness, the power and value and importance of it in our lives. I think it allowed us to create a new life of friendship. It wasn't worth carrying around things that happened in the past."

And when he died? Was there more forgiveness then, I asked.

"When he died, it was as though I had to go through it all over again. Reading those journals, there was a lot I didn't know. I had new anger. People ask me what surprised me when I read the journals, and, truth is, there wasn't much that surprised me. There weren't many things he did that surprised me. What upset me was the prevalence; things were more deep-seeded than I knew. And I never would have cared to know the details of many of these things. It brought it all up again. I had to go through it again, it felt like getting beat up again, like getting punched in the face all over again.

"But when I was done, it was over. I would never have chosen to do it; had he not asked me to do it, I wouldn't have. But now, I'm so glad I did it because it was like Warren's one last confession, one last request for forgiveness. It allowed me to know and to forgive everything. And now I just really miss him. I miss his voice on the phone, the chance meeting somewhere or making plans to go out to lunch or what to give Ariel for her birthday.

"I think a lot about our conversations, things I only told him and never talked about with anyone else. I think about other things, too. What I think about most is that I'm not angry with him anymore. Even when I think about the awful stuff, I'm not angry. Really, what a gift. Had I not read the journals and written the book, I don't think I could be this clear."

Throughout our lives, we suffer the losses of those taken from us, and the loss of those we let go. We judge and hold grudges, or we choose to forgive and move on. But the finality of death takes away the choice of how to handle past grievances or bad decisions. Things we should have said but didn't, or things we did say but didn't mean. They all leave a residue of regret when the other person isn't here to provide resolution. If we're very lucky, as Crystal believes she was, we're given the opportunity to make peace, something that may not erase the grief but at least offers solace to those who remain.

4

NANCY JONES

Within minutes of meeting Nancy Jones, as I ask her to tell me about her late husband and country music legend, George Jones, she begins to cry. Her granddaughter looks on, concerned. "I didn't really want to do this," she admits. "Sometimes it's alright to talk, but other times it's hard. Losing George was the worst time of my life." We sit quietly for a few minutes while Nancy holds her granddaughter. "Grandma's okay," she tells her. Nancy has recently struggled with health issues. She's regaining strength, both physical and emotional. "God put me here to save George. And now he's saved me so I can tell my story. Let's keep going. I'll be alright."

Nancy returns often to the theme of her faith, to the idea that God placed her in George Jones's life to save him. If she has no other purpose, she's okay with that. I think back on my own faith and how it was tested through Kevin's illness and death. It is difficult to continue to believe when all you've prayed for is taken from you. But Nancy remained faithful when George turned on her, when he broke promise after promise to get sober, and when he finally left her after a few weeks' illness. Hers is a rock-solid belief that everything worked out just as it was meant to. Now, she relies on that faith to get her through difficult days without George, believing with certainty that she will see him again.

Nancy and George Jones Courtesy of Nancy Jones

Nancy Sepulvado was a single mother of two living in Shreveport, Louisiana, when a friend talked her into going to see country music legend George Jones. Her friend knew George's manager, and he had invited her to come to a Syracuse, New York, concert. Thinking they may be able to get backstage, she invited Nancy to come along. Nancy really didn't want to go because she wasn't a country music fan.

"I loved Creedance Clearwater Revival. I used to turn on that album on Saturday mornings and clean my house. I loved them and that kind of 70s rock music. I didn't even know George Jones. But my friend said I didn't have to listen to the music, she just wanted me to go along. So, I went. We went backstage, and I met George, and he was such a nice guy. We talked and talked.

"Then I heard his voice and thought, wow, he really is good. I'd never heard anyone with a voice like that. Then, after the show, we met again and talked into the night. The next day, we were in the same hotel, and I saw him and asked him if he'd go with me to the airport. George said, 'no cause you're not leaving.' And I said, 'I have to. I have two kids and I've got a job.' I said 'it's been very nice. I enjoyed it, and you're so sweet. But why don't you go with me to the airport?' And he said, 'I'm not going to the airport because I'm not going to say goodbye.'

"Well, my girlfriend and I took commercial flights home. It took forever to get flights from Syracuse to Shreveport with layovers. George chartered a plane and then got a car at the airport. He was sitting in my driveway when I got home. And that was it.

"He lived in Muscle Shoals, and he begged me to go there. He said I could just come for a week and see what it was like, see where he lived. Well, my boss was upset, he had a fit. He said, 'You're going with this man, he's a bad man. He's a drunk. He's this and that.' But I'd never seen that. George had only been sweet and kind. Well, I went. But that's when I found the truth. I found out he needed help. I suppose I could have left, but something told me to stay. So, I stayed. We met in 1981, and I could have walked away. But I didn't. We got married in March of 1983. I remained and I fought.

"The first few months were okay. Then I realized I was seeing things that I didn't understand. I had never even seen marijuana. That was first. But then it was coke, and then whiskey. And I could see the changes in him whenever the devil took over. But then I realized that maybe I was put here to have a fight with that devil. So we did, we had a long hard fight."

George Jones was born in Texas to poor parents. He found music as both an escape from an abusive father and as a way to make a little pocket change. He began singing on street corners as a young teen. From there, he sang on radio shows and in honky-tonks throughout Texas. His first marriage, to Dorothy Bonvillion, was short-lived, but the couple did have a daughter, with whom George would reconnect as part of his eventual effort to come clean and make amends. He cut his first record in Texas in 1955, but it was his move to Nashville, to record for Mercury Records, that really put George on the country music charts again and again through the 1950s and into the 1960s. Hits like "She Thinks I Still Care" and "A Good Year for the Roses" highlighted Jones's smooth, rich voice, reminiscent of predecessors like Hank Williams.

In the early 1970s, George partnered with Tammy Wynette, both as a singing partner and as a married couple. The two together recorded hits that are country music classics, and their marriage and work together catapulted them both into legend status. Together, they recorded nine studio albums and released fifteen singles. There were also several compilation or "greatest hits" albums that continued long past the time their relationship ended. Their relationship was never easy, but it has become the stuff of music legend, both for how prolific and volatile it was. They loved hard and fought hard, all while George sank deeper and deeper into addiction.

"I get so hurt when I hear fans say, 'Well, he really loved Tammy,'" Nancy says. "They say, 'Oh, they loved each other.' Well, if they loved each other, they would have worked it out. But all they did was fight. I wouldn't be here if they loved each other. Even today, I hear people say, 'I know he's now in heaven with Tammy.' It hurts. But fans think that's the story. He had six years with her, and he stayed drunk most of the time. And I'm sitting here with thirty-two years."

After his divorce from Wynette, George sank even deeper into alcohol and cocaine addiction. Several arrests followed, as did stints in rehab and hospitals. He missed so many performances due to his addictions that he became known as "No-Show Jones." Despite his troubles, he also wrote one of his most popular songs during this time, "He Stopped Loving Her Today," which garnered a Grammy Award and a CMA Male Vocalist of the Year Award.

It was into this life that Nancy would step by agreeing to meet George in Muscle Shoals. She quickly learned that in addition to his addiction issues, he had financial problems and had greatly damaged his reputation. Nancy became involved in George's management, made him reschedule shows, and made certain that he got there. Even so, he continued his drinking and drug abuse. "I was the tough one. I learned to be tough with the record labels, to get what we had coming. I got his shows rebooked. And I knew who would give him drugs and whiskey. Who would sneak it in. I learned all of that.

"But I also knew there was a good man in there. I had met him and spent time with him. I knew I had to get those demons out so the good man could come back. It was difficult. I knew we'd be out, and people would be talking about 'George Jones the drunk.' Well, just wait, we're going to fix that," Nancy says with a quiet determination.

It took several years, during which Nancy endured multiple relapses, broken promises, and even violence. As she stated in an interview with the *Nashville Tennessean* in 2015, "You can't walk around and say I never got slapped, I never got hit. You know that's a lie," she said. "I'd say yes on that one."[1] Still, she also believed there was something in George worth saving, so she continued to try for several more years. Until she decided nothing was working.

"It didn't occur to me to walk away until 1999, when I had decided I'd had enough. That morning, I had found vodka bottles everywhere. Hidden in coats and boots. He had a bottle in the car with him. I'd told him I was through, I had enough. I'm not going through it anymore. I told him, 'I'm not going to put up with it. I'm getting older and I've fought these demons with you, and I think it's best that I leave.'

"He said, 'If you'll just give me one more day. Just twenty-four hours. I've been riding around here in the back pasture, and I asked God to hit me over the head with a sledgehammer if that's what it takes. Just give me time to be able to get through this and quit. I promise I'll quit.' I said I've heard that so much I'm sick of it. But he said, 'I promise, I promise. Just don't leave.' So, he took off, and sure enough, he got hit by a sledgehammer. Actually, something much worse."

On that day, March 6, 1999, as George drove off in search of an answer, he lost control of his SUV and slammed into a bridge railing. Emergency crews worked for two hours to extract him from his vehicle, and he was admitted to the hospital in critical condition. In addition to a collapsed lung and internal bleeding, Jones was placed on a ventilator to help him breath, something that could have permanently affected this voice. It would take three weeks before he could even come home.

"I don't know that he ever would have changed had that not happened," Nancy says. "He'd promised so many times. After all the times that I'd heard him say 'I quit, I quit,' and it didn't happen; I didn't believe him. But he asked to be hit over the head hard enough to make him change, and that happened. Then he said, 'I quit,' and I believed him. Be careful what you wish for, I guess." From that time on, George gave up drinking and smoking, cold turkey. He knew he had been given yet another chance at life and that he'd better not waste it.

"After that, I had *the* George Jones. All the demons he'd been fighting finally left. He was always the type of man that, when things got rough, he'd run. Then he'd come back and say help me make it better. But no one could make it better but him. Finally, he decided to do it. From 1999 to 2013, I had a man that any woman would want for a husband. He had such a big heart, and a beautiful soul. His soul was just so good.

"George never had vocal lessons. He was just gifted. They told him after the car wreck and after he had been intubated that he had to come back to do vocal coaching and rehab. He went one time and said, 'That man don't know what he's doing. I'm not doing that anymore. I'll do my own.' He practiced himself and got his voice back."

From 1999 until his death, George enjoyed life, perhaps for the first time. His daughter Susan from his first marriage lived on the grounds with George and Nancy. He entertained friends and grandchildren, riding four-wheelers in the back pasture.

According to Nancy, the two often went out and entertained, with George remaining sober, never breaking that last promise. People would ask if George minded if they had a drink. "'I'll never touch that stuff again. It doesn't bother me. I'll never do it again,' he'd say. Like there was never a temptation again," Nancy says.

Nancy knows that she had the best of George, a sober, caring man who tried his best to make up for past hurts, but that isn't always the George Jones narrative that gets the attention. Many love to go back to earlier times, but Nancy is secure in their love story. So much so that she encouraged George to reunite with Tammy Wynette for an album and series of concerts.

"I always got along well with Tammy. We were fine. But the two of them. I told him, you need to get along, you have a daughter. But those two. And why everyone thinks they were a couple. But they performed fine, I was glad to see it.

"I loved people, still to this day I love meeting his fans. But they would say, 'How did you live with him knowing he's an alcoholic?' I'd say, you gotta love them first. Then you pray for strength. And I learned how to cope with him. I learned about living with an alcoholic. Do not nag them. Don't argue with them when they're drinking. He often told me he'd never had a woman who didn't argue with him. But I knew better. What would it accomplish? I'm not going to get ahead anyway. He had to come to it on his own. It was God-given patience that allowed me to stay through all that."

Through tears, Nancy begins to talk about George's death. She has been through so much lately herself after contracting Covid-19 and developing a lung infection. Added to that is the feeling that her rock, the one who would have cared for her, wasn't there when she needed him. "After George died, it was the worst time, the worst nightmare of my life. Everything's gone and there's nobody there anymore. You sleep in a bed and reach over and no one's there anymore. Or you look at the clothes. The person who wore them is gone. There's such an emptiness there like I've never felt before. Some days, you want to get rid of everything because of all the memories, and then you don't want to get rid of anything. You just want to hold on to all of it.

Or then you get mad. Then you ask God why. I know, he was eighty-one years old. He lived a good life. But it still hurts."

In 2008, Nancy accompanied George to Washington, D.C., to receive the Kennedy Center Honor for Lifetime Achievement from President George H. W. Bush. He did some further recording but spent most of his time with his family. George and Nancy decided to undertake a "farewell" tour in 2013 that would have George playing with several of his country music contemporaries, including Kenny Rogers and Charlie Daniels. Instead, on April 18, he developed a fever, and Nancy called an ambulance because George was very sick. He spent eight days in the hospital and died on April 26, 2013.

"We were in the hospital with George. He hadn't spoken for several days, hadn't opened his eyes. The doctor said he'd go home, as it was close to George's time. I asked him to come back, to stay with us. We were all in the room at the foot of the bed. And George opened his eyes and looked out and began to talk. I tried to get to him. He said, 'Hello, I'm George Jones. I've been looking for you.' And then he was gone. I know, in my heart, that he was meeting God."

Over five thousand people, including First Lady Laura Bush, attended George's funeral, some from as far away as Japan. Nancy erected a large monument at the cemetery. Unfortunately, she has dealt with fans who misinterpret every move. When the cemetery erected a fence around George's and several other well-known graves, fans blamed Nancy, though she had no idea it had happened. "It's so easy on social media to say things and hide behind the anonymity." She has also had to have ashes of fans removed from the grave site. "That's happened twice. People are cremated and want their ashes spread on his grave. I don't understand."

"I'm not going to say that life with George was always easy. We were together thirty-two years and married for thirty of them. It took me a long time to get those demons out. I can say they were gone. I know they were gone. He got to enjoy life, he knew what it was like to have a family, to have love.

"And now it's been nine years. It's a lonely, lonely time. The worst part for me was at night. I did okay during the day because I'd stay busy, but at night, it's quiet, everything comes back.

"I knew I wanted to carry on his legacy. I didn't want to say, 'Well George Jones is gone so you won't hear anything more now.' I did not want that. He had too many fans and friends. It's still so hard to listen to his music, even today. But I press on, I make sure no one forgets."

For a few years, Nancy managed the George Jones Museum in Nashville. "I bought a place in Nashville on Second Avenue and turned it into the George Jones Museum. That was hard. Pulling out everything. I collected everything. George used to laugh at me that I needed to throw things away. Like his Nudie suits. But I collected everything."

The museum was fifty-thousand square feet and included a restaurant, nightclub, and rooftop bar. Every inch displayed something of George. But it was a tremendous amount of work. "It was so hard to go through all of it as we were setting it up. I'd laugh over something. George was always trying to give things away. He'd tell someone, "Take this Nudie suit, that'd look good on you up on stage.' And I'm like, no, no, no, please give that back! So, I had all of it and we put it in the museum." Nancy sold the museum to a holding company in 2016. It continued for a few more years but was eventually closed after being negatively impacted by both Covid-19 and the Christmas-day bombing that happened just a block away.

Nancy now spends time connecting with fans via social media and planning events in Nashville to celebrate her beloved George. She has also relied on other widows for help and support. "It helps to connect with another widow. Mine is Hazel Daniels, Charlie Daniels's wife. We text every single day. And I wore out poor Brenda Lee. I'd call her and be crying, and she'd say, 'It's okay to cry.' A widow needs someone who's been there that can help, and Hazel has been there. She's also a spiritual woman. She has helped me through. You learn that you can't wake up one day and say you're over it. Unless you have buried the person you love most, you just don't know what it's like."

Nancy recently published a book of her own to tell the story of surviving George's roughest years and persevering with him until he was able to embrace sobriety. "I'm working on a book that tells our story. I want to do my testimony. I want to do a little on my life and a little on George. I want to clear some things up. If you don't say it, people make it up, so you might as well put the truth out there. But then I'm going to write about the spiritual part. The strength that God gave me to deal with all of this and now he has saved me so that I can tell my story."

Despite all the hardship and heartache, Nancy continues to rely on her faith and to nurture the strong belief that she was put here for the purpose of saving George's life. Though there were many days of anger at George, she does not rage at her loss but instead lives in a place of gratitude. Thinking back on George's life, she remembers all the good days they had together. "It was years of hard times, yes. But I also got the best of him. God gave me some good."

5

VERA RAMONE KING

Marriage can be an odd thing if you think about it. Two people, who want to live together, dedicate their lives to each other, not because of a blood bond, but because they have a relationship based on love, mutual attraction, dedication to one another. From a religious perspective, marriage is the joining of two people into one—one heart, one mind; rarely does that actually happen in real life. Instead, there are give-and-takes, sometimes more of one than the other. When I consider my marriage, that give-and-take was sometimes challenging.

Marrying young, we both had dreams and goals not yet realized. We committed to helping each other reach these goals as part of our vows. Yet my goals and dreams were often set aside as Kevin applied to graduate school, decided our first house should be a fixer-upper, became a long-distance runner, add two kids and elderly parents into that mix, and my dreams and goals were set aside for most of our marriage as I rehabbed a house, cooked, cleaned, attended school events, scheduled doctor appointments for kids and parents, and managed other tasks of daily life. So common is this phenomenon that it now had a name: emotional labor. We were not unusual in our struggles. It took months of therapy for us to realize the inequity in our relationship, understand it, and work at correcting it, which Kevin willingly did. He devised schedules, created menus, taught our

Dee Dee and Vera on a flight to London Courtesy of Vera Ramone collection

kids to do their own laundry, and sent me off to grad school. It was working and most likely saved our marriage to face this challenge. But six months later, he received a fatal diagnosis.

Once Kevin became ill, everything that either of us had taken on as personal development or hobbies was set aside. For two years, saving his life was our only focus. I made deals with the universe: I'll give up my dreams of being a writer, I'll drop out of graduate school, if only . . . But his condition only worsened.

After he died, all the things I had once wished to have time for seemed frivolous. I couldn't write without being racked with guilt. I completed grad school because Kevin made me promise I would. I found after he died that he had once written about the "happy places" he traveled to in his head when he was filled with pain and unable to move. At the top was attending my graduation. He supported me more outwardly after our therapy discussions, but of course, he had supported me quietly all along. Had it been him, and the full, busy life we had created together, that had held me back? Or had it been me, all along? Grieving has a way of bringing these situations into sharp focus: loss will stab you in the heart while hindsight whacks you over the head.

I first spoke with Vera Ramone King by phone to plan our meeting. As the former wife of Dee Dee Ramone, the bassist and a founding member of the punk rock band the Ramones, Vera lived through the wildest of the 1970s punk rock movement. Listening to her say their names—Joey, Johnny, Tommy, and Dee Dee—in her thick Queens accent took me right back to New York in 1976. Today, Vera lives in Florida in a peaceful community of palm trees and identical pink condos. Though she still has the spark and spunk of a 70s punk queen, she also exudes a calm resolve, something that came to her in the last few years, first after her divorce from Dee Dee and again after his death. Vera is charming and welcoming as we meet and settle in to talk about her life with Dee Dee.

"After all these years, it's still very painful for me. I grieve on the day of his passing. I celebrate his birthday. I try to keep his legacy alive because that's what I think he would have wanted. I don't want him to be forgotten. And all the boys, they all went so young. Joey was forty-nine, just short of his fiftieth birthday, Dee Dee was fifty-one, Johnny was fifty-five. They never got their due until years later, and then they're all gone so young."

Dee Dee Ramone was born Douglas Colvin in 1951 into a military family, so they relocated often. He spent much of his youth in Berlin, but when his parents split, Douglas moved with his mother and sister to Queens, New York. He began playing music in high school with his friends, John Cummings, Jeff Hyman, and Thomas Erdelyi. After learning that Paul McCartney signed into hotels under the pseudonym of Paul Ramon, Douglas suggested that the band call themselves the Ramones and that they adopt Ramone as their own last names. Though not really related, the band was made up of Johnny (John Cummings), Joey (Jeff Hyman), Tommy (Thomas Erdelyi), and Dee Dee (Douglas) Ramone. Dee Dee contributed several songs to the Ramones discography, including some of their most popular.

Playing their first gig at Manhattan's legendary CBGB's nightclub in 1974, the band was heralded by a small group of fans as something completely new, in stark difference to the staid, overproduced and orchestrated rock music of the day. They quickly became regulars at places like CBGB and Max's Kansas City playing powerful, stripped-down, catchy songs, most only two-to-three minutes in length. The four of them were in many ways and by many accounts the band that was the prototype of the punk-rock movement in the United States. Their music pulled from catchy 60s pop songs, influenced by basic garage rock and filled with quirky pop culture commentary. As their counterparts like The Clash and the Sex Pistols changed British music, the Ramones blazed the same trail in America. Yet, despite constant touring and some amount of radio airplay on alternative stations, the band never seemed to catch on as they should have. Their biggest US hit, Dee Dee's "Rockaway Beach," was their highest-charting single in America, climbing only to #66 on the Billboard chart. Though mainstream radio ignored the band, they developed a steady following through nonstop touring of the United States, the UK, and Europe. "They could never get radio play," Vera says. "The guys worked really, really hard but they never had a hit. They had some success with 'Baby I Love You,' which Phil Spector produced. KROQ in LA played their music, and WLAR in Long Island played them. But whatever success they had was from constant touring."

In the years since the band ended, they have received overdue recognition as pioneers in the fast, beat-heavy, elemental pop songs that fueled both punk rock and post-punk, and which became their signature style. Many of those songs were written by Dee Dee, who played a significant role in the band's impactful career even though he had been replaced in the band by the time they called it quits.

"It was November of 1977. I was upstairs at Max's Kansas City," Vera says about first meeting Dee Dee. It wasn't unusual for her to be hanging out where there was live music. "I've been a music fan all my life. I saw the Beatles at Shea Stadium when I was twelve. I had to beg my parents to let me go. I loved the Beatles. I fell in love with live music. The whole British Invasion—Dave Clark Five, The Kinks, T. Rex. I loved the fashion of Biba and all the 60s fashion.

"I was facing the wall at Max's that was covered in mirrors. There were a bunch of photos on the wall of all the musicians that had been playing there, the Ramones, Debby Harry, others. It was a Sunday night, so they weren't playing, but Dee Dee walked in. I wasn't facing him, but I saw him in the mirror and recognized who he was. I saw him looking at me in the mirror, but I didn't act starstruck or anything. I had a blackberry brandy on the rocks because it was really cold out. And he ordered the same drink. He didn't know what I was drinking, but we just had the same drink.

"After a while he walks up to me and says, 'Hi, I'm Dee Dee.' And I said, 'Nice to meet you, Dee Dee.' But I didn't respond like I was a fan. I acted cool. Then, a few minutes went by, and he came back and said, 'I'm Dee Dee,' like insinuating that I really should know who he was. And I still played it cool. We talked for a while. This was 1977, and they were heading to London to play the Rainbow Room. He said, 'Can I have your number? I'll call you from there. And I want to call you when I get back.' I didn't think much of it. I certainly didn't think he would call.

"But then he called the next day. He told me he was in a phone booth, and he only had a minute because they were leaving. I could hear someone in the background, and it was the woman whose place he was staying at yelling at him that he had to go. She was dragging him out of the phone booth. He kept saying, 'I gotta go, but I'll call you.'

"Then, closer to Christmas, I had been out with friends, and I got home, and my mother said, 'someone named Dee Dee called you from England.' And I said, 'You're kidding! Did he say he'd call back?' and she said 'Yeah, he said he'd call you back.'" So I waited, and finally he called. He said he was coming home in January, and he wanted to see me. I said I'd see him when he got home."

The shows in the UK helped solidify the band's popularity abroad. Everyone from Marc Bolan of T. Rex to the Sex Pistols, Clash, the Pretenders, and the Damned attended those shows. And the members of U2, who were seventeen and not yet a band, knew they were seeing the future of the music they wanted to play when they first saw the Ramones in Dublin. In fact, the Ramones would become a huge influence on U2.

Once they returned to New York, Dee Dee kept his promise and called Vera.

"He was staying at [Ramones's manager] Danny Fields's apartment. That's where I went to meet him, and I moved in about a week later. After that first date, we were inseparable. By the end of January, I was going on tour with them. We toured across the country in a van. We went from New York through Ohio, Chicago, Detroit, all the way to LA. The Runaways were opening for them. We went up the West coast to Seattle and Portland, then south to Arizona, Louisiana, and Florida. It was a three-month tour. From Florida, they started up the East coast to North and South Carolina, but I left because I had to go back to work. I had a regular job and they expected me to come back.

"It was hard, but it was also fun and exciting. We really got to know each other spending all day and all night together. It's really quite amazing to think back on it. The shows every night were great. It really was good fun. So much fun." The Ramones were playing smaller venues during this tour but were well-received by die-hard followers around the country.

"I was surprised to see packed venues in Idaho and smaller towns," Vera says.

When the tour ended in April, Vera and Dee Dee were reunited and got engaged. They were married the following September. "Dee Dee wanted the Dead Boys to play our wedding, but my dad was paying for the wedding, so that wasn't acceptable. Tommy and Joey were there. Arturo [Vega, the Ramones's artistic director], Seymour and Linda Stein [cofounder of Sire Records], Tommy, Joey, the band's tour manager, Monte Melnick and Danny Fields were there. It was very nice.

"For a while after we were married, the other guys didn't want a wife at the shows. Especially Johnny. I think he made a policy about no wives, but of course, we were the only ones married. I had seen them a thousand times, so it didn't really bother me to not see them. I traveled to see them if I wanted to. But local shows, I would go if I wanted to and not go if I didn't feel like it.

"But then when I wasn't going to the shows anymore, the rest of the band started asking me to come to shows because they needed a babysitter. Nobody wanted to deal with Dee Dee when he got out of hand."

Vera tells of Dee Dee's response to going on tour in Europe just days after they were married. "He was so anxious about touring and about being separated from me so soon after our wedding that he showed up at the airport to go to Helsinki after medicating himself with a concoction of Tuinal, Valium, Seconal, and Quaaludes. The flight was delayed, so Dee Dee had to be carried onto the plane.

"Once they started the tour, he would call me five or six times a day reversing the charges. We ended up with phone bills that were more than our New York rent. It was cheaper for me to just tour with the band. I met them in London and stayed on tour. Caring for Dee Dee became my full-time job. Not just the day-to-day caring for him, but also constantly trying to rehabilitate him and get him sober."

The band continued to tour and develop their small but die-hard following. They also recorded, turning out at least one album each year from 1977 through the mid-1980s. In 1979, the band went to Los Angeles to film *Rock 'n' Roll High School*, a comedic movie produced by Roger Corman. They recorded an album with Phil Spector, releasing that along with the soundtrack to *Rock 'n' Roll High School*.

"The first time I saw Dee Dee overdose was in LA while they were filming *Rock 'n' Roll High School*. We were staying at the Tropicana Hotel. I had gone out just to the corner grocery store for twenty minutes. When I got back, Dee Dee was nowhere to be found. Finally, we found him at a party at the back of the hotel behind the bungalows. A bunch of punk bands were there, and Dee Dee and Joey were in the middle of it having a great time. Dee Dee had taken Quaaludes, Tuinal, methadone, and was drinking hard liquor. He was incoherent, running around in a frenzy. He collapsed in the parking lot. The LA sheriffs were called, and they ended up taking him away handcuffed in an ambulance. I went to the hospital the following morning and was just so relieved that he was alive. I cried. I thought we could leave the hospital together and put it all behind us. But, oh god, really it was just the beginning.

"They didn't know how to treat his drug issues in those days. They had him on lithium for a while, and his hair started falling out. I called the doctor and told him Dee Dee was losing all his hair. He said, 'well, do you want him bald or dead?' What a thing to say. Obviously, he's a musician. He couldn't be a bald Ramone. The look was part of his job.

"I'm thinking, my God, those are the things the band is singing about. And sometimes he'd forget to take the medications, other times he'd take too many. If I went out for a while, I'd come home and find him crawling on the floor. I'd say, 'Tell me what you took. Tell me how many.' You could overdose on those drugs pretty easily. It got to the point where I couldn't leave even to just go shopping.

"I was there with him all the time. I took him to meetings. I sat with him in meetings and therapy. I wasn't an alcoholic or addict, but I would be there to support him. I did what I could to try to understand. I could never understand why he was drawn to that stuff, especially the dope."

"Did he feel that it made him more creative?" I ask.

"Dee Dee did his best work straight. Maybe smoking a little weed. But not on any dope. He wrote a lot of good songs straight. 'Pet Sematary,' he wrote, and 'I Believe in Miracles.' He did great work without it.

"The worst was when he locked himself in the bathroom of our apartment and said he was going to kill himself. I tried for hours to talk him out of it. I didn't know what he was going to do, what he had with him in there. And I couldn't get him to come out. I finally had to call my dad and my brother to come help me at three in the morning. He listened to my father and respected him. My father talked to him with kid gloves. Dee Dee had a strained relationship with both his parents, but that night, my dad talked him out of that bathroom. I really owe him for that one.

"Other times he would tell me, he just wanted to die. He would say he's no good and he just wanted to die. Like there was self-loathing. But it was his mental illness.

"When he was good, he was a sweetheart, but when he was bad, oh boy. It was a major part of our relationship. He was a handful. A real handful. He was bipolar, but they didn't know how to treat it. He was on tour, somewhere in Texas, and he called me. He said 'I'm gonna play you something I just wrote.' And he played me 'Funky Man' over the phone. I encouraged him to have an outlet, to be creative, because it kept him from doing drugs. If he was feeling creative and having fun, I encouraged it. I couldn't tell him that he was never going to be a rap star.

"Then he wrote the song 'Baby Doll.' He took it to Seymour, and Seymour loved the song and gave him a contract on the spot to do an album. But it wasn't a rap song, it was a love song. He wrote the song for me. He always called me Baby Doll. It went from there. He started writing playful, fun songs and having fun while he wrote. But the touring and recording, it got to be too much."

As Dee Dee's health declined and his behavior became more volatile, he told Vera that he wanted to leave the band. "He said he wanted to go play guitar in Central Park with a monkey on his shoulder. Or he wanted to be a doorman. Things we both knew he wasn't going to do. But he was tired of the music, tired of the constant touring. He was tired of writing songs about cretins. But that's what the others wanted. Those were Ramones songs, but Dee Dee wanted to grow.

"Caring for him, being a babysitter and a policewoman, I got tired of it after a while. Dee Dee needed to have a partner that would keep him in line, which I tried to do. I tried to support him, but I couldn't go along with the idea of leaving the band with no plan. I told him I wasn't onboard and that I wasn't going along with his idea of leaving the band and becoming wanderers. Which is what he ended up doing. He lived in Amsterdam for a while. He was staying in England for a while.

"We kept in touch, and he would call me from all over the world. He called me once from England, where he was living in a flat with another family living upstairs. He didn't have a phone so he would use theirs.

"At any moment of the day, it would be like a switch flipping, and suddenly you'd be with a different person. And I knew he was getting in deeper, but there was no one to help him since I had left and I couldn't help him. Once he returned to the States, he would still call me to be his voice of calm and reason. He'd call to get opinions or run song lyrics by me. Always asking what he should do or where he should go. I knew it wouldn't last if we got back together. I was thirty-nine, and I needed to be settled. All that drama was just too much for me."

Vera and Dee Dee remained married but separated for five years. She continued to keep in touch with him and tried to monitor his behavior from afar.

"He called me one time and asked if I still had one of the bass guitars he had given me. He gave it to me to give to my nephew. I should have told him I didn't have it, but I said yes, that I still had it. He made me meet him in Queens and give it back to him. He was with a girlfriend. They took the bass, and I'm sure they hocked it so they could get high. A few weeks later, he called me again, this time from a phone booth on Ninth Street, in the pouring rain at 1:00 a.m. I could hear the rain. And he said, 'Vera, I want to come home. Please let me come home.' But I couldn't do it. I told him, 'I can't do it again.' It hurt me. It hurt me so much. I could hear him, sounding so desperate."

Vera sits with this thought for a moment, wiping tears.

"It hurts now thinking about telling him. But I knew I couldn't go back. It was a revolving door, in and out. After that, I didn't feel safe even coming home from work by myself at night. I didn't know if he would be waiting for me or make demands. I never knew what kind of state he was in. So I had to move."

During that time, Dee Dee left the Ramones and was replaced by CJ Ramone. He attempted solo work and joined or formed several other short-lived bands, releasing two albums. Dee Dee and Vera also worked to determine their divorce settlement. A formal separation agreement was already in place.

"He gave me half of everything. He didn't even dispute it. He knew I deserved it. He knew he wouldn't be alive if it wasn't for me."

All that remained was for Dee Dee to sign the papers.

"Nobody I knew wanted to serve him the final divorce papers," Vera says. "Finally, I got someone I was working with. His name was Big Mike, and he had that name for a reason. He was a big guy! He said, 'I'll do it.' Dee Dee was living at the Chelsea Hotel at the time. Big Mike went to Dee Dee's room, knocked on the door, and asked Dee Dee for his signature. Dee Dee thought he was signing an autograph, but he was signing the divorce papers.

"That was another fiasco. Keith Green, the photographer, was in Dee Dee's room, and he said Dee Dee went ballistic when he found out that he had signed the divorce papers. He wasn't expecting that. By then, we were married fourteen years, and he just wasn't expecting it. He thought we'd go on being married but separated forever.

"But after he got served, his accountant referred him to an attorney. And I got an attorney. And then the divorce started, which lasted five years. Going back and forth, back and forth. By then, I had moved on. I was living with a boyfriend who would become my second husband. Dee Dee lived with three or four women during this time. As crazy as they might be, they still couldn't keep up with him, so he'd soon be on to the next one.

"They'd call me for advice! I guess they figured, if I could live with him for twelve years, maybe I could tell them how to do it. But I didn't know what to tell them. He wasn't going to change."

The divorce proceedings carried on, with Dee Dee's attorneys fighting Vera "tooth and nail and getting very expensive." Vera wanted to remarry but couldn't. Tracking Dee Dee down during this time was one of the reasons for the delay. He would live for a few months in various cities around the world and then eventually return to the Chelsea for weeks at a time.

The separation and divorce agreements stipulated that Dee Dee was not to write or speak publicly about Vera or about them as a couple.

"He was fantasizing all the time. Nearly everything that came out of him was a story. You couldn't trust anything he said to be true. I thought, someone will look at this, either now or years later, and think, 'What was wrong with her?' And it was mutual. I couldn't speak or write about us either."

Just before the divorce was finalized, Dee Dee called Vera one last time. "I was living in Florida, and we were still communicating once in a while, back and forth, about divorce things. He called me and told me I abandoned him. He said he was living in the Chelsea Hotel and was miserable. I told him I didn't abandon him. I just couldn't go on living the lifestyle that he chose for us. He thought I would just go with him and live like a vagabond, and that might be okay when you're twenty. But we were approaching forty, and it wasn't for me anymore.

"I tried to talk to him and tell him that I hadn't abandoned him, that I still cared for him and felt close to him. He said, 'Are you coming back to me?' And I said 'No, I'm not coming back.' And then there was dead silence on the phone. He was still hoping after all that time and everything both of us had done. Then I told him I was getting married. Ugh. He took a long, long pause."

At this, Vera pauses as well, thinking of this last conversation with her ex-husband. "After a couple minutes, he said to me, 'Goodbye, Vera.' And those were the last words he said to me."

Vera wipes away tears. We're sitting in her safe, comfortable home in matching chairs, sipping glasses of wine. She has done everything she can to make me feel welcome and at ease. We've snacked on antipasto, laughed at jokes as though we're together at a girlfriends reunion. The feeling has been one of two women telling secrets of their long-ago love affairs—the highlights and the challenges. But with this, the mood becomes somber for the first time. It's clear that she still loves Dee Dee, and there is also a sense of guilt and regret for leaving him despite having done all she could for so many years to try to save him. This extra responsibility in their marriage shouldn't have fallen to Vera, and yet it did, leaving her to sometimes feel that she could have done more.

"Our divorce was final in March. I tried for so long. But he never got better. He got worse. He quit the band, didn't want to take his medications. I told him, 'Without taking your medication, I can't live with you. I'm scared for my life.' He'd get so angry he'd punch a hole in the wall. At a certain point, I realized, I could end up like Nancy Spungen. I didn't want that. And he never stopped that. He could be so easily set off. We were always on pins and needles.

"But that wasn't all there was to Dee Dee. When things were good, he was the sweetest person. He was very giving and loving. Everywhere we went, he held my hand, for years. We stayed together because we loved each other. He was very generous. He would always bring me gifts for no reason. When he was good, he was such a good person.

"And I understood that when he was bad, it wasn't him, it was his disease. I knew that's what it was; I lived with it. Every day. You get to know the signs. I'd know what was coming and then be walking on eggshells waiting for him. Every relationship has ups and downs, but ours were just extreme."

Vera remarried in September after her divorce from Dee Dee was final. She would hear from Dee Dee occasionally, but that came to an end when he married Barbara Zampini, a fan he met while touring in Argentina. Dee Dee and Barbara formed multiple bands and were married until Dee Dee's death in 2002.

"I hadn't heard from Dee Dee in a couple years. Then, out of the blue one day, my sister came by the office where I worked. I saw her pull in through the window of my office, and I thought, I wonder what she's doing here in the middle of the day. She came in and asked if she could talk to me outside for a few minutes, and I said, 'What are you doing here?' I told my boss I was going to go outside because my sister was there. She told me that Dee Dee had died. She had heard it on the radio, and she didn't want me to hear it from someone else. I just kept asking, 'What are you saying? What are you saying?' And then she told me that they were reporting that he passed away from an overdose. And I just remember that I started screaming, 'No, no.' It was so unreal to me. I thought he had been clean. I thought I had gotten him through the hardest part, and now he was going to be clean. And he had been clean for years, six or eight, at least. We all thought he was out of the woods, but I think he just wanted to go back to it one more time. He had been clean for a long time, and his body couldn't handle it. He thought he could do what he used to do, but he couldn't.

"After I learned he died, I called his mother. I kept in touch with her over the years, and we'd talk every couple of months, on her birthday or Christmas. When I called, she already knew. Someone had called her. She asked me to see if we could go to the funeral. We were told it would be alright, so the two of us went, me and his mother, Toni. I was able to have a few moments with him privately. He had bought me a dolphin ring on his last overseas tour with the Ramones when they were in Greece. The tail had diamonds and there were rubies for the eyes. The dolphin has some meaning of eternal love in Greek mythology. I put that ring in his left coat pocket. That was my gift to him. I wanted him to have it always."

Dee Dee's funeral took place in Hollywood, and he is buried in the Hollywood Forever cemetery, not far from his former bandmate Johnny.

"He really had tried so hard to get clean, and I thought he was happy. But you know, he was still troubled. He still had his demons," Vera says. At the time of his death, friends and family estimated that Dee Dee had been clean, especially from heroin, for eight years. He had reunited with his Ramones bandmates just months earlier to be inducted into the Rock and Roll Hall of Fame.

"Dee Dee even told people don't do drugs. That was his message after he got clean. Don't do drugs. Look at me and don't do drugs. I think he meant that. His heart was in the right place, but he slipped up. And that time, he just couldn't be saved.

"I miss him still. I've always felt connected to him. Even when he was living with other people, he still called me. We were best friends; we grew up together. It wasn't that we stopped loving each other, we just couldn't live together. I couldn't live with what he was doing. But we shared so much, and no one knew him better than me. We could look at each other and know what the other one was thinking. I couldn't listen to Ramones music for a while after he passed. It would just make me so sad.

"He's come to me in dreams a few times. Very vivid, very clear. I've never slept well. I'm up and down, awake, asleep, so I never remember dreams. But those dreams, the dreams with him, I remember. In one, we were sitting under a tree, and he was giving me advice and telling me what to do.

"In 2009, after he died, I wanted to write about us, thinking that the divorce agreement was no longer in effect. But his estate still came after me and sued me. It was another expensive and time-consuming lawsuit. But for me, I just wanted to tell the truth about our relationship. I had no ill intent. It was very cathartic to get to put everything down on paper. I didn't want to hurt anybody. The lawsuit went all the way to the Supreme Court of the State of New York. It was ruled in my favor, so I could write my book.

"I've had all the emotions. I think about the good times, and it makes me smile, still. And I think about the bad times, and I still get sad. Writing the book helped me to process and to release all that I was holding inside. I came full circle."

Did it bother or hurt Vera, I wondered, that as much of her time being Dee Dee's caretaker as being his wife, trying to keep him sober or get him well. Though we try to always see such things as acts of love, they can also, with time, come to feel burdensome. And they certainly take their toll on any relationship.

"If I had to change something, I wouldn't change anything," she says, emphatically. "I have no regrets. I did the best I could for as long as I could. I know that. We do our best to care for those who need us. Dee Dee deserved to have that care. And I continue to uphold his memory and legacy as best as I can. I'll never say bad things about him. I want the kids just learning about the Ramones now to remember the best of him. He deserves that, too."

6

ANNETTE WALTER-LAX

It's been a great realization for me that so many of the women I've interviewed were so young when their lives were completely upended by wild circumstances. I think of myself at twenty-one or twenty-two and wonder if I could have kept up, if I could have handled the wild situations or the egos. I know the answer. Though I had dreams of being the rock and roll girlfriend, I now know I never could have handled what these men demanded, especially at eighteen or nineteen, when I struggled just to live away from my family at college.

"Maybe you need to be so young though, to want to pursue this lifestyle," says Annette Walter-Lax, wisely. Annette was the eighteen-year-old girlfriend of The Who's drummer Keith Moon for the last four years of his life. She endured all the insanity for which Keith became famous, along with the torment of trying to save the man she loved from himself.

"If I had met someone like Keith, let's say when I was twenty-five or thirty, I would have thought twice about the whole thing, and probably would have walked away. But at eighteen, I was young and adventurous, and I was always a bit of a rebel. I didn't think about what might happen. I just thought it was all very exciting."

Annette had come to London from Sweden in 1972 in search of a modeling career, just after graduating high school.

Annette and Keith on the beach in Malibu. Photo by Kent Gavin/Mirrorpix/Getty Images

She worked as an *au pair* and sold blue jeans at shops in King's Road and Kensington Market while making connections in the fashion industry. For two years, her career moved steadily as she established herself. Her blonde hair and blue-eyed Swedish good looks were exactly what magazines were looking for, and she kept herself busy with photo shoots. A friend stopped by her apartment one day and noticed Annette tapping the rhythm of a song on the radio.

"I loved music, but I wasn't much into rock and roll. I was more of a disco girl, you know. I loved going out to the disco-theques to dance. So, I wasn't into The Who's music. I remember when the album *Tommy* came out. It was all over, but I thought no, not interested, I can't dance to that."

"I was staying with a friend who knew Keith, and one day he noticed me tapping my fingers on the table to the music, and he said, 'I can introduce you to a real drummer.' I didn't know who Keith was, but my friend took me to this apartment which, oddly enough, was the same apartment Keith would die in four years later. My friend took me up there and introduced us. He said, 'This is Keith. Keith, this is my friend, Annette.' We shook hands and said hello and nice to meet you. He did his whole English gentleman thing, bowing. He was very theatrical.

"And he had a Swedish girlfriend there. I don't know who she was, but it was all very proper. We talked for a while. My friend and I left, eventually. Nothing more was said. I told my friend, 'Well, that was a nice evening. What a funny man.'

"A few weeks went by, and I had a date to go to Tramp, which was the place to go at the time. And there was Keith. He came up to me and wanted me to join his table, but I was on a date, so I told him, thank you but I have a date. We sat down and then, all of a sudden, someone came up to my date and escorted him somewhere. I don't know what was said. But then a waiter came to me and said, 'Miss Annette, we need you to join this table.' So, I just went. I didn't understand what was going on, but that was it. That was Keith's table, and I was there. I asked him, what happened to my date, and Keith said, 'Don't worry, I paid him to take care of that.' I asked, 'You paid who to do what?' I still wonder sometimes what happened to my date!

"Later that evening, we went back to Kit Lambert's apartment [Lambert and Chris Stamp were The Who's managers]. Keith was staying at Kit Lambert's because he was going through his divorce and didn't live at home. He occupied the top floor of this apartment. When we got there, he already had a girlfriend there, the American actress Joy Bang. We got there so late, or early I guess, that Joy was already awake and planning to leave that day to fly back to America. There was commotion about her leaving and going to the airport and how late Keith had stayed out. So, I got installed in a room. I looked around and there was a big waterbed in the room, and I thought, oh, this is pretty decadent. But Keith had to hide the fact that I was in the room below until Joy left. Then, I spent the day with Keith, and I went home.

"The next day, he sent his car to pick me up. This big white Rolls Royce pulled up outside my apartment and there was Dougal, Keith's personal assistant, at the wheel. So, I got escorted back to Kit Lambert's house. We were a couple, right there and then."

I laugh at this. "I can't imagine," I tell her. "Not just getting that kind of attention from someone like Keith Moon, but the matter-of-factness of both his affections and his deceptions." Annette laughs as well. "Oh, that's how it was, that whole time . . . what wild memories."

Keith Moon, the youngest member of The Who, was born just after World War II in Wembley, UK. He was noted as a "mischievous child" by his teachers and got into trouble even as a young boy, his love of pranks and destruction coming through in his teen years. He was playing drums by fourteen, and most could see that he had an aptitude. He began referring to himself as a future rock star during secondary school. Young Keith was often described as hyper, energetic, restless, even out of control. It didn't help that he enjoyed taking drugs, first legal speed and then more illicit drugs, which contributed to his hyperactivity and ability to bang the drums for hours on end. He joined his first real band, The Beachcombers, in 1962, answering an ad in the local newspaper.

Keith soon determined that his Beachcomber bandmates, though talented and doing well on the local circuit, didn't have the desire to be as big as The Beatles or the Rolling Stones. Though he never technically left the band, he did begin looking for other opportunities. Around that same time, another band, the Detours, had just changed their name to The Who and were considering dropping their drummer, a man five years older than the others, who had a wife and child at home and who was tiring of the life of a rock and roll drummer. After auditioning Keith and seeing his talent, The Who immediately hired him as the fourth member. Soon after, the combination of Keith's finely tuned yet wholly erratic drumming and Pete Townshend's angry approach to his guitar (to which he would eventually add arm windmills for full effect) tapped into a frustration and antagonism among the teens in their audience. They knew they were on to something.

Shortly after joining the band, Keith also met his first wife, Kim, a former convent-school student who was working as a model, They met at a show in London and Keith pursued her until she relented and became his girlfriend, and then his wife. Their marriage was troubled from the start and doesn't seem to have ever been settled, even after they had a daughter, Mandy. The band, however, was on a different course. After the success of their first single, "I Can't Explain," The Who's popularity grew alongside other 60s British pop bands like The Kinks and the Faces. They put out a string of hits, including "My Generation" and "Magic Bus," and toured nearly nonstop for four solid years.

The playing and then the touring solidified Keith's reputation as a wild-man, both onstage and off. He trashed hotel rooms, eventually getting himself banned from Holiday Inns after a particularly raucous night celebrating his birthday with fellow Brits Herman's Hermits in Flint, Michigan. His drinking became the thing of legend, even among other rock bands that The Who toured with. And he seemed to deal with the havoc he caused by spending lavishly on houses, cars, and jewelry.

His relationship with Kim, almost always troubled, finally ended when she decided she'd had enough of his exploits, which she had recounted as often dangerous for her and for their young daughter. An infamous photo shows Keith pointing out a champagne bottle he had thrown at Kim that had landed in the wall and had then been framed for posterity. Kim is quoted often, as Annette would later be, discussing the dichotomy of Keith—how he could be sweet and loving, talking her into returning to their home and marriage, and then, often assisted by drinking, how he would become the "other Keith," the aggressive, violent tormenter that she finally decided she could no longer live with.

It was during this time that Keith took up with several women, from Pamela deBarres, one of Frank Zappa's GTOs, to models and actresses like Joy Bang. He loved his time in the United States while on tour and assuaged his loneliness by spending money, taking drugs (leading to multiple overdoses and hospital visits), and sleeping with a variety of women. Adding to this tricky mental state was the news that the band had no plans for touring or recording, leaving Keith with the need to fill his time and deal with the question of who he was without the craziness of being on the road as the wild rock drummer. It was into this environment that eighteen-year-old Annette entered Keith's life, joining him at Kit Lambert's apartment because he had been forced to leave his lavish British estate, Tara, when he and Kim broke up and she filed for divorce.

Annette quickly learned that dating Keith Moon was not going to be a simple, quiet affair. "I think I was in shock for the first few weeks knowing him," she says. "And I certainly thought the way he acted, all the alcohol and late-night partying, was just how rock stars lived. We went to the clubs nearly every night, and everyone there was drunk."

Shortly after meeting Annette, Keith entered a rehab facility, which presented her with a calmer, quieter Keith for a few weeks. Then, in late July of 1974, Annette and Keith traveled along with Pete Townshend to Atlanta, where they joined Eric Clapton on his US tour.

"Pete originally wanted to go join the Clapton tour, and Keith and I kind of came with. We traveled to several cities in the United States. While we were on the road, Keith decided that he wanted to pursue this acting career. I didn't know that when we left the UK; I thought we were on a trip. But he decided to live in Los Angeles. We traveled a lot and went back and forth to London a lot. But we had a house in Malibu where we lived for four years starting in 1974."

Early on in their relationship, Annette began to see the explosive side of Keith, the side that he was known for, *that* Keith Moon. "Almost straightaway, I saw this person. When we arrived in Atlanta, that was the first very long flight for me. I wasn't used to that travel. I didn't go to the Clapton concert because I was too tired. I wanted to stay in the hotel and rest. Keith agreed and went to the show, but when he came back, he became very violent. He wanted to order room service and they had shut down. He got very angry about that, so he proceeded to smash the hotel room. He ripped the phone out of the wall, knocked over the furniture, and broke it to pieces. Eventually, he passed out.

"I was sitting in the corner of the room, quite scared. Thinking, what is going on? I called Pete, but he just said, 'Yes, he's always like that.' But then, the next day, Keith acted as if everything was back to normal. When I brought it up, he said, 'Oh, I did that?' 'Did I?' 'Oh no, did I really do this? Oh wow.' But we looked around and, well, the furniture, you might as well put in the fireplace. It was all broken up.

"You know, I was young, I thought it would stop, that it can't be forever. And part of it was just thinking, 'This is what rock stars do.' But yes, every time I was thinking, this can't keep happening like this. Each and every time."

There is the adventure-seeking, try-anything-once side of being young, but that is also accompanied by naivety. Both clearly came into play with Annette's feelings for Keith. An older, more realistic woman may have suspected that he wouldn't change. She may also have understood the need to leave. That initial sense of adventure fades with age and reality, as does our hope and belief that things will be different. While Annette hoped for things to be different, instead, they continued, and Keith solidified a reputation for being out of control. Though he had episodes of violence against his first wife, Annette maintains he was never violent with her.

"He never laid a finger on me. I didn't know the horror stories about his ex-wife Kim and how he treated her. I hadn't a clue. I've only heard those in recent years. I certainly didn't know then those things had happened. I was there when Keith was destructive, but he wasn't abusive to me, ever. The anger, or whatever it was that motivated him, always seemed to be toward things he could destroy, not hurting me."

After Keith and Annette purchased a house in Malibu, it quickly became the place to hang out. "It was a strange time, with so many people always in the house," Annette says. "Keith wanted the attention; he needed it. We got into this Hollywood thing, and I was so amazed. I remember thinking, how, just the year before, I was just a seventeen-year-old back in Stockholm, and all of a sudden, I'm now sitting in Hollywood, talking to Jack Nicholson about his dogs. It was just surreal. Keith was crazy, yes, but it was just another part of this whole situation that was unbelievable for me.

"But I was concerned about Keith and his health. Four years can go by very quickly. I got concerned after about the first year, knowing that he needed help. He needed rehab, he needed professional help. Dougal and I tried to help. We got him into Cedars Sinai. We also got help from our neighbors, Larry Hagman, the actor, and his wife, who was Swedish, and she and I got on very well. They were very sweet people. They helped us a lot in trying to find a solution. They also wanted Keith to recover. He went into Cedars Sinai for a while, but when he came out, they all knew it didn't work. Within weeks, he was drinking heavily again and spending thousands of dollars to maintain his cocaine habit.

"I wish we had known then what we know now about mental illness, because that was the part that was missing. No one understood it then, really. He was just considered a drunk lunatic that could smash up places. Isn't that entertaining, everyone thought?

"But what we know now is that it is a symptom of something else. He didn't get the right help because it didn't exist at that time. But we did what we could, we tried to get him help. And we all wanted him to get help because he was such a sweet, kind person. He had a very big heart, and he liked ordinary people. But just having him dry out, thinking that, if he could go a few weeks without, he could go for the rest of this life, well, that wasn't the answer." Many of his friends, including bandmates Pete Townshend, Roger Daltrey, and others who interacted regularly with Keith, have talked about his lovable personality, his kindness, but they also understood that he suffered from tremendous insecurity and self-doubt.

Annette believes that along with longstanding mental health issues—Keith had possibly a neurodiversity, or even being bipolar—Keith also struggled with the pressures of rock and roll life. When it was just the two of them together, he could be quiet and calm for long periods. He loved nothing more than to lounge around, reading books and watching television shows. "People wouldn't believe that it was the same Keith Moon that they saw and read about," she says. "And that is what gave me hope the whole time to stay and hold on and hope and hope. Of course, he's going to grow out of this. Of course, it's going to blow over. And this hope is what stayed with me, what kept me there for the four years. Not just because I wanted it, but because I loved him and he really deserved to be well, to get rid of this demon.

"He was always feeling like less-than where the band was concerned. That he wasn't as good as Pete or as popular as Roger. He seemed to love being in Los Angeles, but it meant that he wasn't with the band, and he worried about that. He didn't know what he would do if there was no Who."

"We had two lovely vacations. One in Tahiti. We stayed at a hotel and met a woman who worked there who invited us to her home. She lived in a hut. And we had lunch, this local Tahitian meal. She spoke English, so we had this lovely visit, sitting on the floor. And Keith was so relaxed and sweet. He probably could have stayed in that hut for the rest of his life.

"The summer before he passed, we went scuba diving in Mauritius. The band at the hotel asked him onstage to drum, and he became angry. He didn't want to. I could tell in his eyes that he was really mad. He wanted to be allowed to be on vacation like everyone else. But he did it. He went up on stage and smashed this drum kit, just as they wanted.

"Through the rest of the time, he was so nice, and so sweet. But as we flew back to London, he got drunk on the plane. He assaulted the stewardess. They made a stop in the Seychelles to pick up more passengers, and they threw him off the plane. He got angry and threw his briefcase into one of the engines. He ended up in the Seychelles jail for the night. By that point, I had it. I stayed on the plane and continued to London. A couple days later, he comes back and acts like nothing happened. He came back on Kenyan Air, and he had nice words to say about them because they let him on the plane!

"People read about it and thought, well, that's just typical Keith. Isn't it funny? But I knew there was something more. Why would he do that when he had been so happy just days before? Was it just the alcohol? Or did he not want to go back to London, to that world? It really was two sides of the Moon." On the one hand, Annette believes, Keith craved attention, but on the other, he wasn't equipped to handle it.

As the situation worsened, Annette tells of the two times that she left Keith. "I was completely emotionally and mentally exhausted. I just felt totally drained and needed a break. Worse, I felt like I had failed. Like I had failed him and his needs. We were apart for a few weeks, but then he would turn up again and would cry and beg me to return. I would come back and try again," Annette looks off into the Nordic darkness, and I can't help but feel that she still has some of those feelings of failing Keith, of questioning the actions of her youthful self.

"It makes me wonder, so often, after four years, what would have happened. If he hadn't taken that Heminevrin, what would life have been like? Would the alcohol have taken his life anyway? How long could we carry on like that? The only way was for him to change, and we will never know if he could truly have done that. But I think he tried," she says. Many who knew Keith, including his bandmates, have stated that they believe he wanted to get his alcohol abuse under control and seemed to be genuinely trying to do so at the time of his death.

"Keith was never very comfortable in his own skin. He was restless from childhood. He was the classic hyperactive. You know, not everyone can handle stardom. You can be talented—Keith obviously had significant talent—but not have the ability to handle what comes with it. I don't think he had self-confidence because he knew he was different; he felt different inside, because he had ADHD or something. He felt he wasn't good enough as a person other than as a drummer. He just didn't know how to behave.

"We all tried to tell him, after a while, that he was damaging his own reputation. He was creating a situation where he could lose everything. It wasn't funny anymore. But if someone tried to tell him that he was hurting himself with this behavior, he couldn't take it in. He just had to keep doing what he did, keep feeding the persona. In order to do what he had to do, he had to medicate, but he was using the alcohol for the medication. Alcohol was the core of the problem for him. It became the medicine he used to get the self-confidence. And he just needed more and more."

Yet there were also periods where Keith would stop drinking on his own. The house in Malibu had a small apartment attached to it that became Keith's place of respite. Annette recalls that he would lock himself in that apartment and stay for days, cooking himself meals and refusing phone calls. "He wouldn't come into the main house. He would stay, just reading books, watching television. He wouldn't answer the phone. I'd try to tell him someone was on the phone, and he would say, 'Tell them I'm not here.' He just wanted to be alone. He was really sort of a recluse. A happy recluse in those times in between the drinking.

"And on his drums. He was the absolute happiest behind his drum kit in front of a big audience. That was Keith euphoric. If he could have had that just with his normal self, without all the craziness, that would have been so good. That's what makes it sad that he had this insecurity that caused the drinking. No one knows where it really comes from. I just wish we had been able to figure that out."

As Keith considered returning to London to record The Who's new album, he was regularly drinking multiple bottles of alcohol throughout the day. Annette says it wasn't unusual for him to have a bottle of brandy through the day, then another with a bottle of champagne with dinner, then another bottle before passing out at night. "He once drank an entire bottle of brandy in the limo from LAX to our house in Bel Air. But toward the end, he tried, he really did because he had an ultimatum from the band to shape up. I think Roger and John would have let him go, but Pete wanted to give it another chance. I think Keith really, finally, had the will to change.

"In the weeks before he died, he started getting serious about our relationship as well. We had talks about getting married, getting a place in the country, maybe even having children. I took all of this in stride, too, because I never knew what was real. But he seemed a different person. He was making a real effort. It was an emotional time for me as well, to see him really want to make plans for the future. It was as though he was saying 'I want this, but I don't know how. Help me figure out how.'"

In addition to the drugs and alcohol, Keith was struggling to return to his previous capacity behind the drum kit. He had gained weight and slowed down after heavy drinking and not regularly playing for three years. Those in the studio as the band recorded the *Who Are You* album noticed that Keith's drumming was unusually erratic, something he tried to make up for by thrashing even more. He clearly couldn't keep up. It seems that even Keith was realizing something had to change.

After accidentally overdosing on Valium one night, he was admitted again to another stint at Cedars Sinai Hospital. He called Annette nearly every day and wrote her a series of letters. It was a difficult struggle for Keith, whose withdrawal caused seizures, and for Annette, who watched from afar with Dougal, not knowing whether Keith would survive. He came out of rehab declaring himself fit and ready for reengagement with his bandmates in the UK, only to succumb to free alcohol in the airport lounge as they waited for their flights to London.

"When we came back to London in '78, he was in quite bad shape. He needed to get himself together. I think he tried really, really, hard. It's difficult to say what was going on in his head. His career in LA hadn't materialized like he thought it would, and it was less and less important that he was the drummer for The Who. Even Dougal had given up and left.

"He seemed to have a new desire to get clean. Of course, he tried to do it alone and ended up with another seizure. I got him to the hospital and thought that might really be it. But he survived." It was around this time that he began taking medication to assist with his sobriety.

"People wouldn't tell me that much. I wasn't really enlightened about his medication. His manager and doctors kept that from me. If someone had told me. If I only had known what they were and how they had to be taken, I could have watched out. But I didn't know. I didn't know."

Keith had begun working with a doctor to regain his sobriety after returning to London. It was clear that none of the previous attempts at sobriety had worked, so he became desperate for a new approach.

"He knew he could drink a few bottles of brandy, and then a bottle of champagne, and survive that. So of course, he thinks if he can handle one pill, he can handle more. These pills should only be given to you if you are in a hospital, under controlled dosage by a doctor. But he had a whole bottle of these big, yellow capsules. I'll never forget them.

"All I knew was that they would keep him sober. If only someone had told me what these were and what they could do. But they did seem to be working. He seemed to be getting better."

On September 5, 1978, Keith and Annette attended a party thrown by Paul McCartney, who had recently purchased the publishing rights to Buddy Holly's music. They were invited to watch a screening of the film *The Buddy Holly Story*, preceded by a party at the London restaurant Peppermint Park. It was one of the first times Annette and Keith had been out with a large group since returning to London, and Keith was eager to rejoin his friends and revel in his British celebrity status. He had survived completing the *Who Are You* album without being dropped from the band, though Annette believes he worried that it was still a possibility. They partied through the night, but Keith remained relatively sober, taking the prescribed Heminevrin multiple times. Attendees noted that Keith seemed quiet, even subdued.

The two returned home at 4:30 a.m. and began watching a movie. Around 7:30 a.m., Annette cooked Keith a meal of lamb. Keith finished eating, took additional Heminevrin, and went back to bed. Annette slept until 3:30 in the afternoon. At 4:30, she returned to the bedroom to check on Keith and found him unresponsive. She summoned the doctor who had prescribed the pills, and he phoned for an ambulance. Annette watched in horror as paramedics attempted to revive him. The official autopsy report listed the cause of death as an overdose of Heminevrin, with at least six pills in his system and twenty-six more undigested in his stomach. His blood alcohol level, on the other hand, showed the equivalent of a pint of beer or a few glasses of wine.

In the days and weeks after his death, twenty-three-year-old Annette struggled to face the reality of the situation. "I was numb, I was in a state of shock. I had always thought to myself, one of these days, he's going to kill himself with these crazy stunts he did. It was a fear in me all the time. He's going to jump from a roof, or do some crazy thing, and kill himself. I think I was prepared for that sort of thing to happen. But for him to just fall asleep. I was completely jolted. What was that? How did that happen? It was just such a shock. I was given medication to help me calm down and sleep. I was in a daze for a while after he passed.

"After Keith died, I received great help from The Who. They were very, very kind to me. They looked after me, they took care of me. They paid for a luxury hotel that I stayed in for weeks. Then they rented a flat for me in Knightsbridge. This came out of Keith's estate, but you know, they could have dumped me in the street, and they didn't allow that. For that, I will be forever grateful to Pete and Roger, because they showed that they cared in the best way possible. I wasn't left on the street, out in the cold. They kept this up until I married and moved in with my husband, quite rightly so.

"But I didn't fight for his estate or for our house in Malibu. Someone told me I was a common-law wife in the United States, and I that should fight for my share. But I didn't have any fight left in me. Nothing mattered. I was in shock and pain and grief. I wasn't in any emotional state to fight for anything. It's strange when I think of it now. But then, I simply didn't have the energy after those four years and then his death. And Keith was so in-debt, his estate was a problem. He had very expensive taste, buying cars, and jewelry at Cartier. He came back from tours with less money than he made because he caused such damage. And he lost money, people stole from him, he gave it away. He had little to show for it. The estate is still rolling on today, I suppose, but I have no bitterness about that.

"I've always been a survivor. I stayed with a girlfriend in London; she let me stay with her for a while. I tried to pick up modeling again, but I was down, and it showed in my face. My eyes. I couldn't glow and look happy. I couldn't project that image that I didn't feel. It was difficult for me to try to adjust."

Some have suggested that Keith knew how many pills he could take and that rather than live a life of sobriety, he chose to kill himself. Several people noted that he seemed very subdued at the McCartney party. But Annette doesn't believe this at all. In addition to being with her, and saying nothing about feeling depressed or down, Keith also had a history of purging himself in order to avoid overdosing.

"I am so against the theory some have that he killed himself. Not many people knew that he did this, but he did it, often. It was like a routine. Party, party, and then come home and throw everything up. When people say to me that they saw him swallow ten valiums, well, maybe they did. But they didn't see, ten minutes later, when he got rid of them all. But I did. He wasn't suicidal at all."

In her memoir, *The Last Four Years*, about her time with Keith, Annette writes that the purging came from Keith's fear of vomiting during the night and choking to death. He had lived through deaths of other musicians like Jimi Hendrix who had perished in this way, and he consciously tried to avoid it.[1]

"A few times he would say that he would be dead before he got old. Like the song, yes. But I think it had more to do with him camouflaging what he was doing. That he knew his life was so wild that it couldn't go on forever. Maybe to say that, if he died young, I shouldn't be sad. But it wasn't to do with how he was feeling, just that he couldn't really see himself as an old man."

For Annette, after Keith died, The Who died with him. The remaining members of the band, who had just released the *Who Are You* album and had planned an expansive US tour, made the decision to go on. Drummer Kenney Jones, previously of the Faces, joined the group, along with keyboardist "Rabbit" Bundrick. Just eight months after Keith's death, they played their first show at the Rainbow in London.

Within two years of Keith's death, Annette met and married the British actor Gareth Hunt. They lived in a cottage in the English countryside and, in 1980, had a son, Oliver. "I enjoyed that period very much. Gareth was calm, he was secure in himself. To me, he felt safe. He projected a sense that I needed there and then. I was probably too fragile to realize that I should wait to be in a relationship, because it didn't turn out well in the end. But it was calm and quiet and lovely for a while. Gareth was quite funny and made me laugh. I needed that.

"Things started to fall apart, and he eventually started to show his real self. He would lie and go to parties. I believe, and it felt as though, he used the publicity of my situation. I was getting a lot of publicity at that time, and he got noticed a bit more, and he used that situation to his advantage.

"I felt bitter and sad, so I left. Of course, I was pointed out as the bad guy because I was the one that left. His family talked badly about me to my son, and I wasn't there to defend myself. I tried to rebuild my life in Sweden and thought I could just let them talk whatever they were going to talk. I was twenty-four and needed to get on with my life."

Annette enrolled at the university and studied psychology with the hope that it would help her better understand the situations and relationships she had experienced. Annette laughs, saying, "I hoped someone could explain these situations in my life. Please, give me a book to read about this!"

She became a therapist, helping others but also helping herself. Through talking to others, studying, and reading, and better understanding, she received the help she needed. "I hope I've helped someone, and I've got help, too. I gained perspective. I got to understand. I learned not to dwell, not to go back and worry about old things. That gave me strength that I use to this day. People have opinions or whatever, and I don't let it weigh me down. I let people judge for themselves. I suppose I grew up a lot during that time.

"Grieving with time properly is so important. You have to come to terms with yourself and your life the way it is, without that other person. I was in shock when Keith died. I was looking for him. I would look at the stars and ask, 'Where are you?' Then other things happened to me so quickly, before I was finished with my grieving. Was I naïve about how quickly I could move on? Probably I was. Because I was so young. I didn't have family to go back to, didn't have that support. I did start drinking just after Keith died. I know I drank too much during that time. Eventually, I found better ways to deal with it.

"I don't think I ever stopped grieving him until I started talking to others. I started working and talking to people and could relate to their dilemmas.

"It's like the word 'closure.' People talk about getting closure. No. I just learned to live with the reality, but then I never stopped grieving. With someone like Keith, it never really goes away. Now, there's new interest. Things like social media make him popular again. Some of the most dedicated fans weren't even born when he was alive. I see photos, hear music. Maybe it's been there all the time, but it does seem that the grief surfaces again and again.

"When I see now how popular he still is, and how admired he is as a drummer, I get a bit of anxiety when those memories return, when I think about him. I still miss him, but a long time has passed. I don't know what could have been for him, for us. I know we weren't finished."

Annette has filled her life with friends, both those from long ago and new friends through social media, including fans of Keith and The Who. "Age and experience help as well. You are able to look at people and how they behave and just back off, not get so involved," she says, "Yes, we do these wild, fun things when we're young, but we also pay much more attention to the words and actions of others, especially words about us. There is a lot to be said for having less investment in the opinions of others as we age."

And what would twenty-year-old Annette feel about this more thoughtful, mature version of herself? I often wonder if teenage me would dislike current-day me. We chat about this reflection of our younger selves and why we feel the need to please that person. "Oddly, I feel privileged to have been there and to be able to tell the stories now. It was insane, the things that happened and the ways they happened, and yet, to have lived through it and be able to tell the story. It certainly was extraordinary, especially to be there with just him.

"And I know I got the best side of him. When I think of the best of him, all the other bad things disappear. He was a sweet, sweet man, really. He was just an ordinary boy. Really, in so many ways, it wasn't just me that was young, we both were young. Yes, he, too, was just a boy. Yes."

LOVE

7

GRETCHEN PARSONS CARPENTER

Gretchen Burrell was sixteen years old and already under contract as a model when she met Gram Parsons, the brilliant singer-songwriter who created what he called "cosmic American music"—an amalgam of country, rock, and blues that influenced everyone from the Rolling Stones to the Eagles.

"A tall, thin girl with long blonde hair could get away with a lot in southern California in those days," she says with a quiet inward laugh. We are sitting on the patio of Gretchen's home, still in Laurel Canyon near where she and Gram once lived. Her husband, Bob Carpenter, joined us in the startling sunshine of late spring. It is a beautiful, comfortable home filled with the accoutrements of a happy and successful life—photos of family and friends, small dogs that follow underfoot, and a grand piano lined with Bob's Grammy Awards and CMA statues (he's the keyboard player for the Nitty Gritty Dirt Band and an acclaimed session musician). I get the impression that Gretchen is happy, and that this happiness must be a sort of vindication for her, a storybook ending to an otherwise difficult tale. But I quickly understand that to be a judgment based on outward appearances. All stories are really about people, and Gretchen Parsons Carpenter is still living the story of her life with Gram.

Gram and Gretchen at a party in Los Angeles. Photo by Ginny Winn/Michael Ochs Archives/Getty Images

"Oh, I've been called every name. I've certainly been blamed for everything that happened. I've been sued for thirty years by women who claim they had his baby. I've had every ambulance-chasing lawyer come after me. The hatred or envy, I don't know which. And I can't go online. I once went to a fan site where they were making comments and said, 'You know I can see you, right?' and they just went bananas. I just can't do that anymore.

"Gram's death had the worst possible combination as far as being able to move on from that," adds Bob. "He was young and good looking, a high-profile musician whose reputation has just gotten larger since his death, a tragic death, and a cult following. That cult following will never leave her alone. They'll never stop following and finding her and reminding her. These people feel as though they've had something precious stolen from them, when the person they're accusing is the one with the real loss. This person they're attacking lost her husband, and they think they have this great injury because they listened to his music or read about him in a magazine.

"And of course, Gretchen had to deal with something no one else has ever had to deal with after Gram's death. Talk about piling pain on top of pain."

Gretchen reaches past Bob for a tissue from a box that she brought out with us. "Thinking about talking with you has kept me up the last few nights. I won't get very far before I need these," she said as we left the kitchen.

Sitting now in the garden looking out over the famed Laurel Canyon, Gretchen begins again.

"I was so lost for so long. There were a lot of bad choices after Gram died, partly from my youth, a lot from grief. It's so ephemeral and yet it weighs a thousand pounds. It depends on what catches you, who's talking to you, what music you hear. Someone says something and it sends you immediately to that dark place that still keeps me up at night. Still, even though my life is so wonderful now.

"I was thinking the other day about my father. I'm not sure why he crossed my mind, but he did. My father was my everything, and he had struggled with me to help Gram because we just didn't know which way it was going to fall on any given day. I lost him a few years ago and that loss was so different. It's difficult to explain the difference, but it's just completely different. My grief for my father is a dull ache in my heart. Gram screams—that grief is so powerful it just screams."

Ingram Cecil Connor came to California from his native Florida by way of a semester at Harvard Divinity School. Once in LA, he became Gram Parsons, his last name courtesy of his stepfather, Bob. He'd been in bands since high school and arrived on the LA rock scene with a deep love of country music in his heart and a trust fund in the bank. Born into a wealthy family of citrus growers, Gram's childhood was filled with its own loss and grief. His biological father, Cecil "Coon Dog" Connor, after suffering for years with alcoholism, committed suicide when Gram was just twelve years old. His mother, Avis, then married Bob Parsons. Avis succumbed to her own depression and alcoholism on the day that Gram graduated from a private high school. Gram barely made it through his first year at Harvard, where he formed the International Submarine Band with fellow classmates. He quit school and the band shortly after his first year to move west and pursue music full time.

Once in Los Angeles, Gram set about to create his cosmic American music by joining with Chris Hillman, whose band The Byrds was already making records. Gram contributed his country sensibility and love of the stories of Nashville singers like Merle Haggard and Waylon Jennings to the band. The Byrds's first album with Gram, *Sweetheart of the Rodeo*, is generally considered a classic example of rock and country genre-bending. Gram left The Byrds prior to a South African tour, citing political and philosophical reasons, and soon formed a new band, The Flying Burrito Brothers, in 1969, with fellow Byrds alumnus Hillman along with Chris Ethridge, Sneaky Pete Kleinow, and later Michael Clarke. They recorded *Gilded Palace of Sin* and toured the Southwest and played local gigs. In 1970, the Burritos recorded their album *Burrito Deluxe*. During this time, Gram's behavior became more and more erratic and he was fired from the band. Parsons had experimented with drugs and alcohol before he met Keith Richards, but by 1969, it had reached the level of drug abuse, which he supported with his trust fund. Gram met Keith in Los Angeles while the Stones recorded their *Exile on Main Street* album, and the two developed a friendship that Keith would later write about in his memoir. A photo of the two astride a motorcycle sits framed on Gretchen's piano. It was during that time that Gretchen and Gram's paths crossed.

They met on Gram's birthday after a friend invited Gretchen to a party being thrown by the Stones at the Warner Brothers studios.

"One of my best friends introduced me to Gram. She was a groupie. I was just about to graduate from high school and was already modeling. My friend called me and said, 'Guess what? I got a job driving the Rolling Stones around town. They're here to record an album and don't know where they're going, so I'm driving them around.' She honestly was one of the worst drivers I'd ever met, but she had called me from a pay phone while they were out driving around. She said they were having a party later that night at the Warner studios and asked if I wanted to come.

Well, I'm seventeen, and this is the Rolling Stones. What do you say to that except yes?

"I drove over to Warner Brothers, and they're in this giant sound stage studio. My name was on the guest list, so I went in. The first thing I saw was this boy. This skinny, tall boy with blond hair. I saw him from behind. He was wearing these dark brown suede hip-hugger pants and they had silver conchos going all the way down these ridiculously long legs. I was like, who the hell is that? I knew he wasn't one of the Stones, and that was good because I was only seventeen and not really up to meeting Mick Jagger. But this guy. And it just happened to be his birthday, and Keith was throwing him this party. We went up to Monkey Manor, a house owned by Mike Nesmith of The Monkees."

Gram and Gretchen dated for a few months before leaving the United States to spend time with the Stones in France, living at the Villa Nellcôte on the Cote d'Azur.

"The time in Paris was heaven: making music, hanging out with Keith, living in this castle. We were young and carefree and a little stupid. But I will also say it was a time of tension as well. It was during that time when Hendrix died, Morrison died, and Mick became very paranoid. Really, all the Stones became paranoid. There were days when you could cut the tension in the air with a knife when all that was going down. There was a lot of fear, a tremendous amount of fear, because they didn't know, really, why these people were dying. Did someone give them bad drugs, or what happened? And there were bad people around. We eventually had to leave because of them. But how do you know, because they all tell you they're your friends. You don't know these things at the time. Of course, Gram's story wouldn't be what it is without his connection to Phil Kaufman [a road manager and friend of Gram], but Kaufman was friends with Charles Manson, as was Terry Melcher [an LA record producer who made albums with The Byrds, The Beach Boys, and Bob Dylan, among others]. If you've got money and you're making music, they're around. Oh, the grief these people caused! It's almost as though they deal in grief, and death and pain. To think that people like this are the last people Gram saw, it's agony."

Soon after returning from France, Gretchen and Gram married in New Orleans in September 1971. "We lived in New Orleans for a while after we married. I love it there to this day. It's a place of good memories. Drinking and eating in exquisite places and exploring. I remember the first time he took me to this small town called Algiers outside New Orleans. We walked around and checked out the local record store.

"Gram was so smart and charming. He had impeccable manners, not very common in rock and roll. But he was a charming Southern gentleman. It was really like an innate Southern charm which came from his upbringing. His childhood wasn't pleasant. His father died mysteriously and both parents were alcoholics. It really set him up for his own destiny. Some things are just part of your life no matter what. No matter what good things might happen to you, you take these other things with you, sometimes right to the grave."

Much of what's been presented as Gram's life during that time centers on his drug use, his inability to keep commitments in the recording studio or on stage. But Gretchen remembers good times as well.

"Gram had such a refined sense of everything. We really enjoyed that lifestyle. Fine wines and foods, beautiful clothes, and beautiful women, if I can say so. I remember my first glass of champagne with big fat Australian blueberries. Who ate blueberries from Australia? For a time, we did enjoy life to its fullest. But then, you know the fullness starts to empty out, and you don't know what to do."

After Gram was fired from the Burrito Brothers, he made two solo albums, *GP* and *Grievous Angel*, but his drug and alcohol use caused problems in both his personal and professional life. He toured in support of the second album with his new band, the Fallen Angels, which included a then-unknown young singer, Emmylou Harris. Gram and Harris developed a connection that has been the subject of much speculation through the years. What's certain, however, is that their musical connection was special, and together, they created classic southern California country music. Harris is also credited with getting Gram straight enough to tour for several months behind the album and to go back into the studio. Gretchen accompanied Gram on that tour, but would only speak about Emmylou off the record.

After returning from the *Grievous Angel* tour, Gretchen and Gram's relationship continued to fall apart, with Gretchen trying to handle things but quickly realizing that she was in over her head.

"Using my own money, I would pay the waitresses at the Palomino to not bring him a drink. I was so young, and I had never dealt with anything like this before. It was all fun stuff, until it's not fun anymore. We had a life, we had a home, and then it all started going to shit. You fall in love with the charm, you don't fall in love with the bad parts. No girl does. They're all love and charm and what have you, until they're not. It's such a betrayal."

Some accounts say that the two had separated, that Gram was ready to serve Gretchen with divorce papers. But Gretchen's only hope at that time was that they could work things out, especially since she had recently learned she was pregnant.

"I remember our last conversation. There's much about that time and the months after that I simply don't remember. I've had trouble remembering the day Gram and I got married. I can't remember much about the day he died. I've blocked it. It's my body's way of allowing me to go on. It's what you do, and it's okay. But I remember that last time I saw him. He came by our house, and I told him about the baby. I told him he needed to sober up."

After the news, Gram headed to his favorite place, Joshua Tree National Park in the California desert. Gram had always loved the area and visited frequently. Was he leaving everyone and going into the desert in an effort to get clean and start fresh? Gretchen believes so. His career appeared to be on the upswing. He was making music with Emmylou and the Angels and had reduced his use of heroin while they were recording their album.

Or did he head to Joshua Tree planning to have one last party before settling down with a wife and child? It is known that he brought along his "manager" Phil Kaufman and another friend, Michael Martin. He was also joined by Margaret Fisher, a high-school girlfriend with whom he had started a relationship. On September 18, 1973, after several days of drinking and taking barbiturates, Gram injected himself with a lethal overdose of morphine. Several hours later, Fisher took him to High Desert Memorial Hospital, where he was pronounced dead.

"The first days and months after he died are a blur of pain and agony, and then compounding everything was that whole incident with Phil Kaufman. I just don't know how I got through it," Gretchen says. She leans back in her chair, folding and refolding her napkin and nervously straightening her dress.

The incident to which Gretchen refers is the stuff of infamy. It is the part of the story that has encouraged the cult of Gram Parsons. Gram's stepfather, Bob Parsons was living in New Orleans and, according to some, had hoped to cash in on Gram's trust fund by establishing Gram's residence in Louisiana through burial in New Orleans (which wouldn't have worked). Gretchen was fine with that because New Orleans was where they married and had been happy. It was a place that Gram loved.

Kaufman had a different plan, however. According to him, he and Gram had made a pact that they would save each other from a traditional, maudlin funeral. Phil figured out the location of Gram's body at LAX (as it awaited a flight back to New Orleans), "borrowed" a hearse, stole Gram's body from the airport tarmac, and took him back to Joshua Tree. Once there, Kaufman doused the body with gasoline, lit it on fire, and then left. Gram's remains were discovered the next day. Because there was no law against the theft of a body, Kaufman was charged only with theft of a casket. He held a benefit concert to raise money to cover his legal expenses, saying he was trying to fulfill Gram's wishes.[1]

It is difficult to even write this part of the story. How does a very young woman, who has just discovered she's pregnant and has lost her husband, also survive this level of trespass? The hardest part, Gretchen says, is knowing the kind of people with whom Gram spent his last hours. "They were users and dealers. They dealt in death and pain. It was their stock in trade," she says, wiping away tears. How does someone endure that added pain, then live with it for so many years afterward, watching as it becomes the stuff of lore and legend? Fans still make pilgrimages to Joshua Tree and to Room 8 at the Joshua Tree Inn where Gram died.

Kaufman's act created a situation in which Gram will never have peace as long as the story stays alive. And without peace for Gram, there can never be peace for Gretchen.

"People think it's wild and cool, that it's a cool story. That's where the screaming comes in. That's why my grief over Gram is like a scream. It will never go away, and people don't realize that there are actual people behind these stories. The person who perpetrated this is still out there, doing his job, living his life and never being held accountable."

At this point, Gretchen's husband Bob steps in with a view that is more logical, perhaps more easily stated from his objective vantage point.

"When you're young, on drugs, and have the mentality of a motorcycle gang, that's what's going to happen. There is no thought to other people," he says.

So just how did Gretchen move on from this tragedy? In many ways, she hasn't been able to move on, but in other ways she has by creating a wonderful life with a second husband that clearly loves her.

"I cried for five years, every day. I still haven't completely stopped crying about it. I haven't stopped asking why. There are no tools for this, and you don't know how you'll respond until you're in the midst of it. Some people do well, others go off the rails. People don't know how to respond. I really found out who my friends were.

"I went to Gram's funeral with my friend Claudia Lanier [a back-up singer]. She and I are still close friends to this day. After Gram's death, she was my rock. She was the only friend that would travel with me to New Orleans for the funeral. The only one. And everyone said it was my fault. Even Gram's family said it was my fault, and I was just a child. I was barely twenty-two. Somehow people feel better finding a scapegoat and making others feel less-than."

A few weeks later, still reeling from Gram's death and the aftermath, Gretchen had a miscarriage.

Three relationships helped Gretchen to heal and live again. The most recent is possibly the one that was the greatest help.

"Gram's youngest sister Diane was just a child when he died. Finding her again, because they kept her away from me saying that it was all my fault; like I could handle this character who had alcoholism and drug issues, and me being so young. It wasn't until she grew up and had children that she came to the realization that, wait a minute, that's just not possible. She reached out to me, and it has been such a blessing. Bob has embraced her as well. We are a family together, which brings such comfort."

Her relationship with Bob and the birth of their son were the other two events that helped Gretchen to heal.

"This is the love of my life," she says, pointing to Bob as he excuses himself from our chat. "He is not only my best friend, but he has always been Gram's biggest advocate. That has really helped me. Without that, I'd have continued to be lost.

"When Bob and I met, he told me he was an architect. I had moved to Hawaii, which was a good thing. Not everything I did during that time was a good choice, but that was. I needed to just be away from everything and everyone. I was there for eleven years and spent most of that time grieving. Then I returned to California for a while. My friend [guitarist and singer] Dave Mason was getting married, and Bob crashed the wedding. Bob had studied architecture, so it wasn't too far off to tell me that story. But after we started dating and I was finally invited to his apartment, I walked in, and there's a grand piano, and I thought, well, that's interesting. He knew who I was, and he knew that I wouldn't have given him a second glance if I knew he was a musician. I'm glad he did it; I'm grateful that he didn't tell me who he really was."

As Gretchen tells me about her life with Bob, she pulls out her phone and scrolls through photographs—recent shots of her with her friend Claudia and holiday photos of the family. She finds a photo of her son and smiles brightly.

"This is also who saved me," she says. "Having this child, this reason to think outside of myself is what really got me through. He's so funny. I'm very happy, and some days just can't believe how fortunate I've been. The grace to find someone new and to have a child after losing a child with Gram and then being able to have a whole, full life again, I'm just lucky in so many ways."

As I come back to this idea of Gretchen making peace, of possibly having arrived at a place where she feels exonerated, perhaps even absolved, she is quick to correct me.

"I've said that I worried after we spoke and planned for this conversation. I've lost sleep thinking about it. I asked myself why I would want to sit here with you and go over all of this. I'm so tired. But yet, this is important. It's important that people know." I ask her why she hasn't written a book herself, why she hasn't taken the opportunity to set the record straight. Once again, I learn, it's not that easy. Gretchen understands from experience how futile it can be to try to tell her story. How fans will challenge her truth—*the* truth—rather than accept responsibility for her mistreatment.

With that, the woman who has been very composed for the past two hours begins to cry. "I've never met any of these other women that you're writing about. Isn't that odd? I don't know why, but I've gone through this alone. I feel badly that I don't know their names and their stories. This work, telling our stories is so important. I thought I'd cry over something else, some memory of Gram, but I'm crying over this, over the grief and that I don't know these women who've also gone through so much."

I consider the experiences I had with Kevin's illness and death and how I handled both. I know there were times when I was less than patient, when my anger over our situation made him feel responsible. Yet the only person judging me for that is myself. I've never faced judgment from family or friends. Had I faced that, in the midst of that grief, after feeling like a complete failure for not stopping a terminal illness from taking the life of my husband, I don't know that I would have been able to go on. So much of your life is cut out from under you; so much of grief is grasping for something that can prop you back up. When that isn't there, when it gets pulled away or worse, when people turn away, what is left to keep you moving forward? What strength it must have taken a young Gretchen just to keep going. It is a common thread among nearly all these women—that they are not able to own the narrative around the life and death of the men they loved. Yet so many others feel they have some owner-ship of that narrative because they liked his music, or knew his birthdate, or kept his picture on their bedroom wall.

Gretchen looks at me intently, bringing me back from my thoughts. She puts her hands to her chest.

"I've been asked about writing a book before," she says. "But no one is going to get a book from me, not ever. Not ever. With all this, this landscape that I've lived on, the years that have passed, the lies that have been told, I'm not going to spend time cleaning up their mess. I need to hold my truth sacred. It's mine, and I will decide who, if anyone, I share it with."

8

JANNA LEBLANC

As I packed twenty-six years of a marriage into boxes for a move to a smaller house in a new city, I came across letters and photos from the years that Kevin and I dated. They were an important part of our past life together. They proved that he loved me, that he missed me while I was in school. In one letter, he wrote about visiting my parents and telling them that he intended to marry me, assuaging their fears that his intentions were suspect, especially since they knew he had been in another relationship when we first met. We had broken up and gotten back together a few times over the course of the year that we dated prior to my departure for school.

Within weeks of my leaving, Kevin visited me in Chicago and brought an engagement ring. We had barely finished college when we married. I sometimes worried that I had married too soon, too young, and yet I asked myself, how would things have turned out differently if we had waited, or if I had said no, not yet? We were young, but we were—as attested by those letters and pictures—in love, a love that was celebrated by our friends and family; a love that was never questioned by those people, despite our rocky start. I considered that question again after spending a day with Janna Leblanc. Kevin and I had limited time, and we would never grow old together as we had promised in our vows. I know now the answer to my questions

Janna and Stevie attend President George H. W. Bush's inauguration in 1989.
Courtesy of Janna Lapidus Leblanc

would be even more emphatic, and that the mementos hold even more meaning and significance. Yet, because we married, because we had a piece of paper from our local government, I would never be called upon to use those letters and photos, or other privately shared keepsakes, to prove our love or claim what was rightfully mine. Janna wasn't so lucky.

Janna Lapidus was a seventeen-year-old Russian immigrant to New Zealand when she met Stevie Ray Vaughan in Wellington.

Stevie had just arrived for two shows as part of a New Zealand–Australia tour when he saw Janna walking down the street. They would quickly become constant companions, with Janna holding Stevie's hand through detoxing and the start of his sobriety.

"It was March of 1986, and I was finishing my senior year of high school. He was sitting outside, in front of his hotel, across from the Old Town Hall where he would perform that night. As I walked toward him, I could hear him speaking to me, but I couldn't really tell what he was saying. I got closer and he repeated, 'howyadoin?' in his Texas accent. We laughed and then started talking.

"A few minutes later, Stevie's brother Jimmie came outside, and the three of us walked around the city for a while. I told Stevie I had to leave as I already had plans. He asked if I would come back and see him before the show. I said I would see, but I had no plans to return. Later, my friend Terry and I were walking past the venue on our way to a movie and we saw a line of people waiting to get into the show. As we were walking away, Jimmie was walking into the hall. He saw me and asked where I had been and told me Stevie had been waiting all day for me to come back.

"I went backstage where Stevie was, and we talked until it was time for him to go on. He was funny and easy going. There was plenty of Crown Royal and cocaine, neither of which I had ever tried. I wasn't very familiar with his music at that time, either. I was more into The Clash and the Psychedelic Furs: not really new wave, but more on the punk side, GenX, bands like that. Watching him and hearing him play that night, however, showed me his talent and abilities in an unexpected way. He was so good. But he was also going off on long tangents, and you could tell something was off. It wasn't like a long solo that becomes mystical; something was wrong. After the show, Stevie gave me his black velvet cape, and he took my jean jacket so that I would have to come back the next day to see him."

Janna did return the next day, and spent several hours with Stevie, during which he told her of his constant life on the road and of the difficult marriage that he was ending. He hinted at a realization that drug and alcohol use were becoming a problem. In turn, Janna told Stevie about leaving Russia as a child, having to learn English and adjust to a new culture, and her own struggle with an eating disorder. The two bonded quickly over shared difficulties and a need to find hope in their lives. "He knew, he just knew something right away. He reached out to me right away. When I had to leave, he said 'I want to know you. Come back. Are you coming back?'"

Stevie Ray Vaughan was nothing less than a blues guitar prodigy, but he was a troubled prodigy. Born and raised near Dallas in Oak Cliff, Texas, to working-class parents, Stevie picked up his first guitar at age eight, mimicking his older brother Jimmie, who was becoming a local star. Together, the two learned blues guitar from listening to late-night radio shows that featured their heroes: B. B. King, Albert King, T-Bone Walker, and others. They began purchasing records and teaching themselves to play by ear. By age eleven, Stevie was in a band, playing at beer halls and music jubilees, where, in order to get in, he had to be accompanied by his parents.

Soon, the Vaughan brothers were listening to British-influenced blues and became fascinated with how musicians like Eric Clapton and John Mayall were interpreting blues guitar. And then there was Jimi Hendrix. Stevie became a huge fan of Hendrix, and his influence on Stevie's own sound was unmistakable. Stevie continued to learn from Jimmie until the elder Vaughan turned fifteen, dropped out of school, and left home to play in a popular Dallas band, The Chessmen. That left Stevie at home to fend for himself in a difficult family situation.

"Stevie's home life was rough when he was a kid," Janna says. We're sitting in the sunshine of St. Augustine, Florida, many years and miles away from either 1960s Oak Cliff, Texas, or 1980s New Zealand. "Especially after Jimmie left. He talked about his dad, how nothing was consistent. I do believe it affected him. People were surprised by our age difference, but I believe Stevie stopped growing up, in some ways, around 15. When you start using alcohol to numb your feelings and the pain and grief and sadness and all, you don't learn how to deal."

From the late 60s into the early 70s, Stevie lead, or was a member of, several bands around Dallas. His reputation began to eclipse that of Jimmie's, who would go on to form the Fabulous Thunderbirds and have moderate success. When Stevie grew tired of the Dallas music scene, he headed for Austin, where audiences were more progressive. While there, he reconnected with Doyle Bramhall, whom he had previously met at age twelve. The two would later cowrite music, and Doyle would become lifelong friends to both Stevie and Janna. Janna remembers Doyle's support in the months after Stevie died.

"When Doyle passed a few years ago, that was like losing a piece of my heart," Janna explains. "Because he was the one man who was a real man after Stevie died; he was there for me. And he cared. He and his beautiful wife Barbara, you know, they were the ones who gave me the name for the lawyers to go see, like advising me, saying, 'Janna, you need to go do something.' I thought, oh no, surely not, surely not. Surely everyone will do the right thing. But that didn't happen.

"Doyle Bramhall is also who Stevie ended up with writing material for the brothers' album [*Family Style*]. He was his go-to guy and his best friend. That was the first person who encouraged him, who heard him and said, 'Hey, you're really good, keep it up.' He taught him how to sing. Gave him notes, you know, was a friend throughout, and wrote some of my favorite songs together with him."

For Stevie, a series of events helped to raise his profile shortly after reconnecting with Doyle. After joining and leaving multiple bands in the early 1980s, Stevie put together Double Trouble with Tommy Shannon and Chris Layton. It was this configuration that would bring the level of recognition Stevie's talent deserved. The band frequently played the Austin blues club Antone's. An invitation to play the Montreux Jazz Festival came in 1982, which led to a meeting with David Bowie. A year later, Bowie requested Stevie play on the new album he was recording, *Let's Dance*. Bowie later asked Stevie to join him on tour, though Stevie backed out, feeling that he was on the cusp of achieving his own stardom for Double Trouble. The band was ready to release their album, *Texas Flood*, and Vaughan felt the need to perform a series of dates with Double Trouble in support of that release.

During this time, Stevie also married his first wife, Lenora "Lenny" Bailey. The two had a tumultuous, abusive relationship that began so passionately Stevie named one of his guitars after her and penned one of his best instrumental songs in her honor. Within six years, however, the marriage ended in divorce—shortly after the time that Stevie met Janna, although the separation had occurred more than a year prior. Simultaneously, as Double Trouble's popularity was growing, so was Stevie's alcohol and drug abuse. As Janna had observed during that first night together, every show was fueled by Crown Royal and cocaine.

By 1986, Stevie Ray Vaughan and Double Trouble had released three albums and had been touring constantly. With their record company demanding a fourth album, the band recorded two live shows in Austin that would become the *Live Alive* album. Many around Stevie knew he was in bad shape and that his level of alcohol and drug use was not sustainable. Musically, the concerts recorded for the album were far from Double Trouble's best performances. Despite concerns, the band soon took off for a tour of Australia and New Zealand before heading to Europe.

It was on this tour that Stevie and Janna met. After returning to retrieve her jacket, as Stevie predicted she would, the two spent the day together in Wellington. Stevie traveled with a Polaroid camera, often setting the timer, and taking the 1980s-version of selfies. One such photo, which Janna still has, is a close-up of a thoughtful looking Stevie. At the bottom of the photo, in red marker, Stevie wrote, "Last night I found the best friend I've ever had. Stevie Ray, 3/86." By the end of their second day together, Janna announced to her parents that she was leaving with Stevie to tour Australia.

"They were pretty trusting. They knew I had a good head on my shoulders. I had already done some modeling work away from home, so they let me go. They also knew I was going to go either way. Eventually, one time, I remember my mum saying, 'I hope you have a daughter just like you, someday. You'll see!'

Of course, I now have two boys, but I still see. Parenting under the best of circumstances is still challenging."

Janna flew to Australia with Stevie and traveled with him to six shows throughout the country. She had her own hotel room and tried to distance herself from the alcohol and drug use.

"I remember one person said to me, a roadie, somebody in the road crew, said 'Stevie drinks a lot. Maybe you can help him to slow down, maybe you could be a good influence.' Because they could tell, I think, that I wasn't a big partier. But I just knew that you can't make somebody do something they don't want to. That's something that really has to be up to him.

"Plus, I'm going out, I'm going along to the bars, having these drinks and going, wow, you guys are nuts. You guys are crazy. I can't keep up and I don't want to keep up. But this is fun. You know, it was a fun time to play, too, to experiment, and you know, to see this lifestyle, but it was pretty clear that it was all too much."

By the end of the Australian tour, both Stevie and Janna knew they had strong feelings for each other. Janna also knew that Stevie had real problems that only he could overcome. She felt she had seen enough of the good and bad to know that she wanted to be in Stevie's life.

"I saw some of the bad parts, for sure. He was just getting out of this very toxic marriage. He told me many sad, sad stories about that; he was so straight-up about all of that. He said, 'Here's what's going on with my wife. Here's what happened, we're separated.' That's what I loved about him from the start. A real sense of honesty about everything.

"There were times when he would be very rude. Rude to flight attendants on the plane or rude when I commented about drinking first thing in the morning. When you have to use alcohol to get up, you know things are bad. But Stevie's heart was kind, and I could tell he was searching for the right thing, for some peace. I understood that search for peace."

After the tour dates in Australia, Janna flew back to New Zealand, and Stevie returned to Texas. For three months, he called regularly and talked with Janna about the struggles to extricate himself from his marriage. The divorce from Lenny would be expensive and would prevent Stevie from writing or recording new music for some time. He warned Janna that he may have to stop calling if Lenny made demands. The calls stopped, and Janna, heartbroken, made plans to travel to Italy in December as part of an exchange program. She was certain she would never hear from Stevie again.

Back in the United States, Stevie was dealing with several issues: his addiction, the impending divorce, and family concerns. In August, his father died after years of battling Parkinson's disease and asbestosis. The day after the funeral, Stevie and Double Trouble flew to Montreal for a show and then continued on to shows in Denmark, France, and Germany. Within a month, Stevie was on the floor of a German hotel room vomiting blood, believing he was about to die. Instead, he was treated at the hospital for severe dehydration, but everyone around him knew that wasn't it. The hospitalization also revealed several stomach lacerations, the result of drinking shots laced with cocaine. After playing one more show in Zurich, Stevie flew to London and was admitted into the program run by Victor Bloom, who had helped Eric Clapton with drug abuse issues years before. Once in Bloom's care, Stevie asked first for his mother, and then for Janna.

Without telling Stevie, Janna booked a flight and made her way to London, expecting to sleep in a youth hostel or YWCA. Instead, Stevie discovered her plan when he called New Zealand and spoke to Janna's mother. He sent an assistant to meet her at the airport and booked her into a nearby hotel. Within a few days, Stevie was released from the hospital, provided he remained in London and checked in with Bloom every day. The couple used the time to sightsee, shop, and take long walks through the city, often accompanied by Stevie's mother, Martha.

"There were times when we would be driving around, and he would tell us he needed a drink. 'I need a drink. I need a drink.' He would just repeat it. We could all feel the struggle he was going through detoxing," Janna says of this time. After ten days, Stevie was released to a longer rehab program in Atlanta. Janna returned to New Zealand, while Stevie took a flight to the United States. Having never flown without drinking, Stevie took what would become his last drink ever on that flight, something he confessed to Janna, feeling the shame of letting her down.

In Atlanta, Stevie continued to use the Polaroid camera, taking and sending self-shot photos nearly every day. Photos show him in his room or in a common area playing his guitar. He wrote Janna of his daily struggles and how grateful he was to even be alive. Though the clinic discouraged patients from new relationships, Stevie pressed on with Janna, calling her frequently from a payphone. He asked her to attend Al-Anon meetings in New Zealand to better understand his struggles and the nature of addiction. The two began making plans for the time when Stevie would be released. He would have just one week before starting a tour in support of *Live Alive*, and he decided to spend that time in New Zealand with Janna, meeting her family.

Janna maintained her earlier plans to visit Italy and traveled there in December. Stevie asked if he could join her for a week between concert dates. Though very nervous about performing sober, Stevie had now done several shows in the United States and was becoming more confident in his ability to play a live show. Reviews were positive, and Stevie fell into a comfortable groove with renewed vitality. The trip to Italy provided a needed break from the pressure of maintaining sobriety while touring, and the two embraced the opportunity, seeking out Al-Anon meetings in each location. "Sometimes there would be a meeting in the back of a church, sometimes a meeting tucked away in some anonymous place. But I always made sure we found it and he had that time," Janna remembers. Returning home to New Zealand, Janna packed her things and moved to Dallas to be with Stevie full time. "My parents weren't surprised. By this point, they had met him, they had seen us together. They knew. They could tell."

For the next three years, the couple traveled throughout the country, sometimes as part of Stevie and the band's touring, sometimes vacationing on their own. They rented a house in Dallas and settled in. It became important for Stevie to adjust the crazy pace he had tried unsuccessfully to keep prior to recovery. Tours were scheduled with break periods, and Stevie worked at becoming healthy in other ways, searching out naturopaths and implementing a vitamin regimen. Stevie was public about his recovery, including from the concert stage, where he implored fans to care for themselves.

"He knew he risked sounding like he was preaching, but he really did want to reach even just one person. He felt a real sense of responsibility. He will always maintain a place because of his incredible musicianship, but also his legacy of caring for people. And his honesty about sobriety. It was so brave of him to stand up and do that. I remember he would say, 'Does it seem okay? Is that all right?'" I said, "I know it's a little awkward, but it's your thing, you feel comfortable with it, so do it." Every time it depended on the night. It'd be kind of like, what's his choice of words going to be? Cause he's feeling the crowd and what's appropriate. And sometimes it was definitely a just-show-up-and-play kind of vibe. And then the other times, it totally kind of rippled around, and you could feel that kind of vibration going through right to the audience. And then he just launched into the song, and you know, he'd just floor everyone, whether or not they really listened to him and took it in, they'd stopped for that moment."

He traveled with a bag full of books with daily meditations, reflections, and recovery support materials. Several books had passages underlined or highlighted as Stevie found writing that resonated with his recovery. The two settled into their life together, with Janna furthering her modeling career with work in London and Japan, and Stevie again hitting the road to tour.

Their fourth year together began with Stevie playing at the inauguration of George H. W. Bush in January of 1989, and it ended with a New Year's Eve celebration in New York City, where Stevie played Madison Square Garden. Janna continued modeling jobs in the United States, Europe, and Asia. Stevie, fully released from his marriage, was finally able to complete work on the next Double Trouble album, *In Step*. To keep up with Janna's growing modeling career, the two rented a small apartment in New York. "We were paying so much in hotel bills staying there, that it just made sense to rent a place, especially for me to have when I was there for work."

Stevie spent most of 1990 touring, first in support of Joe Cocker and then on a double bill with Jeff Beck. In August, Janna and Stevie traveled to Australia, New Zealand, and Hawaii. They returned to New York and spent time in the Manhattan apartment until Stevie left to play a series of dates at Alpine Valley in Wisconsin with Eric Clapton. It was the last time Janna saw Stevie. "He called that night after the second show. We had decided to take a different apartment next to the one we had been renting. I spent the weekend moving our stuff. But we hadn't yet moved the phone line. I talked to Stevie after the show. While we were talking, someone asked him if he wanted a seat on the helicopter that was leaving. He decided to take it since it would put him back in Chicago sooner and he could call me before it got too late. I told him to be careful and that I loved him."

That helicopter never made it to Chicago. The weather was foggy, and the pilot wasn't qualified to fly in those conditions. Stevie boarded the helicopter along with three members of Clapton's entourage. Janna waited to hear from Stevie, but after she hadn't heard from him by 1:00 a.m., she went next door to the new apartment, where she fell asleep. In the early morning hours, after the crash had been discovered, various people attempted to call Janna, but without a phone in the new apartment, she remained unaware of the accident until later that morning.

"I first got the news in our apartment from his mother, who was still hopeful that he was wandering around in the hills somewhere there, at Alpine Valley. And I was like, okay, I'm going to hang onto that but knowing somewhere deep inside; well, we both knew, but you don't want to call it that yet. Then, of course, Jimmie, who had been at Alpine with Stevie, had gone to identify the body. So, we're just getting the news coming in. Stevie's AA sponsor called me as well and said, 'I want to go too, I want to go with you to where he is. I want to go where Stevie is.' But everyone was like, no, no. They're bringing the body back to Dallas. You need to go to Dallas; you need to get on a plane to Dallas. But I just wanted to be where he was, where he had been. But they all said no. They convinced me it was better to go to Dallas, so I went.

"Luckily, my [modeling] agency was right across the road, and I had a good friend at the agency. She just came over and helped me. I didn't know what I'm talking about packing for a funeral. I'm completely adamant that I'm not packing for a funeral, and for those first few hours, it was horrible. I even remember standing at the airport in line waiting to board. And I was with Stevie's publicist Charles Comer who became a dear friend. And I just remember standing in the line and just bawling. At first, you're just trying to contain it, and then it would just come and just hit you. And you're just like, you can't even explain it to yourself. You just need to get through this minute."

Once in Dallas, Janna went to Martha's house in Oak Cliff and waited to hear more. She knew that Stevie would be coming back to Dallas, and she wanted to be there when that happened. "I remember walking in toward her house when Jimmie got out of the car, Jimmie had a bag, it was a black garbage bag and it had all the belongings from the crash site, so it had his jacket, his boots. He didn't want me to have it, to carry it. He didn't want me to hold it, and I was like, 'Give it to me, give it to me, that's his stuff. I need it. All these things.' So it's thirty years ago almost, and I still remember I had to insist on it. Was he trying to save me from sadness? I don't know. I don't know what that was, but I remember being really adamant about that and taking Stevie's jacket and sleeping with it on me that night on Martha's couch. And looking through the bag, seeing the messed-up boots, the messed-up hat, the pants that were ripped up, because they had to cut things off. Seeing the shirt that he was wearing, seeing all that stuff, you know. But that was part of what I needed to identify because I couldn't go to the place to see where he was. I needed that. I'm okay with that. I needed to see him. I didn't want anyone to make that decision for me. Everybody is different. I respect that. But this is what I needed. And I will remember him how I remember him no matter what. But I needed to see him.

"And of course, by the time I saw him, they'd done everything they do and had him dressed. And I'm just seeing him, the way I needed to see, being able to feel him, what I need to feel that didn't even feel real. I was doing that, and then Jimmie came into the room because, you know, I wanted to be alone and then him coming in so that I don't know, maybe making sure I was okay. All these things I can look back on and think, gosh, I know what I would've done for somebody in that situation. You know, just leave them alone. They didn't want me to have his things, and yet I was the one that had to go back home—to our house—and find an outfit for him to be buried in."

I listen to Janna describe this experience and think of my own, of all the decisions around what we nonchalantly call "the arrangements." I had help in making these decisions, but they were mine to make. No one questioned me or second-guessed what I decided to do. No one felt that I had no right to make the decisions. Kevin had left some notes, and I followed his directions as much as possible. In the years after his death, I continued to live in our home, to honor him in the ways I felt were best. I surrounded myself with his things until I no longer could. Again, I think of this slip of paper, this marriage license, and how much it changes everything in times like these.

Within days of Stevie's death, Jimmie had made himself the executor of Stevie's estate. With only Stevie's mother Martha having any right to dispute it, it was easily done. Janna stayed with Martha the first few weeks, unable to return to their rented house in Dallas. "Martha and I were very close, and of course, my parents were on the other side of the world. I couldn't go back to our house alone, so I stayed with her in Oak Cliff." At the time, Janna was twenty-two and had just lost the only relationship she'd ever known.

Within a few weeks of the funeral, things began to change. Janna was told to empty out the rental home in Dallas and provided with one month's rent on the apartment in New York. "I was given thirty days to go through our entire life, five years' worth, in the Dallas house and put it all in storage. I was devastated. I had a job in Japan, and when I returned, they had gone through everything and taken what they deemed were Stevie's things, leaving mine. I went to the storage unit and only my things were left. It was like an invasion, really. I could schlep things into a storage unit, but that didn't mean I had processed anything. Then to see that someone had gone through our things, someone who had no idea what was meaningful to us. I don't know why, but the first thing I saw was my bike, there alone. They had taken Stevie's bike and just left mine. I don't know why that crushed me, but it did. To see our bikes separated."

Janna returned to New York and kept busy with work. "The only thing keeping me going was that I was getting calls to go to modeling jobs. But I would get there, and everyone knew my situation. Just seeing their faces and the sadness, it was awful. So much of grief, I think, is just this unbearable pain of being left behind.

"I couldn't understand how I could be in New York, with so many people, and yet feel so isolated and so alone. I kept notes and journals during that time, and it's hard to read them even now. I recently read one and was reminded of a time in the middle of the night, sitting in the closet on the phone with my friend back in New Zealand and telling her how they had gone through my stuff. I could get through the day, but the nights; you're just on your own in the night."

Janna credits the many hours she spent at Al-Anon meetings helping Stevie with his sobriety for also helping her get through the worst of the grief. "I was lucky to have quite a few wonderful tools from learning about the program that Stevie was in through Al-Anon just for insights for life, knowing that this, too, shall pass and seeing how you can overcome; seeing what a one-way road living in grief could become. I was right at that age where my friends could be going off the tracks or the wrong way. Eventually, you end up being sad and yeah, either in jail or alone or whatever. I knew I had to see things through and keep moving forward."

Being so young, Janna was naïve about how things would work with Stevie's estate and his family. She continued to believe that his family would do the right thing by her and by Stevie. She was certain Stevie would have wanted her involved in decisions about him going forward. After Doyle Bramhall had suggested she see a lawyer, Janna consulted his attorney and learned that she had only weeks to decide on legal proceedings. Letters were exchanged between attorneys, and a meeting was set up for Janna and Martha Vaughan (Jimmie Vaughan was also invited but didn't attend). With nothing settled at that meeting, Janna later received a letter from the Vaughan's attorney.

"I read the letter. It said that as much as they care about her, Jimmie and Martha never saw her as family. So, there it was, in writing. Five years together meant nothing.

"I found that I had one year during which to make a claim. One year is nothing. You're not even past the grieving. And what would it bring me? Money? It wasn't going to bring Stevie back. It seemed better just to walk away. The family knew it wouldn't look good for me. They'd cast it as being about money. So why would they do this? Why would they act this way? Why pretend I didn't exist? Because I didn't matter to them? They didn't think we're going to be together? It's like Jimmie got to play the hand of God as I see it.

"And of course, Stevie's mother got caught in the middle. We were very close. I remember sitting in that office with her, and we were both heartbroken. But she knew which side she had to be on. Shortly after all of this, she sent me a large check for my birthday with a letter that said she was sorry. I was headed to Japan for a contract job, and I wrote to her and said, 'You know it was never about this.' I still have the check; never cashed it. I'm sure she never told anyone she sent it."

Janna knew she would never be treated as Stevie's widow, but she had hoped she'd be considered as such when it came to projects like posthumous recordings or memorials. Instead, she has been ignored. "I'd be in New York on my own, walk into a record store and there's this new album staring me in the face, and it just guts you; it floors you. It's like your love is there and this whole new thing is there and it's just a shock. It brings so much back. I never asked for royalties, I only asked to be informed, included in some way."

I remind Janna again that if she only had that piece of legal paper attesting to a marriage, she would have been in the middle of everything. All decisions would have gone through her. "But I have many pieces of paper. Letters he wrote almost every day from the road. Notes where he added Vaughan to the end of my name. But I was twenty-two, I was grieving. I had no fight in me. It was all too raw."

Janna also had her photos. Boxes and boxes of photos taken with the Polaroid and other cameras that documented their time together and a relationship that was very happy and supportive. As one does with such things, Janna boxed them up and stored them away. She got on with her life, one modeling gig at a time, feeling fortunate to be based in New York and to have regular work that kept her mind occupied.

She developed a relationship with another musician, Johnny, who had been a friend in Dallas. They dated for a few years, eventually returning to New York. As with Stevie, Johnny also had emotional health issues and the two parted ways, but Janna credits him with helping her heal from her loss and giving her room to grow up. About a year after the break-up, Janna ran into Karl Leblanc, a friend of Johnny's whom Janna had previously met at a party. Karl had also recently broken up with his girlfriend, so the two started spending time together in New York. Within a year, they were married, eight years after Stevie's death.

The couple stayed briefly in New York. "I'm so lucky to have Karl. It was so special to be able to find a relationship like that. And it helped to be in New York, not in the Dallas microcosm of Stevie and guitar music." The couple moved to Sydney to care for Janna's mother after her father died. There, they started a family and remained until Janna's mother also passed away, at which time they returned to the United States to care for Karl's parents. Janna was happy, with everything she needed. She became a yoga practitioner and cherished her role as wife and mother. In all, she became philosophical about her past life as the woman that Stevie Ray Vaughan had lived with and loved for four years. Until, that is, Stevie Ray Vaughan and Double Trouble were inducted into the Rock and Roll Hall of Fame.

"I wasn't invited to the Rock Hall induction. You know, whatever. But a week before the event, I decided to go. A dear friend had an extra ticket, so I booked a flight and hotel room. I watched from our seats as other inductees were honored. And then it was Stevie's time, and Jimmie accepted on his behalf. I couldn't believe that a part of his speech was about how Stevie hadn't found love or a family to share his life with before he passed.

"I sat there and my heart just dropped. Such an insult. Not just to me, since I already knew how he felt, but to Stevie and the life that we had made together. It was one thing for me to be completely disregarded, but what about Stevie? What a way to honor the last five years of Stevie's life when he was happy. It was complete disrespect.

"After the show, I was outside waiting to cross the street to go back to my hotel. Jimmie and his third wife came out of the back door of the venue with her holding Stevie's statue. She stopped in a small crowd and began yelling Stevie's name. Nobody was saying anything, because they didn't know who they were. She had to hold up the statue and yell 'Stevie Ray Vaughan. Steve Ray,' and then people clapped, and I was just standing there. It was like a moment of your heart completely ripping open again. I can't even explain it. I was just thinking, 'No,' and it was like Stevie and everything was right there with me. He was with me. That wound that was so deep, it was like ripping it open. Of everything that I had been put through, this is the part of it that's the most offensive, really. And it was all just so unnecessary."

Janna went back to those boxes of photographs and created her own book and a Facebook page dedicated to Vaughan. The result was *Four Years in Pictures: Offstage with Stevie Ray Vaughan, 1986–1990*, a public, pictorial glimpse into the four years that Janna and Stevie were together. It was proof, if you will, of their meeting, of Stevie's time in rehab, and of their life as a couple in Dallas and around the world. Proof of their love and togetherness, even if a marriage certificate doesn't exist.

"It was time. It was just finally time for me to honor Stevie and our time together. It's one thing to pretend that I didn't exist. But to wipe away the last years of Stevie's life, to publicly state that he didn't find love was simply untrue. Don't take that away from Stevie. After the Rock Hall of Fame experience, I just felt that enough was enough. I just couldn't take any more.

"So I just made the book, it encouraged me to just say here's the story. I could see it in front of me, so I knew I just had to get it out. Because you know your story. You lived it. Obviously, it wasn't easy to pull together, but I got it together."

Sitting in the warm Florida sunshine, Janna pulls a copy of the book from a cloth bag and offers it to me. Though she provides occasional updates to her Facebook page, it had been a while since she had looked at letters and had paged through the book. "As soon as I started reading old letters, I just started bawling because I hadn't had to look at it for so long and it's amazing how it just takes you right back there. It's always in me, it's just part of your being, but it takes you right there, you know? Like hearing his music. And I did have to delve into those letters for the book, and it was too painful to look at. Now I'm a bit better about it, but sharing and talking about it, I think this has helped. Slowly but surely, we look at our memories and become thankful."

Whenever Janna posts on the Facebook page, people thank her for sharing her private memories of her life with Stevie. Usually, she demurs. "Why wouldn't I? Wouldn't it be selfish of me just to keep it all in a box and never give it the light of day? I want everyone to know what he was about with his messages and how happy he was. But if they can serve any goodness, then my God, that's the best thing. And to serve Stevie and his memory as well. I feel a strong sense of responsibility."

In 2019, authors Alan Paul and Andy Aledort wrote *Texas Flood: The Inside Story of Stevie Ray Vaughan*. They interviewed Janna for the book and quoted her in chapters about his sobriety and his life just before the tragic helicopter accident. It provides a small bit of consolation to Janna, a small level of recognition of their life together. In 2020, as the Covid-19 pandemic raged throughout America, Janna and Karl made the decision to return to New Zealand, where they now raise their family.

It is, to me, as though Janna has suffered Stevie's loss twice. To experience this romance at such a young age, and then to lose it so quickly, is bad enough. But to then have your very existence erased from history is even worse. It is difficult to imagine having the ability to move on when, by our very nature, we are compelled to leave a mark, to show that we mattered, that we were loved and loved others, and especially that we were important to someone else.

I know that there are others who shared my grief for my husband. His mother, his siblings, his children, his many friends. Together, we supported one another. I can't imagine the loneliness felt by a young Janna, on her own in Dallas or New York, thousands of miles from her family, grieving her first love. And of the terrible treatment by her adopted family, that of her true love, Stevie, passing judgment on her with no evidence. What a brave woman she was and continues to be.

My boxes of photos and letters now occupy space in a closet in a new home. I pull them out occasionally and, as Janna said, they pull me right back there, to those times when we were healthy and happy, young and hopeful. They are mine to share or not; I feel no responsibility to let others see them. They carry all the weight, but in many ways, they carry no weight at all, except of love between the two people—one living and one now passed on—who shared those moments with each other.

9

JUDY VAN ZANT

What does it mean to be strong in the face of the worst that could possibly happen? When everything is telling us to curl up and stop living, how do we keep moving forward? I remember being very reluctant to agree with those who referred to me as strong in the months after Kevin died. Well-meaning people offer it up as a token of support or encouragement. But they seldom know how weak and lost a grieving person feels. I don't know that I ever felt strong or courageous in the first years after Kevin's passing. I did what I had to do. I cried often, but almost always alone, apart from friends or family. It seemed an odd thing, this "strength" that they observed. Though others seemed to see it in me, I never felt it in myself.

I had planned to meet Judy Van Zant in Jacksonville, Florida, the town where her late husband, musician Ronnie Van Zant, had grown up and where she and Ronnie had met, fallen in love, and married, but Judy had other plans. When I spoke with her on the phone, she suggested we meet in New Orleans. Curious, I agreed. We could meet there, she suggested, and then drive up to Gillsburg, Mississippi, a small town about an hour north. Gillsburg would have never been known by anyone other than the town's residents but for the one incident that put it into music history: the plane crash that killed Ronnie Van Zant, three

Judy and Ronnie backstage at a Skynyrd concert. Courtesy of Judy Van Zant

other members of the Lynyrd Skynyrd band, and the two pilots of the ill-fated plane. The date on which I had suggested meeting Judy in Florida was just three days after the forty-second anniversary of the crash. If I could rearrange my travel, I could meet her instead in Gillsburg, on the anniversary, at the unveiling of a large granite monument that would permanently mark the crash site. I said yes.

A two-lane dirt road leads to a grassy field where previously there was very little to indicate the significance of the location. But on this day, a few hundred people gathered to mark the anniversary and attend the unveiling. During a brief ceremony, Judy introduced her children and grandchildren and thanked fans for their continued support. As the crowd gathered around the three granite stones that tell the story of the band and the accident, I walked through the field to get closer to the actual crash location. The day was warm and sunny; a line of pick-up trucks marked the start of the path away from the granite markers. Wandering farther, past trees that have now grown tall, I came to a clearing. The previous marker soon becomes visible among hanging vines and undergrowth—a gnarled, knotted tree into which fans and survivors have carved their names along with the ubiquitous Skynyrd tribute: "Freebird."

It's impossible to stand in that space and not feel the intensity of the tragedy that happened there in 1977. Ronnie was killed instantly upon impact, along with road manager Dean Kilpatrick, guitarist Steve Gaines, his sister and backup singer Cassie Gaines, and two pilots, Walter McCreary and William Gray. When I think of Judy—just 29 and with a one-year-old child—making her way to rural Mississippi to bring Ronnie home, I naturally think of strength. How tough she must have been to get through such a tragic event. She doesn't agree and, like my own recollections, she knows she barely functioned during those October days forty-two years ago. "You do what you have to do, but I feel as though, those days, it was almost an out-of-body experience. Like I could stand back and watch myself. You do things, say things, but it was like it wasn't really me," she says. But during the years after the crash, Judy was called on again and again to be strong: to honor Ronnie's legacy and to fight for what rightfully belonged to her and Ronnie's daughters, Melody and Tammy.

"I've been called the Yoko Ono of Lynyrd Skynyrd, which makes no sense," she says the next day, as we sit in a New Orleans café. The weight of the previous day's ceremonies and memories had taken their toll. Judy's family and the family of Steve Gaines are preparing to sightsee around New Orleans, but Judy still feels weary, so we sit in a quiet restaurant discussing our shared understanding of grief.

"I didn't break up a band, and neither did Yoko, for that matter. But people come in and want to run things, and so I had to be the bitch."

"Badass is the term now," I say.

"Well, either one. I did what I had to do."

Ronnie Van Zant was a rough-and-tumble, working-class kid from the west side of Jacksonville. From an early age, he knew he wanted to be a musician, and he brought together friends from various social circles until he had an assembly that felt right to realize his vision. They were fellow blue-collar kids, long-haired hippies without much interest in school. Together, they practiced in their parents' basements and garages until they developed their sound. Heavily influenced by the Allman Brothers, but also British bands like Free and the Stones, the band originally called themselves The One Percent. They were steady players at local Jacksonville bars, including The Comic Book Club. Across the street was another bar where a young Judy Seymour, recently arrived in Jacksonville from Waycross, Georgia, was a bartender.

"I worked across the street from [The Comic Book Club]. My roommate was Dean Kilpatrick. I had another roommate named Mary who also worked with me at the bar. Dean liked to hit The Comic Book Club quite a bit, and he became friends with Gary Rossington and then Ronnie and the rest of the guys. I knew and was friends with Dean first, and then Gary, since he would come over with Dean.

"One night I didn't have to work, and Dean talked me into going to The Comic Book Club with him to see the band. I went in, and the band was amazing. You could just tell right away that they were going somewhere. They were all great musicians and just well-rehearsed and tight. And up front was Ronnie, and that was just it." Ronnie was recently single from his first marriage, which included the birth of his daughter, Tammy.

By the time Judy saw the band, they were sounding professional. As band leader, Ronnie called for day-long rehearsal sessions at a tin-roof camp house along the river. The band christened the building "Hell House" because of the many long, hot days they spent writing songs and rehearsing. Ronnie developed a reputation as a task-master and came into his eventual role as bandleader. "I think they all really wanted to play, to spend their time playing and rehearsing," Judy tells me, "Ronnie was the leader, but they were all dedicated. It really was about the music."

When not there, band members congregated at various houses in Jacksonville. "Dean and I lived in this really cool house in Riverside called the Green House on Riverside Avenue. And then the next block over was the Gray House. That's where the Allman Brothers lived. There were Dickey Betts and Barry Oakley and their wives, and Duane and all. We all lived in that area and hung out." They rehearsed at various houses and moved as needed. Judy remembers having to leave one apartment when the landlord discovered she and Ronnie weren't married.

"In those days, that wasn't cool. So, we spent a lot of time at LJ's [early band member Larry Jungstrom] house; at his parent's house. Larry recently passed away, and I posted [on social media] about spending time at his parents' house. We lived there for a while after we lost our apartment. The others were there, too—Gary and Allen and Bob Burns. They were really like a family. It wasn't like 'Let's get together and rehearse and then go do our own thing.' They were together nearly all the time."

Ronnie was still working for his brother-in-law at an auto parts store. In a move that was a highly unusual sacrifice for the time, Judy told Ronnie to quit his day job and concentrate on the band. "He was driven, for sure. I knew that right away. During that time, he was also working at the auto shop. At that time, long hair was not really accepted, so he would wear a wig to work. He'd have to put his wig on every day and pull his hair up under it. He would do that all day and rehearse at night. I finally just said, 'Why don't you give up that job, and I'll get work. I'll go to work, and you rehearse.' And that's what happened. If you're involved with a musician, you know it's just in their blood. They have to be performing. You might as well support it."

The band knew they had to broaden the scope of their live performances if they were going to make it. They began playing clubs throughout northern Florida, South Carolina, and Georgia. Ronnie and the band were on the road a lot, making a name for themselves and looking for that break. That came with the opportunity to record a demo at Muscle Shoals studio in Alabama. More personnel changes would happen during this time as well, until the nearly final line-up of Van Zant, Rossington, Allen Collins, and Leon Wilkeson (who would leave and later return) were discovered playing an Atlanta club by musician and producer Al Kooper. The band went into the studio with the addition of Ed King, former guitarist for the Strawberry Alarm Clock, and Billy Powell on keyboards.

They recorded their first album with Kooper, who would go on to produce their next two albums as well. Kooper signed the band to his newly minted Sounds of the South record label, which was part of the larger MCA Records. Four years into their relationship, just as Lynyrd Skynyrd was taking off, Ronnie and Judy married. Band income, though not much, was becoming steadier, so the couple bought a small place along an inlet so Ronnie could go fishing, his favorite hobby when not playing music. "I still worked up until probably about this time. Ronnie was a big fisherman, he loved the water, and we had lived in rental apartments all those years, so we decided to look for a house. We bought a house on Doctors Inlet with three acres on the lake. That's where I got pregnant and had Melody. And that's where we were still living when he died."

Pronounced 'Lĕh-'nérd 'Skin-'nérd, the band's first album, was a hit, and the band took to the road in support. "Freebird" quickly became *the* rock anthem, and the band was on its way to stardom. Their first national-level tour had them opening for The Who and served to introduce Ronnie and the band to the wild ways of the road. To go so quickly from small venues around the South to a national stadium tour with The Who was amazing but also frightening. Leon Wilkeson is quoted as saying they were terrified, which caused them to start drinking. By the end of the tour, the drinking was nearly out of control.

"No one in Skynyrd, that I know of, ever did hard drugs. They drank, maybe smoked some weed. But none of them did anything like heroin. They were just kind of hippies. Not into the fast-lane lifestyle so much. You know, they did drink a lot of alcohol and that was their devil. I mean, that's what caused them to start tearing up hotel rooms. You don't do stuff like that if you're zoned on drugs or heroin." Nonetheless, the band acquired a reputation as a rough, brawling, country-boogie band and tried their best to live up to that.

In 1974, they recorded their next album with Al Kooper. *Second Helping* was released to mixed critical reviews but went to #12 on the Billboard charts. Their single, "Sweet Home Alabama," became another anthem, especially in the South, and solidified their standing as powerhouse Southern rockers. They toured in Europe in support of bands like Queen and headlined shows in the United States, touring nonstop from February through December of 1974.

"They were on the road a lot. I hung out with the other wives and girlfriends; we had our wives club, I guess you'd call it. I really wasn't too involved with the band once they became a bigger touring band. They had their managers and accountants and tour managers. I would pick some dates to go out and join the band but never really traveled with them. I went to New York, to San Francisco, but mostly, I stayed home.

"When [Ronnie] came home, it was an adjustment for both of us. I had my life with my schedule and structure, and I did my stuff. Just when I was getting into my routine, he'd come back, and there would be disruption. But when Ronnie came home, he wanted peace and quiet. That's where he wrote songs. He wanted to fish, to hang out, play baseball, go see his family. That's why our house on Doctors Inlet was so good for us. It was secluded and on the water."

And the road lifestyle of drinking and brawling? "When he came home, he didn't do that," Judy says. "I really didn't deal with any of that. When he came home, he was a different person. He knew from experiences on the road that Jack Daniels wasn't his friend. He didn't want to do any of that at home."

The band's third album, 1975's *Nuthin Fancy*, didn't receive the critical acclaim the others had. The album included one break-out single, "Saturday Night Special," charted higher than previous efforts. There were personnel changes as well, with Ed King leaving before the end of their earlier tour and Artimus Pyle replacing Bob Burns on drums. In the fall of that year, the band also incorporated under the name of Lynyrd Skynyrd Productions, Inc., with five band members becoming shareholders and Gary Rossington serving as the corporation's president. Share certificates were issued to band members. "I was never involved in the music or the business end," says Judy, "but after Ronnie died, I had to figure it out. I had to dig in."

By 1976, the band was tired and hardly in the mood to return to the studio but knew they must to fulfill their contract. They ended their relationship with Al Kooper and brought in Tom Dowd to produce. Over several weeks, the band recorded songs with tour dates in between. With the impossible schedule, a new producer relationship, and an exhausted band, the new album *Gimme Back My Bullets* was lackluster. It achieved gold status and made it into the Top 20 but was not as well received by critics. The band took to the road again, playing dates in the United States and Europe. Still without a replacement for guitarist King, back-up singer Cassie Gaines suggested they audition her brother Steve when the tour brought them near Steve's home in Oklahoma. Steve sat-in with the band in Kansas City and was asked to join a few weeks later. A highlight of the year was opening for the Rolling Stones at Knebworth Stadium in the UK.

Lynyrd Skynyrd had made it to a level they had previously only dreamed of, but Ronnie felt burned out. Years of travel, hard drinking, and hard work were taking their toll. For a time, Judy says, he considered leaving the band but ultimately knew he couldn't live without it. Yet, he was also aware something had to change. "Early on, I'm not sure fame was even a part of it. Ronnie just really loved music. He had this work ethic to be very good, but they weren't necessarily grooming for this huge fame that happened. They were just doing what they loved to do.

"Melody was born in 1976, and Ronnie just adored her. He actually named her Melody Rene. He really cleaned up his act after Melody was born. She is basically why he settled down even on the road." Melody came along at a time when Ronnie felt he had to make decisions. He was unhappy with the previous album and needed to reset the band and the rules both in the studio and on the road.

After releasing and touring in support of a live album—a tour that took them to Asia for the first time and then back to England—Ronnie recommitted the band to upping their game for their next studio effort. *Street Survivors* was released in 1977 to better reviews and critical response. Steve Gaines had solidified his place in the band, cowriting multiple songs and even performing a duet with Ronnie. Critics noted that it appeared Ronnie was allowing someone else to potentially step into a lead role, and Steve excelled in the role. Furthering his plan to refocus the band, the album was recorded sober, and the tour, dubbed by several band members as the "torture tour," would be played sober as well. In an interview for *People Magazine* conducted at Ronnie and Judy's home prior to the *Street Survivors* tour but published after Ronnie's death, he is quoted as describing the band's recent past as "five years of alcoholism."[1]

The first dates of the tour took the band to Statesboro, Georgia, then to Miami, St. Petersburg, and Lakeland. "Ronnie wanted to see Melody after that first week, so I took her to the show in Lakeland. He was getting ready to be on the road for a while, and he wanted to see her, so I drove down. We spent the night and hung out. And that was the last time I saw him."

From Lakeland, the band went to Greenville, South Carolina, and was then traveling on to Baton Rouge for the next night's show when the plane crashed due to loss of fuel. The plane had engine problems, but the pilots had assured road manager (and Judy's former roommate) Dean Kilpatrick that the tour schedule would be met. They'd go to Baton Rouge, they said, and repairs could be made once there. Additional fuel had been pumped into the plane to feed the malfunctioning engine, but the fuel mix created a situation in which the engine used more than was accounted for, resulting in quicker consumption. They ran out of fuel over Gillsburg, Mississippi, just ten minutes from Baton Rouge. The plane clipped the tops of the trees and nose-dived into the mucky swamp, breaking apart.

"I had been out that night with [Steve Gaines's wife] Theresa. We had started hanging out together when she and Steve lived near us. We became good friends pretty quickly," Judy says. "We both had young daughters, so we connected and hung out together.

"We had gone out to dinner that night. It was a Thursday, and we had just decided to go get some dinner. She picked me up and then dropped me off. I wanted to get back home because there was a show on TV that I liked to watch. I went in and got Melody settled and turned on the TV. Almost immediately it went to a bulletin or a news break, maybe they called it a news alert. To this day, I think it was Dan Rather, but it may not have been. I remember it that way. The flash was that the plane carrying the band Lynyrd Skynyrd crashed into a swamp in Mississippi and there were multiple fatalities, and they would come back on later with more details.

"Well, almost immediately Theresa called me, because she had heard the same news and she was in a total panic. My first response was to tell her, oh that's not true, it's just bullshit. I'm sure everything is fine. I got on the phone with [band manager] Peter Rudge from Sir Productions and said we just saw this news and he confirmed that it was true. They didn't have any details yet. They were waiting, trying to find out everything, and it seems now like it took forever to find anything else out.

"Theresa found out first, because she called me on the phone, hysterical. She had somehow found out about Steve. She just kept crying into the phone, 'Steve's dead, Steve's dead.' She was just screaming it. She didn't even know about Cassie yet. That news came a little bit later. I think the plane went down around 7:30 at night when I saw the news, and I think it was like 9:30 or 10:00 when I got the confirmation about Ronnie. But I kinda knew. I just knew."

I tell Judy the story of Maria Elena Holly and how she found out about Buddy's death in a plane crash by hearing it on the radio. Maria Elena lost her pregnancy shortly after as a result of that trauma. After that experience, the FAA developed rules around not releasing names to news outlets until next of kin are notified.

"Well, even back then, they just couldn't wait. You know, they just can't wait to get the news out. They didn't mention any names, but they said there were multiple fatalities. Just saying that was still a shock to hear. It put a really nasty light on the press for me. When I got to Mississippi, I had to say firmly, 'No press.' I didn't want the reporters coming around. I think I put the word out to the management company. Tom Wills, the reporter from Jacksonville that went to the crash, was at the ceremony yesterday and he told me that he was told they couldn't interview anyone in the family.

"When I think back now, I felt like I was on the outside watching myself do all the stuff that had to be done. Management arranged for a charter plane to Mississippi that same night. We left at two or three in the morning. It was me and Ronnie's dad, Lacy, and Billy Powell's wife. I think there were others, but I don't remember who. Theresa didn't go. We got on a chartered plane and flew to Mississippi. I remember getting on the plane, but I don't remember anything after that until being in a hotel in McComb, Mississippi, but I couldn't sleep. I remember going to the funeral home. Then we went to the hospital to visit some of the survivors, and it all just continued to feel like an out-of-body experience.

"After we visited the survivors, I just remember feeling like I had to get home. I gotta go home and take Ronnie home and make arrangements. We put Ronnie on the plane, you know, in his casket, and we took him home. My parents came down from Waycross, my dad was there. The minute they heard, they came down and stayed with Melody. My dad went with me to the funeral home to make the arrangements. I just remember being very irrational. There was so much to do, so much involved. We had to put him in the cemetery close to where we lived in Orange Park, but they didn't have mausoleums. I wanted him in a mausoleum because I couldn't put dirt on him. They finally accommodated us and let us do that. I went home and I remember a lot of people being there. I think I went to my room and slept. I hadn't slept in two days."

The weeks and months after were a blur. Judy focused on raising Melody and just getting through each day. She moved out of the house on Doctors Inlet where Ronnie had spent so much time relaxing and fishing. "It was just too painful to stay there. I had to get out," she says. Given the circumstances, Judy was never alone in her grief. In the months after the crash, Gary Rossington, Allen Collins, and Theresa Gaines spent significant time with Judy. Together, they comforted each other. "Once Gary and Allen were healed enough to come home, we spent all our time together. Because, you know, none of us understood what had happened. Our lives had all just completely changed overnight," Judy tells me.

"We were all grieving. Sometimes, a band member would be mad that we didn't help them. How could we? You never expect the worst to happen, and we didn't expect it. We didn't expect it en masse—everyone was either dead or injured or psychologically hurt. And we didn't have support. No one had a support system. Because everyone was in their own grief. We didn't have time or ability to help them out; we were helping ourselves and just barely getting by.

"I couldn't go to Ronnie's parents for support because they were also grieving. Theresa was my friend, but she was grieving as much as I was, and she lost two people. It wasn't like, if just my husband had been in a car wreck, at least I'd have some outside support to seek. But all those other people were also grieving. Gary and Allen were both critically injured, in pain and experiencing loss. They lost a best friend, someone they were closest to, who they lived with on the road. And everyone lost this future they had planned, that they had worked so hard for."

For several years, the former band, now just friends and survivors, struggled to get through their grief and to find purpose. "We really didn't do much for nearly ten years," says Judy. "I didn't deal with the band or even really think about it. There was some income from the settlement, and the music was still selling. We just stayed together. We had to.

"One thing we did do was make a pact. Gary and Allen and Theresa, sitting at my dining room table, we made a pact. They would not, there would never be, another Lynyrd Skynyrd. They would not, and we would not, capitalize on that name. They could, if they wanted to, go out and continue their careers, but they didn't want to. They didn't want to do Lynyrd Skynyrd. So that pact was made among us because we were best friends."

Gary Rossington and Allen Collins eventually formed the Rossington-Collins Band, which, like Lynyrd Skynyrd before them, had several iterations, including most of the guys in Skynyrd. Though they released a few records, they never reached the level of their previous success, and eventually it fell apart. Several band members struggled with substance abuse, depression, and grief-related issues. There were car accidents, boating accidents, and other signs that everyone was struggling.

Ten years after the crash, Gary, Allen, and the other survivors were approached by a promoter to do a series of reunion shows. According to Judy, "Everybody got back together. And Gary Rossington called me up and said, 'We're getting back together to do these dates. I know we said we wouldn't, but we are, and we're going to play the music, but we're not going to pay you. You're still making money from publishing rights, so you're fine.' And I thought, wait, what? So, okay, they did the ten shows. I didn't really do anything at that point. They did the ten dates, made a shitload of money for everyone except Ronnie and Steve. But then after the ten dates, it was like, oh, let's keep doing this. Look at this, we're picking up almost where we left off. Lots of people are coming to these shows, and we're making lots of money.

"I'm still a shareholder in Lynyrd Skynyrd Productions, and they decided to have a meeting and boot me out. I went to the meeting at this hotel at the Jacksonville airport. I took the two kids with me, Melody and Tammy. I thought, they wouldn't do anything if his kids were there. But they sat there in that hotel room, and they voted me out. The only person that did not vote, that said he would not be a part of this, was Allen Collins. And I just got up and said, 'You just made a big mistake.'

"That day, I called someone who turned me on to a lawyer in New York who's been my lawyer ever since, and I filed a lawsuit in federal court in New York. The other band members are saying, 'Well, you're not doing anything. You're sitting back in Jacksonville, why should you make any money?' Well, because you're playing songs that Ronnie wrote. And music and a reputation that he built. You wouldn't be here without him. It cost him his life.

"All through that, Theresa was my right-hand person. She didn't say too much. She didn't have too many rights, but she had some rights, and they didn't want to give her anything, either. She was right with me, probably made six or eight trips to New York. We had a couple of lawyers at our table, and they had eight or nine lawyers on their side. We didn't bring a lot of witnesses. We did have a lot of paperwork. I had to testify. We had a person testify about the idea of a blood oath, which was what we had. And the judge ruled in our favor. We drew up a consent order that covered everything going forward, how the name would be used and represented, all of that.

"That created a lot of hatred. Members of the band screamed at me, called me names in public. People that were my friends. I had never really dealt with the band. After Ronnie died, I still didn't deal. But then I had to deal, and with a lot of it. I lost a bunch of weight. I was down to ninety-five pounds, puking in the bathroom of the courthouse every day during a recess. The band members didn't show up; they sent their lawyers. But I had to be there, listening, and dealing with it every day. Gary and I came around to each other, but it wasn't always that way. I'm glad we're coming around because that's a lot to carry." Gary Rossington passed away in 2023, still friends with Judy.

Judy stood up for what she felt (and the judge agreed) was right, and although it helped her financially and she knew she could protect what Ronnie had built, it still came with a cost: friendships, support, feeling a part of the band. This, to me, is the very definition of being strong, but it's a label and a calling that nobody asks for. "Still, to this day, they think I'm sitting at home, so why should I make money off their tours. Well, because the law says so. And it's the morally right thing to do.

"For so long, it was Ronnie's band. From the very start. It was always what Ronnie said, and no one questioned that. Management talked to Ronnie; they didn't talk to anyone else. He really was the band's leader. And whatever Ronnie said, was what went. I just felt like people started coming in and really manipulating the survivors, so I had to stand up."

Once the court settlement was completed, Judy set about honoring Ronnie in other ways. She, Melody, and Tammy established the Freebird Foundation, which donated to worthy causes around the Jacksonville area. They also built the Ronnie Van Zant Memorial Park, a ninety-acre, multisport facility in Clay County. It includes baseball diamonds, picnic pavilions, volleyball courts, fishing piers, all the things Ronnie loved to do when he wasn't playing music. Judy and Melody also opened Freebird Live, a Skynyrd-themed restaurant in Jacksonville that featured live music. "We started by doing a few little bands on the stage in the corner. We did a few blues bands, Delbert McClinton, Jimmie Vaughan," Judy says.

Three years after the crash, Judy married Jack Grondin, another Jacksonville musician—the drummer for .38 Special. "I knew who Jack was since he was in Ronnie's brother's band. We just started hanging out. I'm sure being lonely had something to do with it. Aside from me and Theresa, everyone grieving had partners or spouses to help. We divorced, but we had twelve good years together and an awesome son. He adopted Melody and wanted to take care of her, which I'll always be thankful for."

Jack helped Judy enlarge the Freebird Live space to accommodate larger acts. The venue played host to major acts, including the Indigo Girls, Merle Haggard, Willie Nelson, Kenny Chesney, and Ziggy Marley. "We had the place for fifteen years. I retired after about seven, and Melody took over full-time. We owned the building, which was one block off the beach. At a certain point, we realized we'd had enough, and we really couldn't do anything bigger without investing a lot more money into the place, so we moved on. There were too many other things to do."

Judy was also active in producing the Live Oak Festival in Florida for several years. "It was fun, but it was very challenging. Festivals are difficult and have become really a money-losing venture in many ways. But the music was great. There should always be music in your life. I have found that being around music has healed many things."

And Judy has needed that healing, multiple times. Like the time Ronnie's brother called to tell her that the mausoleum where Ronnie was buried had been broken into. "Me and Melody had to get in the car and go over to the cemetery in Orange Park. We had to decide where he should be. I didn't want to find a permanent place for him unless Gary and Allen could be there, too. So they put him in something that was somewhat temporary. We had a memorial service and moved him to a permanent marker, and it was absolutely beautiful. I didn't want to bury him, to put dirt on him. But then we had to. We had to put him in the ground and put steel over it." He is currently relocated in the cemetery in an unmarked area. A large marker still exists near his family plot. "They never found who did it. They opened Steve and Cassie's area as well.

"I think I've done the best I can by Ronnie," says Judy. "I know you just don't get over something like this. It is with you always and becomes a part of you. I know that he did come to me shortly after. I've seen lots of signs, but this time, it was Ronnie. It was so real that it woke me up, and his presence was there. I swear he was there. I don't care what anybody says. He told me three things: I'm okay, take care of yourself and Melody, and don't worry about Gary and Allen, they'll be alright. I don't know if I woke up, but when I became aware, I was sweating. It was so real. It was about six months after he passed. He wanted me to know he'd be okay.

"Of course, me and Melody laugh sometimes, because every time we go anywhere, there's always a bird that flies in front of me, or in front of my car. And we'll be in a random restaurant and 'Sweet Home Alabama' will come on. The most disturbing thing for me is that I can't remember his voice. Not his singing voice, but his talking voice. I can't remember what he sounded like other than when I listen to interviews. I can't remember his touch. It's a lot, a lot to lose over time. I've tried hard to remember what he sounded like just talking to me, and I can't.

"I guess what I would like others to know about Ronnie is that he really was a simple man. He was kind and gentle and loved his family. His mother was a great cook, and she'd feed anybody that came in the door, so we spent a lot of time there. He loved his mother, and she was just the sweetest lady. He wasn't like the way he was portrayed. He was loyal to anybody that was his friend. He had friends that he grew up with that he still, when he came home, that's who he wanted to see. Those were the people who he wanted to hang out with, not famous people, not anybody else. Just his family and his friends."

As we prepare to part ways, Judy is joined by her daughter and granddaughter. It is easy to see the resemblance to a young Judy, but also to Ronnie, the father and grandfather they never knew. Judy's granddaughter was diagnosed a few years ago with Type 1 diabetes, and Judy has spent much of her "retirement" time fundraising and working with the local Juvenile Diabetes Research Foundation. The Freebird Foundation was dissolved a few years back, so Judy now spends her time working to help the next generation rather than the previous generation. Sadly, Ronnie's oldest daughter, Tammy, passed away in 2022. The most recent Skynyrd tour has been dubbed the "Farewell Tour," and if it is so, Judy is relieved.

But I get the feeling she will never slow down too much, never stop working for what she believes in, and never take "no" for an answer if she feels it isn't right. Whether she's been that way all her life, or whether she developed that quiet fortitude in the wake of the Lynyrd Skynyrd plane crashing into the Mississippi swamps and Ronnie's death, it's hard to say. But as I leave her, I better understand that continuing in the face of grief does take strength and courage, and it can reshape your very essence into a badass warrior if you let it.

10

JAMIE WEILAND

In our marriage, Kevin and I had always picked up slack for one another—I often feared the unknown, which kept me from taking risks. Kevin pushed me and reminded me of the rewards of taking a chance. Kevin had grown up with little support, which kept him from feeling confident. I supported his efforts and often told him he was more capable than he thought. We were fortunate that, prior to cancer coming into our lives, we didn't have to support each other through anything more challenging than these shortcomings. There were no breakdowns, no substance abuse, no lashing out. Had there been, would I have been expected to stay (as I was with his cancer diagnosis) or expected to go? Once cancer arrived and I did more and more for Kevin, eventually doing everything, I knew our marriage would forever be changed, regardless of how long it would last. But I never questioned that I would do it. I knew he would have done the same for me. I took our vows—in sickness and in health, for better or for worse—quite seriously. If you commit to loving this person, you do it through good times and bad, right?

I settle in on the sofa of Jamie Weiland's California home. She moved there suddenly after her late husband, Scott Weiland, founder and vocalist for Stone Temple Pilots and other bands, died of heart failure. Leaving quickly, she brought the small

Jamie and Scott in a quiet moment. Courtesy of Jamie Weiland

number of things she could after realizing that most of what she and Scott had shared would be entangled in legal disputes with Scott's ex-wife and children. "In the midst of grief, I had to just walk away," she says, sitting across from me in a room filled with her art and photographs. Jamie and Scott's dog, Buckley, a big but charming pit bull, snuggles at my feet and begins snoring loudly enough that it registers on the recorder. It's a homey, comfortable tableau, almost too calm for the stories I'm about to hear.

Scott Weiland was a highly creative, intense, confident, yet deeply troubled man. Jamie Weiland learned this early on yet remained with him until the end because she loved him. Though it may seem impossible to understand from the outside, it is easy for Jamie. "I saw how vulnerable he was. He was so vulnerable, especially during difficult periods. Nobody really took care of him or had his back or had his best interests at heart. I got glued into his professional relationships so quickly, it was like quicksand. He was like quicksand. I couldn't leave. I couldn't. I loved him," she says.

They met when Jamie was hired to take photos of Scott for his Christmas album, *The Most Wonderful Time of the Year*, released in 2011. "A friend asked if I wanted a job as a still photographer on set while they were shooting videos for the album. I had never done that kind of work. I did mostly portraits and had photographed kids. I was a food photographer. But I had never been a still photographer on a set. But I just thought sure, I'll do that.

"But the night before, I kept asking myself why did I say I'd do this? I was wondering if I could call in sick, but I showed up for the first day at his studio. It was a full music video set. There were tons of crew and people, management, people from the record label. I kind of hovered in a corner. Scott was three or four hours late. We're all just sitting around waiting.

"Finally, he walked in, and he was wearing a long black coat. He had the collar turned up and he just kind of glanced at me, and it was like, hmmm, okay. For the rest of the day, I was documenting everything around these videos."

Jamie smiles remembering that day. She laughs, "You know, he wouldn't look at me. I would kind of catch him glancing at me, and I'd look at him, kind of study the scene to take a photo, and he'd quickly look away. There was a time when he was being interviewed, and they wanted me to document that. In the photos from that time, there's just a look in his eyes like, 'I don't trust you.' He really was so shy and quiet. He walked past me as we went to our cars, and I said, 'Have a good night,' and he didn't even respond. Just kept walking.

"The next day we're shooting at a house, and the [record] label specifically asked for photos of him posed in front of a fireplace. I'm watching everyone around him, and they're all like, 'Excuse me, Mr. Weiland,' and I'm trying to get these last few photos I need so I can leave. So finally, I'm like just yelling, 'Hey Scott!'" He turns and I said 'The label needs me to take pictures of you. I just need five minutes over there by the fireplace.' He's wearing a tuxedo with the tie undone. I said 'What you're wearing is fine. I just need a few pictures.' He leaned in front of the fireplace, but he was so stiff and awkward, which is funny because it's so out of character. This guy was incredible in front of the camera, but he was so nervous.

"I had to ask him to tuck in his tummy. He'd been drinking so much—I know now—that he'd developed a bit of a belly, and I had to ask him to tuck in his tummy so the pictures would look better. He started laughing. It was clear no one had ever talked to him like that.

"Afterward, we were leaving, I was getting in my car, and he came over and said, 'Thank you so much for everything. You were really great.' I told him thanks and said it was great meeting him. And he gives me a hug. And that hug lingered. It was a little longer than you would just give someone that you'd spent a day working with. So . . ."

They had no further interactions for a few weeks. Jamie continued to do photography work, not really thinking any longer about her two days on set with Scott. When no one from his office followed-up with her about the photos, she reached out to his assistant.

"I called his assistant to see if he'd selected photos. He wanted a contact sheet, which no one ever asks for anymore. When she came to pick it up, I said, 'Tell Scott I said hello and it was great working with him.' And she's like, 'Oh, I forgot to tell you, here's Scott's number and he wants you to call him.' So I texted him just 'hello,' and he called me right back. We ended up talking on the phone until four in the morning. And I knew, I just knew this was my person.

"We met again after about a week of these late-night phone calls. He had a show at the El Ray, and I went backstage. We eventually were alone in his dressing room, and he kissed me. The manager came in and told us we had to leave. We got a ride to drop me off, and I remember, it was cold and rainy. He wrapped me in his coat and kissed me again. He looked at me and said, 'You know, I'm gonna fall in love with you.' The next week, I went to New York with him. He did a series of Christmas shows on the east coast and I came along."

For several weeks, the couple lived a quiet life getting to know each other. At the time, Scott was performing with his supergroup, Velvet Revolver, which included Slash, Duff McKagan, and Matt Sorum from Guns N' Roses, and Dave Kushner from Wasted Youth. Jamie mostly stayed out of his performances and band involvement in the early days of their relationship. Instead, the two grew to know each other together away from the rock and roll life.

"We didn't go to restaurants. We didn't go to parties. I loved to cook, and he loved to eat, so I would go to his house, and we'd cook, listen to music, drink wine, watch movies, have sex. We were in our own little bubble. It was very normal. Well, maybe normal would've been going out on dates, but I never missed that. It was a lovely time. It was quiet, it was sweet. He was just Scott, not rock star Scott. He was quiet and thoughtful. We talked about everything.

"At this point, I had only seen him singing Christmas songs. Then, I think, it was New Year's Eve and Velvet Revolver played a benefit at House of Blues. Scott was singing, and I was in the crowd. I had never seen this Scott—rock star Scott, in the tight pants, slithering across the stage with the megaphone. All this started happening, and I'm watching him. I was with a friend, and I turned to her and started grabbing her arm because I'm freaking out. She looks at me and says, 'Oh, he's so hot.' But I'm like no, no, no, you don't understand. I felt sick to my stomach seeing him. Everyone was asking if it was amazing to see him on stage, and I'm just thinking, no it wasn't. This isn't the guy in my bubble. This is like a completely different person. It was eye-opening that he could be so different on stage. I just kept wondering who this guy was. But at that point, we had started spending all of our time together."

Scott Kline was born in California, but he moved to a suburb of Cleveland after his parent's divorce. The relationship between his birth father and his stepfather shaped Scott in many ways. After his mother remarried, his stepfather, Dave Weiland, adopted Scott, changing his last name to Weiland. The school year was spent with his mother and stepfather and the summers with his biological father, Kent, in California. Photos from Scott's memoir, *Not Dead and Not for Sale*, show Scott as an all-American, midwestern kid. He wrestled and played football and baseball, was a bright student, and developed a close relationship to his younger stepbrother, Michael. He also grew up

Catholic and wrote openly of the strength of his faith. By high school, the family returned to California, and Scott was introduced to music, forming a postpunk band with classmates. Soon after, he was having his first run-ins with his parents, school authorities, and psychologists due to substance use—alcohol, pot, and, occasionally, cocaine.

Stone Temple Pilots was formed in 1991 in Los Angeles. Scott enlisted Robert DeLeo on bass, and together they brought in Eric Kretz on drums and recruited Robert's older brother Dean on lead guitar. After a few gigs in LA with this lineup, Atlantic Records offered the band studio time to record an album. The result was *Core*, an album that wasn't well received critically but became a huge success with fans. The album sold over eight million copies and generated four Top 5 hits, with "Plush" going to #1 and "Creep" peaking at #2 on the charts. The band quickly established itself as one of the most popular of the 90s grunge era. At the band's first big post-album-release show in New York, Scott wrote in his memoir, people backstage were putting in orders for China White heroin. Believing he couldn't be in the "major leagues of alternative rock without at least dabbling with the King of Drugs,"[1] he placed his order and snorted before going on stage.

At this time, Scott was married to his first wife, Janina, but was also spending time with the woman who would become his second wife, the model Mary Forsberg. In his memoir, he writes that heroin "took me to where I'd always dreamed of going,"[2] leaving him unafraid, uninhibited, and without doubts or fears. It is simplistic to reduce Weiland's drug use as a rock and roll thing, although it took a somewhat shy, athletic, religious kid, and allowed him to feel free and spontaneous on stage, the one place he most longed to be.

From 1990 to 2013, STP's line-up remained the same. The band released five successful studio albums, but an attempted tour in 1997 was ended when Scott entered rehab. Over the previous several months, his behavior had become more erratic and his drug use more constant, making it difficult for the band to remain together. The band split temporarily in the early 2000s, with members doing solo projects and working with other bands. During this time, Scott released two solo albums, *12 Bar Blues* and *Happy in Galoshes*.

The band toured and recorded on and off through 2011, taking time away for Scott's solo projects, like the Christmas album he was working on when he met Jamie, and another stint in rehab. Finally, in 2013, Kretz and the DeLeo brothers fired Scott from STP, citing his increasingly erratic behavior. Lawsuits and countersuits followed as Scott fought to prevent the remaining band members from being able to tour as Stone Temple Pilots. Jamie tried to be a source of balance and calm through the last two years of Scott's life, which were filled with band breakups, lawsuits, countersuits, and forming new bands. At the time of his death, he was touring with another band, The Wildabouts.

Though seeing him play live had been an eye-opening experience, the introduction to deeper mental health issues and drug use followed shortly after. She quickly realized that "rock star Scott" needed help.

"I was starting to see some things with him that were odd. Like a lot of paranoia and a lot of suspicion. He always had the curtains drawn in his house. Always. I'd come over and open the curtains, and he'd follow me around closing them. I found odd things like a cigarette put out in an electrical socket. Things that were more than just eccentric.

"One night, he mentioned something about my divorce being finalized. I'd been separated since before we met, and the divorce was proceeding. We'd been to a mediator, and things just needed to be wrapped up. I tried to explain that, but Scott just completely flipped out on me. He was angry but acting more like he was hurt and could no longer trust me. Or like he felt that I had been keeping this big, dark secret from him that I wasn't yet divorced.

"I asked him, you know, I'm with you every night and most days. Where do you think I am? I'm not going out on you.

"I started seeing that distrust. There was another time that he was having trouble with a smoke detector at his place. I went over to see what was going on and called the alarm company. The repair guy comes out and takes it apart and says, 'Is this paint?' Scott was obsessed with paint ball guns and, apparently, this smoke detector was going off, so Scott shot it with his paint-ball gun.

"We would sit in his bedroom in front of the fireplace talking, and he would sit with his paintball gun, shooting it into the fireplace. And that was kind of a normal evening. It was so bizarre to me. And I was crazy about him. So crazy about him that I looked at this like, okay, this is a new adventure. You know, I'd wake up in the morning, and he'd be in bed with a bottle of whiskey and smoking. I asked him if he really had to smoke first thing in the morning, in bed. He looks down and says, 'If you're going to be with me, you better learn how to live in a saloon.'"

Scott was also going through a divorce from Forsberg and dealing with alimony and child support negotiations. Jamie realized very quickly that he was being poorly managed because everything was a mess, from the business side of his music to divorce arrangements. Scott consulted Jamie on his business dealings because she was one of the few people he trusted.

"One of the first things I said to him was, I'm here to be your girlfriend. I'm not going to get involved in your business. I don't want to be your manager. Well, that lasted all of thirty seconds. He quickly brought me in to the fold of managers and lawyers and assistants and all that. They quickly realized that I was the best way to get to Scott because he would just not answer his phone. Or he would lose his phone. Or he'd be suspicious that the phone was tapped, so he'd throw it in the fireplace and his assistant would have to get him a new one. In the first two months that we were together, he had six different phone numbers. But at the same time, he was so sweet and so brilliant."

"You know," I ask, "This has to lead to the question of why you stayed if you saw his situation early on."

"Well, he wasn't always doing that kind of stuff. He was also brilliant, one of the funniest people I've ever known in my life, so affectionate, so adoring. So, so, smart, about things that you wouldn't think a rock star would be brilliant about. I joked that, you know, if the rock star thing doesn't work, he could be a professor of philosophy or history. He just knew so much.

"He had a strong sense of style. We're both style people, both artistic. How we decorated and how we dressed; it was an art form. And we shared that. And he was very passionate, we had chemistry. We had chemistry that was unlike anything I'd ever experienced. I don't know that I even have words for the passionate, physical connection we had. We always felt like we had already known each other. We both felt so familiar to each other. His soul, his mind, felt familiar to me.

"And then I saw how vulnerable he was. Although he had this circle of people around him, no one ever really had his best interests at heart, no one ever really had his back, unconditionally. He didn't really have a lot of friends."

Scott lost his brother, Michael Weiland, in 2007 from cardiomyopathy related to drug use. His parents, with whom he maintained a good relationship, lived in Colorado, so in many ways, Scott was on his own. Jamie felt strongly that his management team wasn't looking out for him. "I had a friend who worked in the management office, and she would tell me things that were going on," Jamie says. "I knew things they were saying about Scott. I couldn't leave him exposed like that, knowing what I knew.

"And I loved him. There was fun, light, loving parts, too. We traveled. We did fun things. But, you know, it didn't take too long to realize that a lot of the dark part had to do with his mental illness. And whether Scott was on his meds. At first, things he did or said just seemed, um, quirky. But then things did become disturbing. There was one time when we were driving someplace, and he was watching me. I'd do something like this [Jamie rubs her nose] and Scott would say, 'Who are you signaling?' And I'd say, 'No one, my nose itches.' And he'd say, 'Really, because your nose itched two minutes ago, and the same car drove by. Why are you sending signals to those people?' And I said, 'Really, that didn't happen.' And then another time, we were driving, and he said that he kept seeing the same license plate on every car. And I'd tell him, 'No, babe, you don't, that's not happening.' But there was no reasoning.

"One day, we were going to the beach, and I wanted to take photos of him. But by the time we got there, I was in tears.

He was so suspicious and so paranoid. 'Why did you do that? What are you doing?' If I got a text, he'd demand to know who it was. I tried to calm him. I said, 'Hey, we're just going to the beach, babe. It's a beautiful Sunday afternoon. Just relax and try to enjoy it.' But he couldn't. That sweet, funny, affectionate, brilliant guy, just gone. If his meds were off, or he wasn't taking them, that person was gone. He even looked different. His eyes would be different, his speech would change. I could glance at him and know that something was off, and it was a constant effort to keep things in balance.

"He would forget to take them, or take too many, or not take them at the right time. Or eventually, they'd just stop working. And then you're on a six-to-eight-week cycle to see if something new would work. And it's fine for everybody else to say, 'Hey, maybe change his meds, maybe something else will work better. Try this or that.' But who was there holding him? Who was at his home dealing with all of it or trying to protect him from all of that behavior when he was in public or on stage. It was all on me. How could I leave? I couldn't. I couldn't."

Despite all of it, Jamie knew she was in love with this man. Scott and Jamie married on June 22, 2013, at their home. Soon after, they moved to another house, which further exacerbated Scott's mental health issues.

"When I met Scott, he was living in a cute little house in the Valley. But his manager convinced him to sell that house and move into a house in a gated community in Bel Aire. It was a huge, hideous house. He had a mortgage on the house in the Valley, so he was building equity. But they sold that house and convinced him to rent instead. The thinking was that a gated community would make Scott feel safe. Except what it ended up doing is that it fucked him financially. He was paying more than ten grand a month to rent this house. It needed significant work for what he wanted. It was just a bad move all around. And I don't think he ever felt safer.

"I moved into that house with him just before we married. Shortly after I moved in, he went off his meds and came after me. I had to lock myself in the bathroom with the cats because I was afraid for all of us. I don't think he would have come at us physically, but he was raging at that point. I was more concerned that he would throw a door open, and the cats would run out, or he'd break glass, something like that.

"But after that, I did decide that I needed to move out for a while. I got a place of my own for a while. A few weeks later, we got back together, and then we married in June."

Also at this time, Scott was leaving Stone Temple Pilots and forming his solo band, The Wildabouts. He began touring with them shortly thereafter.

"The whole thing with STP had become a problem. They wanted him out of the band. They didn't want to try to tour with him anymore, so that turned into a huge legal issue and lawsuit. And his response was to form the Wildabouts. He seemed to settle into that a bit, but it wasn't long lasting."

Looking back, Jamie believes the first year of their marriage was probably their best. But there were problems caused by being in the Bel Aire house because being there seemed to exacerbate his paranoia rather than calm it. "So much bad stuff happened there," she says. "Scott had a lot of paranoia in that house. The house just had something wrong with it. We all saw things and felt bad energy. I believe that impacted Scott.

"Then money started becoming an issue. We were stuck between a rock and a hard place. I was terrified for Scott to be out on the road. If anyone saw him in that state that he could be in, they'd automatically assume it was drugs, and then that would harm his career even more than the precarious place he was already in. Those guys had to work hard to get him to shows and to stay on tour. They get a lot of props for that. It wasn't easy at all because they were also putting their own careers on the line by keeping Scott and working with him. He was volatile. But if he didn't tour, we didn't eat."

Jamie had given up her own career to care for Scott full-time. In exchange, Scott agreed to remunerate Jamie for her lost income. More often than not, those payments were forgotten, something that would later come back to haunt Jamie.

"I had quit working because he became my fulltime job. I was his day-to-day manager and his personal assistant, and I was the go-between for everyone and everything that had to be done. At least half the time he was on tour, I was with him. So yeah, I had no career during that time. It got shelved.

"Which I was happy to do in many ways. It was often really fun to be around the creativity, to be around his genius. It was magnetic and intoxicating. It was so exciting to be around the music. I often told him, if I was the only one that heard the music, I would be completely mesmerized by it and by him. It had nothing to do with the success of the music or the level of stardom, and everything to do with the person who created it. He fascinated me."

During this time, Jamie maintains, Scott was not using drugs, although he was drinking. The mixing of meds and alcohol made him erratic. "You know, he had a backpack full of meds. He was never without his medication. But I'm pretty sure none of them were supposed to be combined with alcohol, which, at that point, he was consuming in large amounts," she says. She also worried about the formation of The Wildabouts, as the four men together were potential trouble.

"Oh, they all liked to have fun. And that fun could be destructive," she says. "And the drinking certainly made things worse. Not just the combination, but he would drink and forget to take his meds, or he'd take too many, or he'd pass out and miss them altogether. Managing that, juggling that, was the hard work.

"When we lived in the Bel Aire house, he did get sober. He went to rehab for a little while. He came back from rehab and was doing great. He was feeling hyper, so he started seeing a psychiatrist, and she put him on something to calm him down. But he had a bad reaction to that. I had to leave the house and call the police."

How do you continue to believe your love will be enough? Especially with a person who can become volatile and dangerous without warning. When do you find it to be time to leave? In reading Scott's memoir, it becomes clear that this is a person who is, time and time again, really trying to figure himself out. When an addict checks himself into rehab twelve times, do you give up on that person or do you give credit to that person for continuing to try? Or do you understand, as Jamie feels she does, that the drug and alcohol use stemmed from a root cause so deep and so destructive that no one can be more frustrated and disappointed than the person caught in the constant loop of trying to get well. At these questions, Jamie begins to cry.

"He tried. He really did. It was just so hard to watch him try. When he was sober, he was the best person. You would have loved him. So creative, so caring. He had such a big heart. A really big heart. And I watched him go to rehab four times in the three years that we were together. He came out the last time and said he'd never go back; it just wouldn't work. He knew it wouldn't. He didn't say, 'Oh it won't work so let's go party.' He said, 'It won't work, and I don't know what else to do.' So where do you go from there?

"We had a therapist once that we both saw together, and then Scott saw her a few times on his own. And she called me and said that if I continued to live with him, she wouldn't see me. She felt that I needed to leave. That was just so shitty. This is someone who should have been working with him to get better; he just needed to be on the right meds. Instead, she gave up on him. Whenever anyone asks why you put up with being locked out or having to lock up his stuff, the answer is that he was sick. When you found out your husband had cancer, did you think, well, that sucks for you? I'd love to stick around and help, but I'm going to take off? See ya. No, you stayed. Scott was sick. Maybe I could have left before I was too deep into it, but I just couldn't leave someone who was clearly sick and who needed someone with him.

"You just hope, you keep hoping that something will work. I have friends that have been sober for years, who don't care about the drugs or the alcohol. They don't go to meetings; it was just something that was a part of their lives that isn't anymore. But Scott could never get there.

"I mentioned to a friend who is a recovering alcoholic that I had been drinking a little too much during the holidays, and I needed to stop for a while. I remember she looked at me and said, 'You can do that because you don't have the -ism.' I can't really explain the term, but I see what she meant; you know, some of us can drink and then stop drinking. Others start and can never stop because, according to her, they have alcoholism, the -ism. They can't turn it off. Scott couldn't turn it off. He was always wondering where his next drink would come from."

Jamie and Scott moved out of the Bel Aire house once the lease was up. "We never fit in that neighborhood, as you can imagine, in the gated community. Our pit bulls, tour buses. Scott used to ride his motorcycle on the walking path. We clearly did not fit in there."

Instead, they found a smaller house in Laurel Canyon, one that Jamie used to drive by before she met Scott and tell herself she would someday own. "That was *the* house," she says. "The one I always wanted. It went on the market, so we bought it and moved in in early 2014.

"We were happy there for almost two years. We were both just happier in the canyon. Scott was doing great, but then his drinking got bad. Really bad. I had to take away his phone, his keys, his wallet and lock them in a safe so he couldn't go out to buy alcohol or call anyone to bring it to him. At one point, he's crawling on the kitchen floor to open the freezer to see if there's vodka in the freezer. He couldn't stand up. Shortly after that, he bottomed out and then was doing a lot better for a while. Then he went on the tour, and I think he was trying hard, he seemed to be doing better. He was drinking, but not nearly as much. Even the guys in the band and the crew were saying that he was doing better with the alcohol.

"I was with him for most of that tour. I was there through September and October, and then I came home. We were together in New York on November 27. Then I came back home, and he died a week later."

Just before the tour started, Jamie began feeling that something major was going to change, that something wasn't right. Possibly, it was a premonition. She had recently started painting, in addition to her work as a photographer, she told me. "I had a little studio in the house, and I started painting on paper bags, and canvas and wood. A couple days before Scott died, I started getting that feeling again that something was going to change. I felt compelled to take pictures all around the house and document how everything was at that time.

"That day, on December 3, I had been painting, and I knew he was probably sleeping. He was on the bus. He slept in really late. He texted me the night before and said, 'I'm so in love with you my beautiful wife.' That was the last thing he ever said to me. The next morning, I texted him and just said, 'Good morning, babe,' but I didn't get a response. I tried calling him a little later and nothing. So, I'm texting and calling and getting nothing. I sent him a picture of the painting I was working on and no response. I sent a text an hour later and said, 'Well, I guess you hated it because you haven't said anything.' But still no response.

"By late afternoon, I called his manager, and he said they had been out all day at Mall of America and Scott was just sleeping on the bus. I told him he needed to go check on him because it wasn't like him to sleep all day. He would have at least gotten up to call me. And at that point, I just knew. I knew there was something bad. I tried calling his manager back, and it was going right to voice mail.

"I was in the kitchen and my son was with me and we were making dinner. I got a call from Maxey, Scott's in-ear monitor on stage. He calls me and says, 'Sweetie, Scott's dead.' Tour managers always talk like this, twangy and direct. I fell to the floor and just screamed and screamed. My poor eleven-year-old son is just staring at me. I don't even remember if I said anything else to Maxey. But my son said 'Mom, it can't be true. Scott loved you too much. He would never leave you.' But I knew, and I said 'No, he's dead, he's dead.'

"Then my son came to me and held me. He said 'Mom, you can't let this break you.' And I just couldn't believe my son, so young, but he was there comforting me with these grown-up words. And then the phone starting ringing. Oddly, one of my closest friends was driving from Sonoma to LA. She got this eerie, cold feeling, so she turned the radio on to have some music, and it was the announcement that Scott was dead.

"Friends started arriving, and the house was just full of people. I'm sure someone stayed with me. I think I took something to sleep. But then there's that feeling when you wake up the next morning where you know something's not okay, but you don't know what, and then you remember. That split second where you've forgotten.

"When I said goodbye to him in New York in November, that day was so odd. It was Thanksgiving, and we were staying at the Grammercy Park Hotel, which was our favorite. We spent the whole day locked up in the room just being together. It was like we felt we had to pack everything into that day. We made love all day, and it felt like we were never going to be together like that again. We didn't say it, but we were just so connected.

"They came to get him about 1:00 a.m. to leave and we said goodbye. I'm watching him walk out the door, and we both felt like this isn't just saying okay, see you in a few weeks. There was something bigger about it. I couldn't explain it. It just felt different. I think back now, and I wonder, should I have run after him? What would I have done? Would it have been better if it happened some other place? If he had been sleeping next to me when he died? Would that have been easier, or even more traumatizing?

"One of the worst things was that I made him go see a doctor to get a physical. I was fanatical about our health and seeing a doctor regularly. We had an appointment with a cardiologist in mid-December for when he got back from the tour. If we had only gone to that appointment first, they could have found the blockage in his heart. Why didn't we do that first? Why didn't I think of that? He was a drug user, a chain-smoker, a heavy drinker. How did I not think to have his heart checked? How did his other doctors not require that he see a cardiologist?" Like many in this situation, the questions and second-guessing plague Jamie.

"And then, just a few weeks after he died, it was Christmas. That was our holiday. It was the reason we met and were together. I love Christmas, but Scott *really* loved Christmas. And for it to be Christmas without him. It was the time for love and being with the one you love, and my person wasn't there. I went to see our neighbors; they were so helpful during that time. I walked in and they had their tree up, and I just stood and cried. She came over, put her arm around me, and said, 'Tomorrow we're going to the lot and getting you a fucking tree.' That

Christmas was really rough. Everything was just hollow; I felt nothing."

Within days, it was clear that Scott had never sorted out his estate or planned for something like this. "Within a day or two, I was being told what I can and can't do, what I can and can't say. People wanted to come into my home, where I had lived with my husband who had just died. There were threats of jail from his former wife. Plus, all the stuff in the press and the statement to *Rolling Stone*. When she [Forsberg] did come over, she started going through his things and looked at me and said, 'Why didn't you throw his clothes outside and set them on fire? That's what I would have done?'" [In 2007, as Forsberg and Scott Weiland were breaking up, Forsberg famously put $80,000 worth of Scott's clothing outside their home and lit it on fire. After Scott's death, she made a statement published in *Rolling Stone* in which she admonished fans to not make a hero of Scott.][3]

The situation left Jamie without many options. "I signed a prenup, which took away a lot of my rights when Scott died. And Scott had paid the monthly amount we agreed to exactly twice. At the time of his death, he owed me over $68,000. And all those times when Scott was too sick to work, I paid for our living expenses. All with the promise from him that he'd pay me back. So not only had I shelved my career, but I also had no money.

"I could have gone to court to take it all over, but at the time of his death, he was involved in multiple lawsuits, including with STP. He owed money to everyone, including the IRS. The studio was a mess. To take that over would really have been just dealing with a complete mess that eventually would have benefitted his kids, not me. Instead, I chose to walk away and move on with my life. The business manager called me and made me leave the Laurel Canyon house three weeks after Scott died. I had very little and couldn't afford to keep that house on my own. Between us, we had books and art and clothing, a lot of things that we had collected together. A lot of it was taken, but there was still stuff that had to be moved, all within days. I was just shellshocked. It brought on anxiety that I'm still dealing with. There's a feeling that just hovers around that something bad can happen at any minute. It's something I still work on.

"What people don't realize is the added stress of it all being so public. And I stupidly agreed to do interviews when I wasn't in my right mind. Everyone wanted to talk, and I felt like I needed to clear the air and explain things. I felt that his fans deserved to know. I certainly misspoke, I said wrong things, said things I shouldn't have said, didn't say things I should have. But I was a mess. And the media loved to butcher my story. They didn't do anything to pay tribute to Scott. Platinum record sales, albums, and singles at #1, sold-out shows. Why wasn't he on the cover of *Rolling Stone*?"

Jamie also battles the publicly reported cause of death. "It wasn't an overdose," she says. "He had minute amounts of drugs and alcohol in his system. The main ventricle of his left valve was ninety percent blocked. His heart gave out. Was it from years of abuse? Yes, but it wasn't an overdose. Even my son is going to school with kids telling him his stepdad was a drug addict, 'Your stepdad died,' they taunted. He goes on the internet and sees pictures of himself because of who his stepdad was.

"And people were awful around what I had to do in the days after. I had no money, nothing. I had to sell my engagement ring. The world hated me and asked how I could do such a thing. But I had to do something to get by. I had to find a new place to live within days. People say things like I should get a job waitressing if I need money. Or they think because I was married to a rock star, I'm set for life. They have no idea. Everything is so public. There's no anonymity, just a big old window for everyone to watch how you respond with your broken heart."

Jamie asks if I'd like to see her photos of Scott. She pulls out a box—one of the few things she was able to bring from their home—and flips through snapshots of the two of them, or portraits of Scott. There are letters he wrote, telling her how much he loved and missed her. There are selfies of the two of them from their day at the beach. In them, he looks more vigilant than relaxed. In one, his brow is furrowed. It is clear he had a difficult time ever feeling at ease.

Living with Scott could be described in many ways, but peaceful isn't one of them. Has Jamie found any peace now? "Not really," she says. "I know he's gone, but he's always around. I hear his voice; his voice will always be in my head. I look at things, at life, with the Scott filter. What would he find funny, what would he think looked good? What would scare him or piss him off? I think about what his reaction to things would be. I have moments where I think of things that he said and did, and I just crack up. He still makes me laugh. He still makes me mad. I'll probably always be mad at him. So much of what he did was really selfish. But there is forgiveness, too.

"A lot of it is forgiving myself. Especially around how mad I would get at him. He could be such a jerk and deserved to be yelled at. But when I would do that, it would hurt him so much. He didn't get mad, he got hurt. I don't know if that was legitimate or manipulative, or maybe both. But there was always this scared little boy in there. Always. And he had so many defense mechanisms that he developed. But if you were close to him, if you knew how he felt, you could see past those. He was, in so many ways, a giant kid. He was great with kids, and he loved his children; he really did worship them."

In Scott's memoir, he wrote about his Catholic faith. It was surprising to read of the importance he placed on organized religion given his wild lifestyle. Upon his death, ex-wife Mary Forsberg wrote in her statement that Jamie had turned him against his faith, saying, "Our once sweet Catholic boy refused to watch the kids participate in Christmas Eve plays because he was now an atheist."[4] When I ask Jamie about this, she bristles.

"I was respectful. I told him I would respect his religious beliefs. I think what he liked about Catholicism was that it was something he could trust. It was always the same; there was a structure that he could rely on. It didn't matter what he did, it was always there to forgive him. It was a solid constant for him when he didn't have many solids. He could rely on his parents, his religion, his passion for what he did. But he never went to confession or to mass, so I'm not sure what he was taken away from.

"You always wonder, with an addict, what is it that compels him to have to quiet the voices in his brain. I'm creative, too, so I understand it. There are times when I just want my thoughts to quiet down. But Scott had so much going on all the time. He was never quiet. Religion, for him, was peaceful, safe, and orderly, but he didn't go to mass or pray, and he never went to confession. It was just a personal closeness. I would ask him if he went to mass or did confession, and he would say no, but he was still Catholic. I never told him he shouldn't believe. I just had my beliefs, and he had his. At some point, he started saying that he was wandering away from his religion. I guess his faith wasn't that strong if he eventually wandered away.

"He was spiritual, and that I connected with. And I think his faith was also a connection to his family life, his parents, his past. He was a nice boy who sang in the choir. He walked away from a lot of that past, but some things he wanted to remain connected to."

Was Scott ever really able to reconcile being that nice, suburban boy with the stage persona that consumed his life—the drug addicted, screaming, writhing, rockstar screaming lyrics through a megaphone? Was he able to exist as both the good and the bad, especially since the bad made life so difficult for everyone around him? These were all questions I asked her.

"Scott was always going to have an identity crisis," Jamie agrees. "Everyone could see the different looks he had through the years. He was always going to have difficulty being comfortable in his own skin. Couple that with a nonstop drive to create and you get a pretty difficult life. And that included the music he created, the way he dressed, what he did with his hair. It was everything about him. Constantly changing.

"He talked about how he was so driven, but said that once he had a platinum album, he'd be happy and satisfied. But then he gets it, and that's not enough. Then a second platinum album, still not enough. He gets a Grammy. And then another. Still not enough. Sell out Madison Square Garden and most people would think they've made it. But he never did. It wasn't that he didn't think he should be successful, it wasn't imposter syndrome. He knew he was good. When he dropped out of college to become a rock star, he didn't have a backup plan because he didn't need one. He knew he would be successful. It was a constant drive.

"His confidence on stage and in the music world, was amazing. And his whole fuck-them attitude. That was on the outside, but internally, there was this unhappiness that he wasn't as successful as he thought he should be. The drive to keep doing more. His parents were so proud of him, so it wasn't about some external acceptance. It was very much internal. He was on fire. He had all these ideas. He wanted to do all these projects. He still had so much to do. And felt he had to accomplish it."

With someone whose every move was so often in the spotlight, were there ever times when he wasn't "rockstar Scott?" I asked.

"He loved *Lord of the Rings* and all things Tolkien. He must have watched the films fifty or sixty times. Once, for my birthday, Scott asked me what I wanted, and I said a cat. Instead, he brought home a bull mastiff–pit bull puppy. So now I have these two giant dogs that can't be left alone together. He also gave me a motorcycle for my birthday, even though I can't ride it. He loved sports, he loved martial arts. He was a big Notre Dame football fan. There were many parts of his life that were exuberant and happy and just normal."

And if he'd lived, I asked, would there ever have been a time when Jamie wasn't Scott's caregiver, when the balance in their relationship would have shifted such that they would just care about and for each other, equally? I think of my own situation and how my husband, knowing his time was limited, kept telling me, "I'm not done yet. I have so much more to do." It's a painful remembrance to have not been able to give him those added years.

At my question, Jamie shakes her head. She's certain it would have happened had they just taken care of his physical health issue. "I'd like to think he would have gotten healthy," she says. "I'll always think, if we'd just gotten the heart issue taken care of, I know he would have gotten clean. He just needed a little more time."

11

SANDY HELM

Driving through the northern New York countryside to take in the site of the Woodstock festival before heading home, many thoughts and questions kept crossing my mind. I'd spent the previous evening with Sandy Helm, the widow of Levon Helm, drummer, lead singer, and founding member of The Band, a group so popular in their time they needed no other name. Starting as Bob Dylan's backup band, they eventually became, simply, The Band, and Levon was quite often, the voice. Songs like "The Night They Drove Old Dixie Down," "The Weight," "Up on Cripple Creek," sung masterfully with heart, and just enough country twang, from behind his drum kit.

As we sat in the dining room of Sandy and Levon's home, music was playing in the adjacent studio that Levon built (and rebuilt after a fire). Levon's daughter Amy was preparing for a holiday show in a space that's been occupied by everyone from Bob Dylan to Marcus Mumford. The air felt different in that space—laden with a heaviness from the history contained within it. The history, not just of one man but of a group, a genre of music, a couple, a family, and all the heartache that comes with those.

"My parents had big band music, people like Tommy Dorsey. Lee had all that music from the South when he was growing up—gospel, R&B, and rock music from the 50s," Sandy

Sandy and Levon on their wedding day. Courtesy of Sandy Helm

says as we sat at the table. "I was listening more in the 60s. We had the best music. We were really blessed to grow up on the best music ever."

But the song I'm thinking about as I consider my interview with Sandy is actually by Neil Young, a friend of Levon who appeared at The Band's last concert, which was filmed for the documentary *The Last Waltz*. That song is "My, My, Hey, Hey," and it included, in particular, the phrase, "It's better to burn out, than to fade away." The Band's members, their stories, their friends (starting with Bob Dylan), and their drugs are all legendary, as was Levon's life. And Sandy was there for most of it, the good and the bad. The life of touring, wealth, and fame, but also the life of playing to nearly no one, sadness, in-fighting, scraping by, suicides, a fire that wiped out everything, and finally Levon's cancer diagnosis. Did Levon and other members of The Band fade away? Definitely not. They still burn bright despite all but one of them now gone.

But where does the widow, often left to deal with the fall-out, find her solace? For Sandy, it is with her unabashed and still-constant love for Levon. When she talks about him, it's like she's twenty again. Her eyes sparkle and her voice breaks. It didn't matter to her whether he faded; what matters is that the legend that was Levon continues to live on through his music and films. What matters is that she does what Levon asked in his final words: "keep it going."

"I had gone with my Aunt Joyce to see The Band in D.C. at Constitution Hall. I knew their music. The first time I smoked pot, The Band's album was on the turntable! Music from *Big Pink*, I think. It was so wonderful. I'd never heard anything like it," she tells me.

"So here we were a while later at their concert, and I'm watching, I'm looking down at the stage, I see this braided rug and this Tiffany lamp, and I hear this voice come out and I'm looking at center stage. You know, you want to see the singer and it's always the guy up front, or maybe the guitar player. And I'm looking and thinking, whose voice is this? Is it the drummer? I've never seen a drummer that could sing."

Their meeting a few years later was completely coincidental and happened when The Band was performing sold-out shows and Levon was enjoying being a laid-back LA rock star. "We met at the Sunset Marquis, where we were both staying. It was a pretty far place from his home in Helena, Arkansas, for sure," Sandy says with a grin.

Levon Helm was born Mark Lavon Helm in Helena in 1940. The son of sharecroppers, his first job was bringing water out to those in the cotton fields. He grew up with a variety of music all around him: gospel, old-time country, rhythm and blues, and Delta blues. With his family, he attended minstrel shows and tent gatherings of traveling musicians performing in the back of flat-bed trucks. Arkansas was a confluence of music because of its proximity to Memphis and even Nashville. As a result, Levon was able to take in shows by Elvis, Bo Diddley, country music stars like Conway Twitty, and one of his biggest influences, fellow Arkansan, Sonny Boy Williamson.

In high school, Levon was recruited by Ronnie Hawkins to play in his band, but his parents made him complete his high school education before allowing him to join Hawkins on the road. Though Levon portrayed himself as the class clown, Sandy later found that he was a star student.

"I never thought he would've been senior class president. Yeah, right. He never, ever told me. He was always such a humble man. His mom told me that he had taken drama and been in a couple of plays. And I'm thinking, well, there's the acting. He was in 4H and on the football team. You know, and he never did brag. He never talked of himself in that manner. He really thought of himself, even as a musician, that it was just his job. Making people dance and feel happy."

Playing with Ronnie Hawkins provided Levon with a significant music education, not only in live performance but in band behavior and the drudgery of living on the road. Levon became accustomed to that life and lived it until the end. While traveling and doing shows in Canada, Hawkins recruited the Canadian musicians who would later become The Band: Rick Danko, Richard Manuel, Robbie Robertson, and Garth Hudson. Together, they played a grueling schedule along the Eastern seaboard and into Canada, with occasional shows in the south.

It was while the group was touring in this formation that they were contacted by Bob Dylan. Dylan had recently "gone electric" and was looking for a backup band to perform with. The Hawks, as they were known then, joined him onstage touring through Europe and the United States. For Levon, this was a difficult time. Fans, for the most part, hated Dylan's decision to electrify his sound. They saw him as an acoustic singer-songwriter, not a rock musician, and they voiced their displeasure at shows, often booing him loudly. This caused Levon to become disillusioned with the new world of rock and roll. How could a fan love someone like Dylan one day, then boo him the next, especially when he was making a decision for his own life? Levon left the group then and returned home to Arkansas.

In the summer of 1966, Bob Dylan was in a motorcycle accident, an event that would change the course of Levon's life. Dylan bought a house in Woodstock, New York, and settled there to recuperate from both the accident and his last difficult touring experience. Members of the Hawks settled there as well, and Levon decided to join them. Together, bandmates would spend long hours with Dylan, jamming and recording. Living together in a nearby pink house, their jam sessions would become the impetus for the album *Music from Big Pink*. Known around Woodstock as "the band," or as Dylan's backup, the name stuck. Working with Dylan's manager Albert Grossman, they shopped the album around, getting a contract with Capitol Records and heading to New York to record the songs previously sung in the basement.

"When The Band became a group with the five players, it was supposed to be called The Band, just like The Doors was The Doors, not with one person's name on it. That's how Levon and Rick envisioned it. Everybody sings, plays an instrument. They all make music together. Nobody out front. Though it didn't stay that way," Sandy says, alluding to the troubles that would later besiege the group and become a partial cause for their breakup.

Over the next eight years, Levon remained with The Band, recording multiple albums, and crisscrossing the world for months at a time. In 1970, Levon met singer Libby Titus. The two never married, although Titus accompanied Levon on many of their tours in the early 1970s and they had a daughter, Amy.

"I actually met Amy before I really got to know Levon," Sandy says. "He was thirty-six, and I was twenty-six. I had come out west with friends from Virginia and the D.C. area, where I grew up. We had moved out west and were living in Lake Tahoe and working at Harrah's, but it wasn't like we thought it would be. My friend Judy was dating a guy named Rusty, who was managing Doug Kershaw. So, she says, c'mon, let's move to LA. And I thought, sure. I love movies and movie stars. Let's go. It was 1973.

"Well, I'm at the pool at the Sunset Marquis doing laps at eight in the morning. As I'm doing a lap, I can see this person standing at the end of the pool. And then I see a pair of Palomino cowboy boots. Well, out east it was loafers, and in LA it was sandals. Nobody wore cowboy boots. I kinda looked up, and he was bent over, in his Levis. He said, 'Hi, I'm Lee from Arkansas,' and I said, 'Hi, I'm Sandy from Virginia!' I figured he thought I was the biggest hayseed ever.

"Well, then, what really made him think, that was when he asked me, 'What are you doing today, Sandy from Virginia?' And I remember, I said, 'I think I want to go see the stars' homes!' Could I have been more of a tourist? But then he said, 'Well, I can take you.' He was just so sweet. And he said that we could go see the stars' houses and then go have some raw fish. Of course, I had never had sushi before and couldn't imagine eating fish that was raw. I couldn't figure out why this guy in cowboy boots and Levi's from Arkansas didn't want fish that had been coated in cornmeal and deep fried in oil. But boy, I started at the boots, and the farther up I looked, the better it got!

"But then he walked away, and Judy said, 'Don't you know who that is?' And I said 'Sure, it's Lee from Arkansas.' She told me, 'No, it's Levon Helm from The Band,' and I said, 'Levon, the singing drummer?' But I was so happy that I didn't know who he was, and he knew that I didn't know him beyond just being Lee from Arkansas. He told me he was Lee and not Levon so that I wouldn't know he was the famous drummer. I'm glad he didn't think I was some groupie who just wanted to glom on and hang on him or ask him to listen to my tape.

"Then, when I found out who he was, I didn't go out with him. I told Judy, 'I'm not gonna be another notch on his drumstick!' Thank God, I didn't say that to him!"

Sandy had a boyfriend at that time who had proposed, but he wanted a traditional wife. That wasn't for her, so she kept putting him off. Meanwhile, she couldn't get the handsome drummer in cowboy boots out of her mind. Six months later, she was still thinking of him.

"Some friends from Virginia had moved to LA to try to make it as a band. I asked one of them if he had heard anything about Levon Helm, and he said yes, that Levon was wild and getting into fights because he was hitting on other guys' wives. But of course, it wasn't really true. It was the reputation they all had.

They all thought that's how musicians should act. My friend told me Levon was staying at the Miramar Hotel in Santa Monica and that they also had Shangri-La, which was a house out between Malibu and Zuma Beach. Lee was going between the two.

"I just got up my nerve. I hadn't heard from Lee after he asked me out, and I didn't want to go because he was a musician. But then I called the Miramar and asked for Levon. They knew he stayed in the bungalow by the pool because that's where all the stewardesses hung out. So, they put me through. When the phone rang, I asked if Levon was there. Rick [Danko] answered the phone. Lee wasn't there, but Rick was and Ronnie Hawkins. Rick said I should come on by, but that Levon wasn't there, that he had gone to pick up the children. Well, then I'm thinking, oh no, he's married, he's got baggage. And he has children. How did I not know? I'm talking myself out of it, but I just couldn't get that man out of my head. I was going back and forth, but Rick told me to come on by and that Levon would be glad to see me.

"And you know, it turned out that he wasn't married. They [Levon and Libby Titus] had never married. And one of the children was Amy's stepbrother, not Levon's child. Amy was an only child, so it was just her. She was four when I met her.

"When I first got there, they weren't there yet. It was just Ronnie Hawkins, splayed over a king-sized bed with his beard. And Rick left to go back to Malibu. But then Levon gets there with Amy, and it was almost as though Amy sensed it. Levon never really had her around any women. Either The Band was on the road, or, if they were in LA, Levon stayed at Shangri La or at the Miramar.

"So, Levon walks in, and I looked up and saw him, and I thought, oh my God, I just love this man so much. It was love at first sight. I said, 'Hi, do you remember me?' and Levon looks at me and smiles and said, 'Hell yeah, from the pool.'

"And then Amy kind of sidles over to me and says, 'See those curtains? There's a man behind them named Mr. Johnson, and he's going to come get you.' And then she takes me to the little kitchenette in the back of the suite, and she says, 'This is where my dad makes me wash all the dishes.' And I see room service trays and carts everywhere. Nobody was washing dishes there. She really just wanted to scare me off.

"We met in '73 and didn't get married until 1981. Nell [Levon's mother] would always say to Levon, 'Son, you're just not doing her right. You need to marry her.' So, finally, we invited friends up, and we got married here in the studio."

By the mid-70s, The Band faced multiple internal and external challenges. Robbie Robertson grew tired of nonstop touring and had departed upstate New York permanently from Malibu. During this time, it also came to light that Robertson was receiving the majority of royalties because he listed himself as the writer or cowriter of most of The Band's songs. Levon disputed this claim, causing further stress within the group that would soon prove too great to overcome.

The worst of times during Levon and Sandy's dating came when The Band was performing their last concert on Thanksgiving Day in 1976. The concert was *The Last Waltz* and became the film of the same name by Martin Scorsese. According to his book, *This Wheel's on Fire*, Levon did not want to end the band, but with Robertson's decision to quit, there wasn't much choice.[1]

For Levon, recording and performing live was the only life he knew, and it was a decision that left him angry and bitter. In his book, he says he purposely left Sandy out of the band's affairs during that time because he wanted their relationship to be separate from the worst of the rock and roll life. After selling millions of albums and creating songs like "The Weight" and others that would outlive the group for generations, The Band disbanded in 1983.

For Sandy and Levon, most of the challenges to their relationship seemed to come from outside, not within. "Everybody always asked me what I was possibly thinking marrying a musician like Levon," Sandy says. "So many people put it into my head that he had to be womanizing that I became jealous over nothing. They couldn't believe, and didn't believe, when I told them that Levon was true to me, and we were happy." Once Levon decided to keep performing with a reconstituted version of The Band, he hit the road again, now with Sandy joining him.

"I remember going home to visit my family and my dad telling me that my former boyfriend, the one who had asked me to marry him, had stopped by. He had asked my dad how I was doing and where I was. My dad told him I was dating a farmer in Kansas! He didn't want to tell him that I had married a rock and roll musician and was traveling the world!"

Together, Levon and Sandy picked up the pieces after *The Last Waltz*. Sandy traveled with Levon across the country all through the 1980s. The breakup of the band had caused the members to lose their primary income, so Levon kept them on the road. Furthering the animosity between Levon and Robertson, when money was almost nonexistent, was the fact that Robertson bought out Danko's and Hudson's publishing rights for $10,000 each, a pittance. The contractual set-up caused lasting divisions, causing Levon and Robertson to never speak again.

"You can say whatever you want to say, but just listen to the songs. Every one of those songs is about Levon's childhood. Annalee, Jack the Dog, Crazy Chester. They all came from stories of Levon's childhood. It just isn't fair. And that publishing gets handed down to others' kids and grandkids. Something about that isn't fair. It got to the point where Levon wouldn't speak his name. And now, I don't speak it, either."

Their financial struggles led to drug use, which made things worse. By the early 1990s, Levon and Sandy had gone through a series of losses, including Levon's mentor Henry Glover, the death of a family friend while visiting their home, and the suicide of The Band's keyboardist Richard Manuel, which greatly impacted Levon.

"It was just such a difficult time. So many deaths, and the barn where Levon had played so much music burned to the ground. Rick and all of us are on heroin, there's drugs everywhere. And Richard's death was pretty overwhelming for Levon.

"They were opening for Crosby, Stills and Nash on their tour," Sandy explains. "And Richard and Levon had gotten together after the show in Florida and talked well into the night. The rooms were next to each other but not adjoining. They had been talking about the small places they'd been playing on their own, the dives. They were depressed about where they were playing. They felt degraded. They had been on top, with others opening for them. Now they were opening for someone or playing small venues. Richard's piano would be out of tune all night. Levon said they laid across Richard's bed until early morning talking about all of it. Lee left and went to call his father on his birthday. He told Richard he'd be right back, but then he fell asleep. It was about eight in the morning, and Levon was woken by the screams of Richard's wife shouting, 'He's dead, he's dead.' Lee went in and found Richard had hung himself in the bathroom with a luggage strap. He and Rick had to get him down.

"Richard and Lee were so close. He always called Richard the lead singer. He was so talented. It really hit Levon hard."

By the early 90s, Levon and Sandy knew they had a problem with their own drug use, and they asked their friend Ringo Starr for help. Ringo was able to pull some strings and get them both admitted into rehab together.

"Once we were in rehab, we both went through counseling. We were separated and only saw each other at lunch and dinner. Neither of us had ever talked to a therapist about all the things that happened over the years. But they also wanted to know about all the womanizing he had done and how I coped. I had to tell them that it didn't happen. Jealousy is not what caused the drug use. They didn't believe me. They think, Levon's a rock star, he had to be involved with several women and cheating on me.

"I wasn't big on drugs when I met Levon. One thing he did do was introduce me to Thai sticks. And then we went to harder stuff. I'm so glad we knew we had to stop it. And we did."

Through the 90s and early 2000s, Levon spent months at a time on tour. In 2003, he developed a raspiness in his voice that wouldn't go away. The diagnosis was cancer of the vocal cords. Many thought he would never sing again.

"In 2007, The Rambles [concerts by musicians in the barn to raise funds for his treatment] were just starting to take off, and I was diagnosed with breast cancer. Levon told me immediately that what he learned with his cancer was to starve it, give it no attention. He felt that since he never talked about it, or worried about it, it didn't come back."

Levon continued the Midnight Rambles for four years, bringing in significant musicians to play along in The Barn studio, artists like Elvis Costello, Emmylou Harris, Mavis Staples, My Morning Jacket, Mumford & Sons, Gillian Welch, and others. The money raised paid the medical bills and also paid off the mortgage on the home and studio, allowing Levon to rest a bit easier. "I remember Lee being in the studio with Rick and they were talking about singing a song for a friend's birthday. And Rick said to Lee, 'You know, we have to figure out a way to have shows in our living room, so all we have to do is play and then walk out to the mailbox to collect the check.' And Lee thought, you know what, that's a damn fine idea.

"Really, they should have been sitting back collecting royalties for their music, which is still on the radio. But that couldn't happen because of those earlier deals."

In 2007, Levon recorded the album *Dirt Farmer*, his first solo album since 1989. It was released to critical acclaim and won a Grammy Award for Best Traditional Folk Album. He then won a second Grammy Award for his next album, *Electric Dirt*.

In 2012, however, the cancer did come back, and Levon declined pretty quickly, Sandy tells me. "He died April 17, and the strange thing is that he had just had a thorough exam at Sloan Kettering in February. We were all with him in the waiting room. They said then that everything was fine. And then April hits, and he got so frail. He was sitting right there where you are, and he said, 'I can't get a breath. I can't breathe.' And that was it.

"He couldn't tackle the stairs after the cancer came back. It hurt so bad in his back and his chest. He got so frail, but he kept doing those Rambles. The last one was with Los Lobos. And everyone could see the shape he was in. He got down to ninety pounds, but that was what he did. If he had given up performing, he would have died sooner.

"And I knew, I always knew that, with the ten years difference in our ages, Levon most likely would go first. You try to prepare yourself for that, but you can't. And I'm so thankful after that first diagnosis that we had ten more years. What a life he gave me. Travel, music. He was such a good person.

"I had so hoped we could bring him home. We could bring hospice in, but it never happened. I just got a phone call telling me to get to the hospital because they're inducing a coma. I got to go in and tell him I loved him and say goodbye, but it happened so quickly.

"After several days, I finally asked the nurses if I could stay after-hours through the night with him because there were always people in and out all day. That first night that I stayed with him, it was just the two of us, no nurses, no one else. I walked over to him and told him, 'I love you so much. You know, honey, you don't have to hang on for me. I'm okay, Lee, I'll be okay. Just let go. Fly away. Release that pain and go,'" Sandy says, her voice breaking.

"I went and sat down in the chair and looked over, and his foot started moving. At first, I thought it was a convulsion. But then I could see it was in rhythm. His feet were in rhythm, like he was playing his bass drum. I think he was telling me that he heard me. What a gift. And then I wasn't sad.

"And then one afternoon, a few days before he died, I got a call from Amy that Robertson was there and wanted to see Levon. She asked if it was okay. Well, I said yes because I didn't want that on me. He can see him, but Levon hadn't spoken to him in years by that point. She said he went in and stayed for about a half hour and was maybe crying and whispering to him. Then he left the room and went right out into the hallway, got on his phone, and started insinuating to the world through social media that they made up. Lee was in a coma! I was glad that after the documentary about Lee came out (Jacob Hatley's film *Ain't in It for My Health*], when we went to the premiere in Greenwich Village, there was a question for Barbara [O'Brien, Levon's former manager]. It was a packed house. The first question was, 'I heard Levon and Robertson made up,' and Barbara said, 'Well, that's not exactly true. Actually, Levon was in a coma.' And the whole audience just gasped. They felt like they'd been betrayed, I guess.

"All those years and the bitterness and the hatred. There were feelings of blame and vindictiveness. Who was responsible for everybody being on drugs and broke? Who's responsible for a suicide? There were so many bad feelings that didn't have to be."

As we continue our conversation around the Helm's kitchen table, with music from the house band coming from the studio downstairs, the phone rings, and Sandy excuses herself. She talks for a few minutes about seeing a friend in a nursing home on Christmas. The situation sounds bad. Multiple times she says, "That's so sad." But it isn't just any friend they're going to visit. It's Garth Hudson, Levon's former bandmate They're hoping to visit so he's not alone during the holidays.

"He doesn't get too many visitors," she tells me. "They told me that before when I visited him. He's the sweetest guy. Lee always called him Brother Garth or Honey Boy. When we'd be so broke, Garth would say, 'Levon, I want you to borrow this book and read it later.' Lee would wonder what he was doing because he didn't really read that much. We'd get home, and he'd open the book and inside there'd be two $100 bills.

"You know, you think about rock stars, and rock star life, but these guys were broke. After all the music, they were barely getting by. They struggled, and it wasn't fair. Thank God their music lives on.

"And they're saying Garth may be having problems hearing. He can't hear his music. I'm thinking, we'll bring him some earphones so maybe he can hear. Garth was the one who studied music. There'd be no band without him. He played every instrument. He's a genius." Garth's wife Maud, who was a singer who performed with musicians like Dr. John and Emmylou Harris, had been homebound for some time and sadly passed away on February 27, 2021.

"And then there's another member that's sitting in Malibu. That person can go to Switzerland to get the best doctors if he gets sick. Why is that?" Sandy asks, referring to Robertson. (Author's note: Robbie Robertson passed away on August 9, 2023, one year after this interview, leaving Garth as the only surviving member of The Band.)

After Levon died, Sandy was lost. She fell back into using pills and alcohol. She had also lost her parents just prior to losing Levon, which added to her pain.

"I got into therapy, which really helped, and I've kept up until recently. My therapist helped me get through the drug problems and deal with the grief. I also rehabbed myself by taking a French drug, Suboxone, which weaned me off the dope. It doesn't make you feel high, but you just don't crave the drugs. It's not readily available here, and I don't know why. Today, I only take a drug for acid reflux," Sandy says with a chuckle.

"But I still find myself staying alone. I isolate. I have shows going on right next door here, but I don't go. And then I worry about aging and getting old alone; I get insecure about my white hair. I want to do it gracefully, but you know. Levon aged and it was fine. Why is it men get to grow old and be distinguished but not women? Women are labeled eccentric.

"As hard as it is, I'm so lucky that I have a group of friends that were Levon's friends that stayed loyal. They could have gone away after Levon died, but they didn't. They still stick with me out of loyalty to Levon. It still feels like family. I'm very fortunate to have them and being able to live here, with all the music and the memories. So many people who've been here and in the studio."

It's evident talking with Sandy that her love for Levon is still as great as it was when he was with her. She takes me through the house to look at photos of them, some from far off places Levon played, others from their wedding day, photos of Levon playing drums, Levon and daughter Amy on stage in the studio. Sandy tells me she has boxes of photos taken all over the world, with musicians from Dr. John to Emmylou Harris to Ike and Tina Turner. "It was just so wonderful to be married to someone who loved me for me. He never wanted to change me or tell me I should be different. It's so great to have someone that loves the way you laugh or loves everything about you. I remember I used to feel like I had to get prettied-up to go to their shows and Levon would say, 'Sandy, we're not going to no fashion show. Just be yourself.' Oh, he was just the best, and I just miss him so much.

"To think that a man like that, so sweet and kind, would love me. He gave me such a good life, travel, music, the best people."

A storied life, for certain, and, as Sandy has realized, a life that could have taken many other turns. Levon somehow, always with Sandy's help and devotion, managed to turn around the most difficult parts of that rock and roll life and re-create himself again and again.

Levon enjoyed fame at a height few achieve, and his influence was and remains significant. But he also saw much of that fame fade away, along with the income it generated. What happens when one doesn't quickly burn out but rather fades away? How difficult it must have been to remain standing when your brothers leave, through irreconcilable differences, suicide, or simply the body giving out. And for Sandy to bear witness as yet another talented and once-influential musician battled to get by, struggling financially and mostly alone.

She isn't sad, though. "I have my days," she says, "But I just believe I'll see him again. I believe wherever he is, he's not in pain. He's playing music, reunited with so many people he loved. I feel his presence everywhere in this house, all the time. And I just live for when I'll see him again."

LEGACY

12

CATHERINE MAYER

Is there an easy way in which to lose the love of your life? Or a way that is at least less traumatic? One that reduces the grief that inevitably follows? Does the ability to hold his hand, to say all that needs to be said, or to plan for what should be done afterward, make the grieving time any easier? Many of us will never know the answer because we won't have that experience. Kevin's decline took months, during which he never seemed to lose faith that he would be cured of Stage IV cancer. It was either a brave fight, or a complete avoidance of the truth born of fear: I'm still not sure which. But the lasting result is a cloud of regret that dims my memories still. I couldn't initiate the discussions around what may happen because that was akin to giving up on his ability to fight and overcome his disease. So we marched on, to our last day together, never saying what needed to be said.

Much of the reason we avoid these discussions is our fear of death and inability to face our own mortality, says Catherine Mayer, widow of Gang of Four founding member Andy Gill. Catherine is a powerhouse of endeavor and accomplishment. Her success as a journalist, author, blogger, activist, and events creator was equal to her husband's success as a songwriter, band founder, guitarist, and producer. "It was that equality that allowed us to have our own pursuits, quite separately, and then come back together and truly be together. I've always thought

Catherine Mayer and Andy Gill. Courtesy of Catherine Mayer

that was good. Relationships with musicians can so often be unequal. If one member of the couple isn't a performer, and certainly if there are children or other caring duties, one gets left behind to hold the fort while the other person does what they do," she says as we chat in her London flat.

Just two years after Andy's passing, Catherine has become active in a Covid Bereaved Families for Justice group, is developing an annual symposium on death called The Death Festival, and has coauthored a book on grief with her mother, Anne Mayer Bird, who also lost her husband, Catherine's stepfather John, just weeks before Andy died. As journalists do, Catherine has stepped back and looked at death: how we react to it; how we avoid discussing it, especially in light of our experience with Covid-19; and how we do or don't deal with the aftermath of loss.

"Andy dealt for years with chronic illness. The worst was during his last tour of America. It wasn't just that he was in denial that he was ill and would have to leave music or change his lifestyle. He was also in denial because he didn't want promoters to see him as a bad bet. He didn't want them to believe that he was in decline. He wanted to believe that this was a one-off and he would recover and get better.

"When Andy entered hospital, he was afraid of word getting out because it would cause the cancellation of tour dates and interest in the new album, and he made me promise to tell very few of his situation. He only accepted visits from people who were involved in projects. For ten days, and just before he was intubated, he was on his laptop, working on the Gang of Four covers album that I would have to finish after he died."

Andy Gill was, by all accounts, a post-punk pioneer, one who was often called a genius. As a founding member of Gang of Four, he created a band that took the best of the ska, reggae, and punk music of the time and added his trademark stark, slicing guitar. As Catherine's work after his death brought into clear focus, he was a significant influence on many younger musicians, from the late Michael Hutchence to Flea, and to bands like Nirvana, REM, and Rage Against the Machine. It was the sound of underground music: combative in its politics and beats, but brought into the light with cerebral lyrics full of cultural commentary.

Andy started the band with Jon King, Hugo Burnham, and Dave Allen. Andy and Jon were classmates in secondary school, hanging out in an art class that allowed students to be expressive in whatever way they felt drawn to. For Andy, it was music, and it happened at a time when significant changes were occurring in how music was made, produced, sold, and appreciated, and during a period of great social and political shifts to the right. Together, it became a great time for breaking the rules. Andy found that to be fertile ground for his music, as was Leeds College, where he matriculated the year after Jon King did, both studying in the college's art school.

After recruiting Allen and Burnham, the four (named after the radical leaders in China who fueled the Cultural Revolution) created a sound that felt like a natural progression from its punk roots, adding just enough room and danceability to be a true descendant. While other bands began smoothing the sharp edges of punk to create the new wave sound that would fill the early 80s airwaves, Gang of Four stopped short, and the result was a sound that defined that middle generation. Andy's contribution on guitar was a seemingly impossible blend of aesthetic rhythms and electrified anarchy, often reaching the point of screeching feedback.

Together, the band released four albums and toured the world. By late 1980, only Andy and Jon remained as original members, bringing on a new bassist and drummer and releasing another album. In 1983, the band went on hiatus, with Andy remaining in music but focusing on other projects and dealing with a health issue. He produced the debut album by the Red Hot Chili Peppers and released a solo EP, "Dispossession," in 1987. In the 1990s, Andy and Jon regrouped as Gang of Four to record two albums, and once those projects ended, Andy returned to production, working closely with Michael Hutchence to cowrite and produce his 1999 solo album, which was posthumously released after Hutchence's death. Andy and Catherine became very close to Michael and his girlfriend, Paula Yates. After their deaths, just two years apart, Catherine now realizes that both she and Andy struggled with their respective grief.

It was between Gang of Four gigs in the early 90s that Catherine and Andy met. "I was supposed to be going to a different gathering, but my sister rang me and said there was going to be an A-to-Zed party. They were these little books that were city maps. The people who were invited to the party were supposed to all live on the same page in the A-to-Zed. I didn't live on the right page, but my sister invited me to come with her. It was in this converted warehouse apartment that some architect friends had made. They specialized in these extraordinary interiors where they would suspend swimming pools that would become part of the wall of the room. They were doing this in the boom years of that kind of showy living in the late 1980s. There was a suspended swimming pool that created the whole wall of the living room, so it felt like a human aquarium.

"I was looking at this aquarium wall, and then I noticed this ridiculously handsome man in a frock coat standing next to the aquarium. But I also noticed that he had an entire bowl of trifle, a serving-size bowl tucked under his arm, and he was eating it by scooping it with his hands. I started laughing at him. There was a big buffet, and he explained that he was unable to find a clean plate and a spoon. Someone else might go wash up a plate and spoon, but Andy just took the bowl and dipped in.

"At the point I met him, he was intimidatingly handsome. I'm not sure I would have found him attractive or would have introduced myself had I known who he was or just saw him standing alone. I would have just thought that he was too arrogant. Because I saw him doing something so funny and humanizing, I went up to him and talked to him. And then I found out he was in Gang of Four. Though I didn't know what the members looked like, I was very familiar with their music and I loved it. We just started talking. Eventually, we ended up on the rooftop terrace. We talked more up there, and he serenaded me with 'Up on the Roof.' And even more unlikely, we saw a shooting star, which in London is just bizarre and unusual to see any stars.

"That was a Saturday night, and we made plans to see each other the following Saturday. And, basically, we never parted again after that. And this was before social media and messaging, so there hadn't been any flurry of messaging between our two times together. And I don't remember going to the second date with any kind of expectation. But that second date was all it took.

"Around that time, he had a flat in the East End. We ended up at his flat that night. I hated it because it was so cold and wasn't centrally heated. But he loved that flat. Because I thought that Gang of Four had critical success but not commercial success, I assumed he was broke. So, I made him come to my flat because I was this established journalist. I was writing for *The Economist* at that point as a foreign correspondent. I just assumed that I should pay for everything as well.

"As a feminist, I insisted on paying my way, but I also thought I should help him. I bought my first flat at twenty-three and had a car. I was used to being the only one in my group of friends that had regular income. And I assumed Andy fell into that group as well. But Andy didn't like coming to my flat, which I thought was perfectly comfortable. Unlike his flat, mine was comfortable but very basic. I later realized that it probably offended his sense of aesthetics on so many different levels. He was such an artist, if he didn't like a design, it became almost a physical pain for him.

"My flat was perfectly nice, but it was the flat of someone who was never home. As a foreign correspondent, I was just never there. One day he told me he was going to buy us a flat; he was already planning for me to move in. I thought, that's interesting. We went down to Tower Bridge, and he showed me this spectacular flat, and I was like, 'How are you going to buy that?' And he said, 'Cash,' and I said, 'Really? You can afford this?'

"I sold my flat and rented another. I think I paid for that rental for a year and spent one night in it. We were never apart from then on.

"I say never apart, but of course, we were apart all the time. Andy had got back together with Jon King, and they had made an album and were planning to tour around the UK and other countries. And I would also go off and report from around the world. There was a time when, after we married, we were trying to purchase this home, and we had to explain to the financing people that Andy was a musician, and I was on the phone with the mortgage office calling from the middle of a riot in Northern Ireland that I was covering. I remember saying, 'I don't think he's going to think we're a good risk!'"

Andy and Catherine continued their together-but-separate relationship, with each of them pursuing their respective loves of music and writing. Shortly after they married in 1999, Catherine joined Gang of Four on a tour of Brazil. While Andy and the band performed shows, she went in search of stories in the most dangerous parts of Sao Paulo. "I would get up to pursue these drug lords at 5:00 a.m. after being at a show that didn't even start until 10:30 the night before. But the alternative would have been sitting around hotel rooms and during endless sound checks. That wasn't for me." It was their home life that provided them with a sense of reprieve and a peaceful routine. They would spend long hours together talking and would make certain to be home together on Sundays when they would take long walks around London, holding hands and catching up. "We rarely did nonwork things separately. When we were together, we were together. But that also freed us up to do whatever project each of us wanted to do."

In the late 1980s, before he and Catherine met, Andy received a cancer diagnosis, followed by surgery and treatment, which led in part to the Gang of Four's hiatus at the time. The surgery left him with a scar from his sternum to his groin. He never had a recurrence of the cancer, and Catherine believes that after the surgery and treatment, Andy probably never thought that his life was in danger. "What it did do, I think, was that it kept him from being arrogant about his fame or his music. He had such success, so early on. And that could have made him a very different person. But I think, coming just before that surgery, it grounded him. He was about as far from the arrogant rock star image as you could imagine. He cared about people. He never thought he was more important than others. Performers are often surrounded by people who tell them they're important and looking after them, but that didn't affect Andy.

"Sometimes that arrogance happens in people who are insecure about being as good as everyone says they are but feeling as though they'll never live up to the hype. And he never had that insecurity. He was really secure in who he was. He didn't care about judgment. He was as lovely as he was because he knew exactly who he was and was very secure in that.

"We did have our rough patch. I defy anyone who was married as long as we were to not have a rough patch. Aside from that time, I believe he was very secure in me and in our relationship, and he made me feel very secure in him. I think that is very unusual in these relationships. It's perhaps more obvious with him in that he was going around the world and touring and was a magnet for certain kinds of fans, but I didn't lack for opportunity either. But that risk just wasn't a thing with us.

"Andy was once playing a festival, and when we went to check into the hotel room, there was a very surprised woman lying in the bed waiting for him. She had not anticipated that I was going to turn up with him. It was all strange because she appeared to be very young and had on very large shoes which made her look like a child. And before she left, she handed me her camera and asked me to take a photo of the two of them. My one bit of meanness was to take their picture, but I cut their heads off, which, because it was a camera with film, she wouldn't know until she got them developed."

For more than ten years after his diagnosis, Andy remained healthy, pursuing various music projects, moving into their new home and building a studio in the basement. Then, he had a health-related episode that affected his sight. It turned out to be sarcoidosis, a disease similar to autoimmune disorders like rheumatoid arthritis but which instead attacks various tissues in the body, most commonly the lungs. Each new attack left scarring on his lungs that appeared as striations. Doctors began watching for a typical pattern of deterioration in Andy's respiratory system.

"In some people, it attacks once and never returns, but in others it comes back. The problem is that the steroids they give you to treat it only work for a time. Then they try other drugs to find something that works, and each drug has side effects. In Andy's case, he was fine for years afterward, but he would have flare-ups. When he had one, he would have to up the dose of steroids, which he hated because of the side effects. He ended up with that steroid puffy face, which he hated. The drugs also gave him diabetes, which he also had to control with other drugs.

"It was all very much under control until the year before he died. That year, Gang of Four went on tour in America, and I came along for the beginning of it. We developed coping mechanisms over the years for tours. Mine was that I wouldn't be on the tour at the end because the bus would be so disgusting by the end of the tour. So I only went for the beginning. It should have been warm because it was California, but it wasn't. There was the polar vortex, so it was cold. He seemed a bit ill before I left to return home, but as they traveled east, Andy got more and more ill. Finally, he couldn't go on stage in New York. But he did get better after he returned home and made a full recovery. The show in New York was the only one he ever had to cancel.

"His specialist gave him a portable oxygen machine, but he never used it. He was absolutely fine after that one episode. This whole idea that he had underlying conditions that then got trotted out after his death was simply not true. Our twentieth wedding anniversary coincided with a gig he was doing in Athens. The European tour had been delayed, and they were making up those dates. We went ahead of the band and had a lovely twenty-four hours in Athens to celebrate. Then they performed this absolutely storming gig in Athens and came back home before a few more European dates. Then they went on this extended tour to Australia, New Zealand, China, and Japan. Andy was ill by the time they got back from that tour."

While he didn't need the oxygen tank for the tour, by the time he returned home in December, he needed it every night. As the month wore on, he became worse. "We had decided to go to Italy for New Years to celebrate his birthday because he has a January 1 birthday. He got worse while we were there and could barely walk through the airport when we came home."

In her book about the grief she suffered after Andy's death, Catherine writes about these days and nights, with Andy doing things like looking at real estate in warmer climates, saying he just needed to live some place where the weather's warm. He continued to book more tour dates and work on music projects, but Catherine came to believe he should never tour again and wondered what it would take to convince him. To treat the symptoms, Andy took higher and higher doses of steroids, and when the doctor told him he should be in the hospital, he refused.

She writes:

"On 18 January, I find Andy slumped in a chair, conscious but colourless. Finally, I tell him I am calling an ambulance and even then, we bargain. First, he must have a bath. Then he asks for a glass of Puligny-Montrachet. I refuse and will always upbraid myself for that pointless rigidity. The paramedic suspects sepsis and summons a blue-light ambulance to take us to St. Thomas hospital. Even then we delay its departure. Andy wants his computer with him, external hard drives, address book. He's planning already to work from his hospital bed. This, too, he will do right up until the moment he is forced to stop. He will cease building a fictive future only when he can no longer breathe."[1]

Reading that line takes my own breath away. How different yet similar our situations are, I think. In Andy's case, there was some kind of illness, but they didn't know what it was, only that it was worsening its attack on him. Yet, he couldn't face the fact that he needed to seek medical intervention or consider the possibility that this could be fatal. I am immediately reminded of Kevin's penultimate day, which I described to Catherine. That morning, he met with his boss. While I anticipated a conversation in which Kevin would thank his boss for all his help during his illness and tell him that he most likely would not be returning, I instead overheard him say it would take just a few weeks to get back into the swing and he was looking forward to returning to the office. I had to go along with this, as doing anything else would have been seen as having lost faith in Kevin's ability to defeat this disease. Like Andy, he would cease building a fictive future only when he could no longer breathe.

Just weeks before Andy's health began to decline, Catherine's stepfather John was also admitted to hospital and passed away suddenly with what was determined to be "hospital-acquired pneumonia." "My mother and he had been married for forty years, so he was a large part of our lives. We were both grieving that loss," she told me.

Andy's diagnosis was pneumonia, which the doctors thought was treatable. They suggested he would be in hospital for a few weeks after the ICU, then into a rehab unit before returning home. But despite several days of hospitalization and treatment, Andy never improved. By mid-January, he was intubated. Several days later, while Catherine was on her way back to the hospital after trying to get some rest at home, Andy was put into a medically induced coma. Though she ran to the hospital and through the halls trying to get to him, she realizes later that "no matter how fast I move, the destination will be the same."

"I would not have gone, but I did," she says. "I feel that one mechanism of turning grief and experience into something useful is to campaign on the things one learns. Whether it's just in terms of your own close group, getting them to discuss death and end of life and what's involved, or whether it's to larger groups. I've been campaigning to several people, including politicians, about amending some of the laws around death to make the end of life and the postmortem process easier for survivors. It's just so unnecessarily complicated and mad. And I've urged my friends to stop pretending they're immortal and to make wills and appoint attorneys, to give power of attorney to people and to express your desires around decisions to switch off machines so that it doesn't fall to one person to do it."

That last experience, however, did fall to Catherine, just days after Andy was placed into a coma. His organs began failing and he was judged too weak to tolerate the machines that oxygenated his blood. She met with a counselor and determined that Andy's final day would be February 1, 2020, a date that would allow time for family members and Andy's bandmates in the most recent incarnation of Gang of Four to arrive. Thereafter, they kept a vigil, never letting him be alone. "There's never going to be a good way for any death to happen, but I believe people do underestimate the importance of being able to be with someone for those last moments. It's not just for the person whose dying, but for the others who remain," she tells me.

Although it hadn't yet swept in and caused so much turmoil in health care delivery, cases of Covid-19 were beginning to emerge during Andy's time in hospital. Just weeks after his death, the world would be shut down by the pandemic, and the numbers of dead would multiply daily. "It didn't occur to us to believe that this could be Covid because all the first reports, and indeed the Chinese government still maintains, that Covid didn't manifest until late December and then only in Wuhan. It wasn't supposed to have made landfall in Europe until January. When he was admitted to hospital in mid-January, and by that time very ill, they did ask him about traveling to China, but when he said he wasn't in Wuhan, they dismissed it and called it pneumonia. They were able to detect a strain of pneumonia through bloodwork and began treating it accordingly. Never at that point did any of us think that it was Covid. We were all thinking just that Andy was dying, and we needed to figure out why.

"Even after that time, we only talked about Covid as something that was fast. It wasn't until later that we saw that people could be ill, then seem to be okay, then get much worse. In May of 2020, I was sent an article in a French newspaper that said the French authorities had decided to test blood samples that had been taken at the end of 2019 to see if there had been Covid in France prior to the established timeline, because they were finding much to suggest that Covid had arrived in Europe earlier. Sure enough, they found Covid in blood samples that had been taken in 2019.

"I was shocked when I read this. I emailed Andy's specialist, who said that they had been doing their own investigation. They found that the lung scans they had done when Andy came in did not look as they expected with the striations. They looked like what we now call Covid lung, which is very different. There were other reasons as well. So, they could never say it one hundred percent, but based on other observations, they do think it could be Covid. They also couldn't understand why he didn't respond to treatment as he should have. And the way that all his organs shut down, which isn't something that happens with pneumonia. And they couldn't get his oxygen up. These are all things they now recognize.

"As I tracked what happened to others, I found that their tour manager, after returning home, had gone straight into hospital with severe respiratory failure. Once I started talking to others around Andy, many had Covid-like illnesses. I didn't really want to go public about it at all, but as soon as I realized that Andy most likely had Covid, it made me realize that all the official timelines were wrong and all the public health response to Covid had been based on incorrect information. The only way you can tackle public health issues is to have the right data. I felt it was my duty to go public, but I hated doing it. I didn't want to associate Andy's name with Covid, because Covid is such an ugly thing and Andy was such a beautiful person. But when I did that, others came forward as well. People who were testing positive for antibodies without having had it. There's a great deal of information now that Covid was around before we realized."

With the Covid pandemic exploding so soon after Andy's death, Catherine spent much of her earliest weeks of grief locked down, away from family and friends. She began meeting weekly with her mother, Anne, who was also suffering her own grief at the loss of both Andy and her husband. They met in the garden, socially distanced from each other. We discuss the added fear that hovers over those who went through all those months of Covid on our own, how frightening and lonely it was. Soon after Andy's death, Catherine made the decision to convert Andy's studio into one that could accommodate the recording of audio books. "It felt like a particular reproach for Andy's studio to be so quiet after his death and with the silence during Covid, I felt the need to bring life to it in some way," she said.

With Andy having been in a band rather than a solo artist, there were, of course, issues with the surviving members, legal and otherwise. Making that situation worse was that the band had parted ways, then reformed, then added and lost members over the years. The relationships often became tumultuous. They had also created new music, some with Andy, some without. Very quickly, attorneys began issuing communiques on behalf of the three surviving original band members.

"After Andy died, I knew I didn't want to be known as a widow. And I particularly didn't want to be called a rock widow because of what I felt were the negative connotations. But then, because of the nature of what began happening with former band members, I had to get over that. I had to assert his legacy in different ways. The only way to do that was to go out publicly as Andy's wife. It felt almost schizophrenic. I had spent so many years developing my own identity as a writer and journalist. I had people tell me after Andy's death that they had no idea he was my husband. I had spent years making sure that I wasn't defined by him. Because of the nature of the worlds that we both inhabited, we had these separate lives. I remember once he came to a State dinner with me and had to wear white tie and tails, which is not what anyone would expect a post-punk legend to wear. But he did, and we went to dinner with the Queen and the royals and politicians. Because of my work, I knew all of them, but Andy didn't, and they didn't know him. Our worlds just weren't contiguous.

"But after he died, I had to sort of come out as a rock wife and now widow. It's been an odd process. But I was approached very aggressively by the three other former members of the band. Their insistent desire to start legal proceedings nearly the moment Andy died was just the worst thing they could have done. There was literally no way that I would have not defended him. It's a complete misreading of the way grief and widowhood works. There was an assumption that I would just roll over, and it made me much fiercer than I might have been because he couldn't speak for himself. It was a sacred duty for me to defend him and it remains for me."

Catherine found herself painfully in the middle between band members with whom Andy had disagreements. She tried her best to balance what she thought was right given the circumstances and what Andy would have wanted. Honoring Andy's wishes, which weren't stated as there was nothing in writing, was the highest priority. To act as though there had been no previous animosity felt like a betrayal. It was impossible to do without anger flaring on all sides. The three former members of the band wished to come to Andy's funeral, a desire they communicated via an attorney. There were also issues with music rights, issues that Andy had been aware of and had fretted over prior to his illness. And finally, there was Andy's work in progress: an album of Gang of Four covers by artists like Gary Numan, the Red Hot Chili Peppers, and Tom Morello. Almost immediately after Andy's passing, Catherine was thrown into these battles, with many in charge telling her to sit down and leave it to others.

"It's not just band members, but managers, the record company, all those people who would say to me, 'Oh, you just don't understand the music industry.' Really? I've lived in the music industry for thirty years, and you think I don't understand it? I've produced a music festival. The combination of the misogynistic music industry and the wider misogynistic framing of widowhood is quite something. And I just thought, how incredibly lacking in their understanding of grief they all were. I would have always been a lioness in defending Andy, but how much more so when he was no longer here to defend himself. It takes a very myopic industry to look at someone like me, a journalist and researcher whose business it is to understand what's happening. But the real myopia is in not understanding that grief makes you stronger, more committed. It doesn't cut your legs out from underneath you: it makes them sturdier. Anybody who tries to take his name or legacy in vain, I will defend against. And I'm not doing it for money or fun. I'm doing it for Andy." Though it took two years and considerable back-and-forth with multiple attorneys, the group was able to settle most issues.

"I haven't stopped finding ways to memorialize Andy. And I have my own projects that I can work on as well. I can memorialize him, which many of the Covid bereaved haven't been able to do. And I can write. I began work on a novel in 2018, and I think I will return to that." She also plans to return to working on the Women's Equality Party and planning the next Primadonna Festival, as well as a new festival celebrating death. "The Death Festival will be in Brighton, and we'll have panel discussions and music all around the issues related to death and dying," she told me.

"I believe I will always want to memorialize Andy. I still want to talk about him, which sometimes makes people uncomfortable. But I do, and I think I always will. I'm pretty unapologetic about it. It might make some people uncomfortable, but that's how things are. And there's so much of what I've come to call 'sadmin.' All the time-and-emotion-consuming administrative things that have to be done. I've gotten through much of that, but it's so difficult. Every few days, I catch Andy looking at me from his portrait, done by Shephard Fairey, and I look at it and say, 'I'm trying my best.'"

"And in the future?" I asked. "I'm trying to make myself understand that I don't really know what my life will be like going forward. I don't want to make decisions that will define it in one way or another. I need to figure out what I want to do. It was almost a relief meeting Andy, because I suddenly had a home. Before I met him, I always thought I risked spiraling out of control. I always have so many projects, there always seemed to be that risk of going in so many different directions. But Andy made me come home. He gave me a reason to come home, to be quiet. Before, I had so many relationships with so many people because of my work. And you look at those relationships and think they are substantial, but they're not. That one relationship, the one that brought me home, that was the one that mattered."

Catherine lives with the regret born of not being able to say goodbye to Andy, of not being with him when he went into a coma, of turning off life-sustaining machines that perhaps in retrospect, if it was Covid, could have changed the outcome, even the regret that she should have given him that last glass of wine. All of this is speculation that only worsens the pain. Catherine admits to these regrets in her book, saying what I have felt for over ten years, "Things done or undone, things said or unsaid: some percentage of grief is always contaminated by regret. Well-meaning people will try to reason your regrets away, but this is neither possible nor, I suspect, desirable."[2]

Until we are able to perfect the art of dealing with the last moments of life, which I am doubtful will ever happen, we will always wish for them to have been different or somehow better. And we will live with regret that they weren't. As the ones who remain, we think about it to the point of obsession. We wish, mostly we rage, not against our loved ones who, after all, handle their end in the only way they're capable of doing, but instead against our shortcomings, decisions, or imperfect actions. And to what end?

Later, as I walk through London looking at the River Thames, I recall a photo of Kevin, having stopped half-way across the river on Westminster Bridge. He is smiling. We were in London as newlyweds, the future so big ahead of us. And now, I'm here as a widow, finding a new way and a new future. "Leave it here," I then think to myself, "Leave the regret, the guilt, the cursed hope for some other ending. Drop it all in this river and walk away." And so, I do.

13

INGRID CROCE

I remember bristling at comments people made telling me how well they thought I was handling my grief, or how proud they were of my ability to move on, to accomplish things like a master's degree or publication of an essay, or getting my children off to college, or selling my house. Also known as starting all over. But I would look around and think, what choice did I have? There is stasis, which is where I wanted to be every day—curled up, not thinking, not feeling. And there is also forward momentum—cooking meals, earning a living to pay the bills, caring for those for whom I was responsible at that time, whether my children or my elderly parents. Putting one foot in front of the other, never mind that the ground beneath me felt as though it would give way with each step, was the only choice I had. We do what we must do; it's really that simple.

There's another enduring memory I have, this one from childhood. Growing up in a middle-class family in Detroit, there was always music, though most often it came to me from my older siblings rather than my parents. On one particular Friday evening, I remember the conversation turning to the news of the day. My sister asked if we had heard about the singer/songwriter Jim Croce. He had died the night before, and his death was all over the news. "He wrote one of my favorite songs," I remember her saying, "It's called 'Time in a Bottle.' It's about

Ingrid and Jim at their bridal shower in Philadelphia. Courtesy of Ingrid Croce

how we don't have enough time in our lives to do what we want to do. That's what the words say. And now, just as a bunch of his songs are popular, he died. It's so sad." Our parents were older, and we seldom shared a common interest in music. But we had all heard Jim's music, his intricate guitar playing and sensitive lyrics, or the bawdy storytelling of "You Don't Mess Around with Jim" and "Leroy Brown." His songs were played on stations from rock to easy listening, even in a recent *ABC Movie of the Week*. From the outside, he seemed like an overnight sensation. There aren't many moments of dinner conversation with my parents that I remember, but I somehow remember that one. Jim's death was the early loss of someone whose music had meaning for me.

And although Jim Croce's time as a hit-producing musician and songwriter seemed brief (it wasn't, of course), he and his work have never left the pop music lexicon. We still hear him on the radio, his songbooks are still some of the most popular among guitarists and those learning guitar, and his short life is the stuff of legend. And behind all of that is his widow, Ingrid. "Ingrid has always been a driven person," says her husband of thirty-five years, Jimmy Rock. "Any of her friends or family or colleagues will tell you that she always has been. She was going to be successful at whatever she did, and, after Jim died, much of her attention was focused on making sure he was recognized for all he had accomplished in his short life. And she has certainly done that."

Jimmy, Ingrid, and I are meeting in San Diego, the city that Ingrid and Jim Croce moved to just weeks before Jim's death in an airplane crash in Louisiana in 1973. The crash that took Jim Croce's life left Ingrid in a newly adopted place alone with their two-year-old son, A. J. The sense of loneliness she endured, in addition to overwhelming grief, fueled in Ingrid a powerful desire to do, to create, to build, to revitalize, to remember: to always remember. Her list of accomplishments is significant. It's impossible to consider all she has achieved without words like "strong," or "brave," or "driven" coming to mind. And rather than bristle, Ingrid takes these accolades in stride, accepting the way in which she responded to the devastation of Jim's death, just as he was being recognized for being the talented musician and composer he was. With a shrug she says what I feel: "I had a child to care for. I had no other choice."

But rather than tell me about those times, I've instead, for the most part, read about them in books and articles. Today, I hear about them from Ingrid, but also from Jimmy Rock, who has generously done much research into the life and times of Ingrid and Jim Croce as part of his marriage. And although Ingrid is a perfectly lovely, caring host on my visit, we are unable to have much back-and-forth discussion because Ingrid has recently been diagnosed with aphasia, a progressive neurodegenerative disease that makes it difficult for her to speak. This woman, who has always been so full of energy, and who has so often directed that energy to tending and telling Jim Croce's heroic story, is now muted by this condition. She has survived more cruel strokes of fate than most of us could endure, not just Jim's death but other very personal losses as well.

And yet, here she is, living life and brimming with a frenetic vitality that is palpable throughout our afternoon together. I never realized how much energy we expend when we tell stories through talking. Now, struggling with an inability to easily do so, Ingrid's passion, her love of Jim Croce, her absolute belief in his talents and in their deep love story, seems to almost roil within her. The memories are there; it's just very difficult for her to share them, to get them out. I'm saddened as I leave her, and think that I should write about the unfairness of this latest development. But then I realize that unfairness is like a pebble that keeps getting into Ingrid's shoe. She will simply sigh, take a moment to stop and fix it, and then continue putting one foot in front of the other, despite it all. If I'm certain of anything, it's that she will keep moving.

Jim Croce met Ingrid Jacobson when he was twenty and she was just sixteen. It isn't possible to tell the story of Jim's rise in the music business without also including Ingrid, who was with him through every frustration, setback, and eventual triumph. The year was 1963, and Jim was a student at Villanova University in Philadelphia. Ingrid was a high school student who was already singing with vocal groups and on that day was participating in a singing contest sponsored by the student radio station where Jim was a DJ. The two were smitten from the first moments, and Jim asked Ingrid if she'd like to join him as a duo. They began dating, with their early lives centered on their common interest in folk music. "As he played the old folk song, 'Cotton-Eyed Joe,' I felt more intimacy with him than I had ever experienced with anyone," Ingrid says. "Jim finished his song and asked if I would like to try one together with him. He picked up his twelve-string and started to play. He taught me the harmony to Woody Guthrie's 'Pastures of Plenty,' explaining it was just like the melody 'but different.'

"I liked everything about him," she continues. "His broad open smile, his strong hands, his slim body, his medium height, his voice. He was seductive but secure."

Jim came from a tight-knit Catholic, Italian-American family in Philadelphia, and Jim's father disliked his son's plans to be a musician, feeling instead that it should be a hobby and not take time from the pursuit of a 9–5 job he had prepared himself for with his college degree. His father's lack of faith in his musical ability would torment Jim until his father's passing, just as Jim's songs were beginning to climb the charts. In Ingrid's family, Jim found an openness and trust that his own family relationships lacked. Ingrid's parents had divorced, and Ingrid's mother passed away when Ingrid was fifteen. Moving multiple times to live with one parent or the other, Ingrid became used to upheaval in her life. Ingrid was also Jewish, another point of consternation with Jim's family as the two became more serious.

"Jim was welcomed into my family. My father was a psychiatrist, and he loved Jim. It was a magical time, the folk period and the 1960s. There was the anti-war movement, so many changes in music and culture."

Just as Jim completed his studies at Villanova, Ingrid was accepted to the prestigious Rhode Island School of Design and went there to study painting and pottery. Though the separation was difficult, the two maintained their relationship. Jim struggled to find permanent work in music but continued his pursuit of a career by writing and taking gigs in bars and restaurants while doing other things like trucking and construction. Quite often, Ingrid would sing with Jim and work with him on songwriting. "I sang with Jim; I grew up with Jim," Ingrid says. "And I always recognized him as a star. He had that charisma, even at twenty. And he lived for music. He'd play until he fell asleep, then wake up and start playing again." During her first year at RISD, Jim proposed to Ingrid, and the two began planning their wedding.

Soon after, Ingrid's father was diagnosed with pancreatic cancer, causing her to return to Philadelphia and enroll in the Moore College of Art. Ingrid and Jim were married after Jim converted to Judaism, and within weeks, Jim began bootcamp in the National Guard Reserves, again separating the two. It was the height of the Vietnam War, with Jim hoping his National Guard duties would prevent him from being sent to fight in Vietnam. Though miserable at boot camp, he would call Ingrid every week and write letters every day. "Tonight, it is getting cold and windy," he wrote in one, "but the memory of you is the fire within that keeps me warm."

When Sid Jacobson died of cancer, Jim took a hardship discharge. The couple rented a small apartment in Philadelphia, and Jim began a job in radio. That spring, Ingrid received a fellowship to study painting and ceramics abroad. She decided to study in San Miguel de Allende in Mexico, in part because it was affordable for the couple, who were struggling to get by. Arriving in Mexico with a friend, Ingrid first traveled to Acapulco for a few days' vacation before starting her studies. Instead, she was brutally raped by a University of Mexico student who had talked the two young women into going to the seaside to watch divers.

Ingrid was tormented by her assault. At turns, she felt guilty and shameful. She had no idea how to tell Jim, who was due to arrive in Mexico a few weeks later. Jim did not respond well to the situation. "The next morning, after Jim arrived, I haltingly told him the story. He initially reacted with detached curiosity. Like a reporter, he pressed for all the details. Slowly, his demeanor changed. 'Why were you with those guys in the first place?' he demanded. 'You ruined everything! You're a whore,' he shouted, 'an adulterer!'"[1]

It took years for Jim to understand that Ingrid was not responsible for the assault against her and for Ingrid to realize that he may have never come to terms with it. The two seemed to work through this difficulty, although Ingrid would understand much later, while volunteering at a rape crisis center in San Diego and working on her book about Jim, that his feelings about the rape hovered over their marriage for years. "I really didn't understand how my rape, when I was newly married, had affected our relationship," Ingrid said in an interview in 2012. "I knew that it affected it, but I really didn't recognize the extraordinary impact that it had, the anger that Jim had, and the passiveness that I felt as a result of his anger; I felt responsible, even though I knew I wasn't. The guilt and the interplay between people who love each other. Rape is an aggressive act, and Jim felt perhaps also responsible [in] that he wasn't there. There were so many things that occurred as a result of that happening that I wasn't really aware of," she says.[2]

Following Ingrid's fellowship, the two moved to New York, where Jim once again attempted to make it in the music business. Jim and Ingrid signed a contract with people he knew from his earliest days performing in vocal groups at Villanova. Terry

Cashman, Tommy West, and Phil Kurnit became powerful in the music industry, in part due to Jim's success. They encouraged the couple to sign the contract without legal consultation. Although they were unaware of it at the time, however, signing the contract allowed the three men to own the rights to the Croce's music "from 1968 to perpetuity." Jim and Ingrid cut an album together, *Jim and Ingrid Croce*, and traveled across the country playing college campuses and bars. The album was rushed to press but never received promotion or support. Their financial struggles in New York seemed constant, with nothing to indicate a better future.

Feeling frustrated and defeated, the two left New York for farmland in rural Pennsylvania. There, the couple entertained local singers and musicians, developing a circle of friends that helped them through it, including Bonnie Raitt, Arlo Guthrie, and James Taylor. Back in New York, however, Cashman and West continued to renew their options on Jim's contract, preventing him from seeking a better deal or exposure elsewhere. "If you have a talent and a passion for making music as much as you can, you're not thinking about the business end of what's going on," Ingrid says, "Jim was at the point of selling off his guitars. It was never going to happen, it seemed, that music would be the thing that would help us financially. Music was the thing that brought us joy, but it seemed it would never support us."

It was soon after moving to Pennsylvania that Ingrid learned she was pregnant with their first child. For Jim, this became a now-or-never moment. "I remember when I told Jim we were going to have a baby. The look on his face was a combination of utter fear and sheer ecstasy. Though he was excited about building a family, his big brown eyes registered panic and a look of, 'Oh my God, more responsibility!' Once Jim got over the initial shock of becoming a father, he found a new sense of urgency to make his career successful as a singer and songwriter." That night, he sat at their kitchen table and wrote "Time in a Bottle," which would soon become a #1 single. "The thought of having a child, there was a sense of immortality that inclined him to write about mortality. It was a turning over of his life into another life. The whole album became a gift to this new life," she explained. He completed several other songs, sent them off to Tommy West, and things quickly began happening. The album, *You Don't Mess Around with Jim*, recorded for ABC Dunhill, went gold, and Jim headed out on what would become two years of constant touring.

After being home long enough to help deliver his son, Adrian James Croce, Jim returned to the road, where he traveled and played over three hundred shows in a year, including television spots, small venues like the Troubadour in LA, college campuses, and arenas. As Ingrid remained home in their farmhouse, she painfully endured a longer separation than had ever happened before. "Waiting at home with A. J., I was so lonely. After eight years of performing and being with Jim constantly, I found the separation very painful. I missed him terribly. It was as though he was no longer ours anymore. He belonged to the road.

"And the longer he stayed on the road, the more we felt the strain on our marriage," Ingrid admits. But it would take a full year of constant performing to promote the album and respond to his new-found stardom. During this time, Ingrid also understood that Jim was relying more and more on drugs to help him through long hours of travel and shows, or to help him sleep after the show was over. She also had her suspicions about Jim's relationships with groupies that he encountered. It was difficult for her to realize how big a star he had become while out on the road. "By the time 'You Don't Mess Around with Jim' reached #1 on the charts, Jim started getting a whole lot of recognition, not just within the industry, but on the street. He was a real star. As grateful as he was for the acceptance of his music, he was shy about being famous," she told me. He would also come off the road and beg Ingrid for forgiveness for behavior he couldn't talk about, something to which she always acquiesced.

Ingrid then learned she was pregnant with their second child. Jim was completing a tour in the United States and heading to several dates in Europe as Ingrid worked on her own to care for A. J. and herself. When Jim would come home for a few days, he was often tightly wound and unable to relax and settle in with his family. During one of those times, they decided to move to San Diego. Living alone in rural Pennsylvania was difficult for Ingrid, and Jim wished to be closer to Los Angeles. Ingrid traveled to San Diego to find a home and then returned east to pack up and get ready for the move. Days before leaving, and at just six months pregnant, her water broke and she went into labor. Ingrid called Jim in Amsterdam from her hospital room. "I called him and told him, 'I'm afraid we might lose the baby,' as tears rolled down my cheeks. I asked him to please come home. 'I can't leave the tour,' was all he said. I hung up, feeling as though our marriage was over."

Ingrid gave birth to a premature boy, Max, who died in her arms later that night. The next day, she checked herself out of the hospital and returned home to finish packing. Within two days, she was back in the hospital, suffering from septicemia, an infection of the bloodstream caused when a portion of the placenta is not properly removed. The hospital struggled to get the infection under control with antibiotics, and Ingrid grew weak. Finally, a family friend placed an emergency call to Jim in Amsterdam, and he flew home. It was a realization for Jim, who admitted to a friend that he hadn't been treating Ingrid properly.

Jim and Ingrid were still living on a few hundred dollars a month they received in allowance from their managers, despite Jim's growing superstar status. Ingrid's many pleas to Jim to determine where his money was going went ignored. Though he had several Top 10 hits, the couple was barely getting by, living on food Ingrid grew in their garden and outfitting Jim for tours in second-hand shops. "He came home to visit that last weekend after A. J. and I had moved to San Diego. He was so discouraged and completely drained from life on the road. He was threatening to just leave. Leave behind the record deals and the constant touring. I told him he couldn't just go away. 'Talk to them,' I said. 'Make them listen.' But he couldn't. Jim was at a crossroad. I believe he was doing his damnedest to find his way home.

"He was ready to just get out of the business. He hated it so much. He hated the touring and all the contrived things that were a part of the business. The pretense. The lies and all the things that had been promised to him over the years, how he was going to make money and it would all be okay."

In a letter, Jim told Ingrid that they should leave it all behind and travel to Costa Rica to live in peace. He had reached the pinnacle of stardom, but felt he had no control over his life and was utterly exhausted and missing his young family. He completed his third album, *Photographs and Memories* and had only a few more weeks of touring before he'd finally get a break. As he traveled to Natchitoches, Louisiana, for a show at Northwestern State University, he phoned Ingrid and once again promised to be home soon. Yet just after the show, he was informed that more dates had been added to his tour.

The show in Natchitoches, though, would be Jim's last. After the show, on September 20, 1973, he and his friend and guitarist Maury Muehleisen and several others climbed aboard their chartered plane and waited for the pilot, who had overslept and was late arriving. After planning to call a cab but finding that there were no cabs in Natchitoches, the pilot walked and ran over three miles from his hotel to the airport, eventually catching a ride with the sheriff. By the time he arrived at the small airstrip, he was disheveled, sweaty, and out of breath. He did no safety inspection and instead took off, heading south. The plane's lift was insufficient, however, causing it to clip several trees and crash. Eyewitnesses reported debris scattered through a large area.

At 4:35 a.m. Pacific Time, Ingrid received a call from her stepmother in Pennsylvania. "I first thought it was Jim. Then my stepmother said, 'No, it's Mom.' I asked her what's the matter. She said, 'Oh Ingrid, I was just watching the *Today Show*. There was a terrible plane crash last night.' She paused, and I said, 'And Jim is dead, right?' She said, 'Yes, Ing. His plane crashed.' I asked about Maury, and she said that everyone had died."

Jim was buried at Hayem Solomon Jewish cemetery in Frazier, Pennsylvania. Because of the impact of the crash, Ingrid never saw Jim's remains. Concert promoter Doug Nichols was called upon to identify the bodies. It would be years before Ingrid learned for certain that Jim had not been decapitated, a cruel rumor that had continued to be spread over the years since the accident. She returned to San Diego days later and found a letter from Jim in the mail. In it, he apologized for his behavior and promised to do better. "I now want to be the oldest man around, a man with a face full of wrinkles and lots of wisdom. . . . When I get back everything will be different. We're gonna have a life together, Ing, I promise. . . . Remember, it's the first sixty years that count and I've got thirty to go."

Ingrid returned to San Diego feeling completely bereft. Within a few years' time, she had lost her father, her baby, and now her husband, with whom she had been since age sixteen. "I had a lot of anger when Jim died," Ingrid says. "A lot of anger. I was angry at Jim; I was angry that he died. I was angry at the whole business."

"It was such a tremendous loss for Ingrid," adds Jimmy Rock. "Jim was her lover, her best friend, the person she had grown up with. She was also very close friends with Maury, Jim's guitarist who also died in the crash. She was best friends and still is with Maury's girlfriend, Judy. So, there was tremendous grief. She was lost. And then there was litigation."

A. J. became her reason to continue. "I had a child to raise. He became my motivation to get up in the morning, just to make breakfast, lunch, and dinner," she says. "I had this child. I had to keep going. Mealtimes put continuity into my life."

In early 1974, Ingrid made her way to Costa Rica, believing against all odds that Jim was there, that he had planned the crash as a way to get out of his contracts and had made his way there to start over. She received two separate calls from friends suggesting she travel there. "Our friend Corb Donahue from ABC Dunhill called and suggested a trip to Costa Rica, saying that shortly before Jim died, they'd made a plan to meet up there. He said that land was cheap, and we could live there.

"To me, it explained the comments Jim had made the weekend before the crash when he said that he wanted to go away and hide and that I'd see him in six months. It was the only explanation," Ingrid explained. She traveled to Costa Rica and looked everywhere for Jim, her grief propelling her to search for some kind of answer to what had happened. She and A. J. spent months in Quepos, living without a plan or agenda. "It took me years to accept Jim's death, several years. When we returned from Costa Rica, I received a check for $5,000, more money than we had ever received from royalties. After all his years of hard work and traveling, Jim had died with just his work shirt on his back and with no bank account."

She phoned the record company and attorneys to check on the progress of settling Jim's estate, demanding an audit. She wished only to receive the funds due her from Jim's record sales and hundreds of concert appearances. Thus began a ten-year odyssey of lawsuits as Ingrid tried to get a proper accounting of Jim's earnings. In addition to lawsuits against record companies and managers like Cashman, West, and Kurnit in New York, there was a wrongful death lawsuit against the company who chartered the plane from Natchitoches to Dallas, and the huge task of settling Jim's estate in San Diego. Lawsuits consumed Ingrid's life for a full decade after Jim's death. "I had to make serious spiritual and ethical decisions about litigation. Having had plenty of experience with attorneys and courts around my parent's custody battles, I didn't want to have to fight in that arena. I hated it! But sometimes there are values you must honor. I felt it was the right thing to do. Jim and I had worked too hard to let someone take it all away from us." Eventually, ninety attorneys were involved in getting back what was hers from the start. Today, students of contract and entertainment law look to Ingrid's cases as cautionary tales of how entertainment contracts can be problematic and unfair for those who wish only to pursue their dreams.

Ingrid also found herself being preyed upon by unscrupulous people who believed she had come into wealth from Jim's success. She also suffered terribly when A. J. was stricken with a tumor syndrome that caused blindness. "That was when I wanted to perish. After all I had been through with Jim, watching my child suffer was the hardest thing I've ever had to do." Though the situation was averted before it became too late, A. J. became very shy and sensitive.

Thinking that returning to music would help her during this time, Ingrid wrote some two hundred songs in the months after returning to San Diego. Besides becoming a prolific songwriter, she also put together a band and recorded two albums. It provided a comforting outlet for her grief and her energy, as music brought her closer to Jim's memory and was something she had spent her life doing. But this life path, too, was cut short when, yet again, Ingrid was faced with bad news. Cysts had developed on her vocal cords. Through two painful surgeries she remained hopeful, but both were unsuccessful. The cysts were surgically removed, but she would never sing again.

With A. J. growing and becoming more independent, and once again looking for a way to create a new life for herself, Ingrid turned to food. She remembered all the times she had spent around the Croce family table sharing Jim's mother's Italian specialties, as well as the times she had spent with her own Russian grandmother making treats. It also reminded her of their happiest times together, when Jim and Ingrid lived in rural Pennsylvania and friends would gather who would talk and sing, while Ingrid baked bread or made pots of soup. When a friend suggested she open a shop making blintzes from her grandmother's recipe, Ingrid agreed and opened Blinchiki in San Diego in a condemned storefront that she rented for eighteen cents a square foot.

From there, she expanded, opening Croce's, a restaurant dedicated to Jim's memory and a spot for good food and live music. The business helped to reinvigorate the mostly empty Gaslamp Quarter in downtown San Diego and was located in a storefront that Jim and Ingrid had passed on their last date before Jim left for the show in Natchitoches. "Being Jim's widow, being Ingrid Croce, almost became my calling card in San Diego. A. J. and I were the focus of people's love of Jim. Fans feel closer to him through us. I've never felt that as a burden; it's always been something positive for me, never a negative."

For the next thirty years, Ingrid would expand the restaurant, adding other concepts like Croce's Top Hat Bar & Grille, which featured blues music. As A. J. developed his musical talent, he played at the nightclub each Sunday. Ingrid authored two cookbooks, *Thyme in a Bottle* and *Photographs and Memories*. She became a fixture in San Diego's downtown renewal and in the food scene, establishing San Diego Restaurant Week and earning awards from state and national organizations. The restaurants flourished under Ingrid's energetic and exacting guidance. They also provided the location of a fateful meeting with a regular customer, attorney Jimmy Rock. Ingrid was formally introduced to Jimmy after he helped one of her employees get out of trouble. They began dating shortly after the new year, and Ingrid quickly felt that this was the right person. "Just when I'd given up on finding a mate, Jimmy came into my heart, as if he'd always been there. He was secure and adventurous. He pursued me with courageous gentility, always calling when he said he would, always arriving on time. I was extremely lucky to find a combination of strong convictions and intelligence in such a kind and gentle man."

It is easy to see Ingrid's continued conviction to Jim Croce's memory and legacy, and just as easy to see Jimmy Rock's equal conviction to Ingrid and all that she values, including Jim's legacy. They are true partners in every sense. Of Ingrid, Jimmy tells me, "She has always had an artistic vision, which she has pursued in different formats, either visual art and collage, songwriting, music, or food. She's never been someone who would lie on the floor and cry. She may cry, but she does so while moving forward. It's just who she is. She has overcome so many obstacles in life just by doing."

Before leaving their home, the three of us take in Ingrid's visual art and collage work. Taking many pieces of loosely related items—photos, drawings, writing—she pieces them together into stunning works that are a visual representation of Ingrid's thoughtful energy. "Ingrid is often shy about her artwork, though I tell her she shouldn't be. She's not shy about anything else," Jimmy says. But I understand. With so much of herself out in the world, focused on others, this representation of her earliest desires to be an artist, this beautiful and deep self-expression, is something she wants to hold close, just to herself. She is deserving of so much, but especially of this moment of privacy.

It is not possible to be in Ingrid Croce's presence and not feel her energy, her love for the three men in her life, and her dedication to life here today, and the legacy of yesterday. To see it represented in visual art, to hear it in music, to feel it as she moves through her kitchen, still making sure this visitor feels not just welcomed but at home. Though the words are few, she is, as Jimmy Rock notes, "fully present and accounted for." She is vibrant and animated, still dedicated to her singular purpose of taking those forward steps.

14

SANDY CHAPIN

The epitaph on a stone taken from Harry Chapin's family's summer home in Massachusetts and placed on his grave on Long Island quotes from his song "I Wonder What Would Happen to This World": "If a man tried to take his time . . . and prove before he died what one man's life could be worth, I wonder what would happen?" Harry attempted to prove what his life could be worth by almost single-handedly bringing both political and social attention to the issue of hunger. He was well into that work when he was killed in an auto accident in 1981 at the age of thirty-four.

His wife Sandy Chapin was left to carry on that work and spends much of her time chairing and running the Harry Chapin Foundation. Since its formation shortly after his death, the foundation has given over $1.9 million in grants to over four hundred different agencies and nonprofit groups, especially those that address hunger, education, arts education, and environmental issues.

Sandy is soft-spoken but cheerful and I can easily envision the smile on her face when she tells me about her children and grandchildren. She and Harry had five children at the time of his accident, ranging in age from six to seventeen (the oldest three were from Sandy's first marriage). But I sense the smile fading as she tells me about the stone that marks Harry's grave.

Harry and Sandy Chapin vacationing in Mexico. Courtesy of Sandy Chapin

"We purposely put Harry at a very public place at the Huntington Cemetery. At one time, it was the highest spot. People are very respectful of his grave. They'll leave little plants; oftentimes they write him notes, sometimes they leave other mementos. There are many stones; people love to leave smaller stones on top of the big rock.

"It is strange sometimes to think of all these people who visit, and I don't know who they are. I don't know them. When I go there, it isn't a place just for me to 'be with Harry,' it's a place that's very public. I think of all these people who keep visiting, and I can almost hear them saying, 'Where is she? Why isn't she here? Why doesn't she come here every day and mourn with us? What is she doing? And I think, well, I can't carry on Harry's work and be at the rock every day. I can't do both, so . . .'"

I talked with Sandy at a time when I was thinking about legacies. Have I done enough to honor Kevin's memory? Every step moving forward seems to also be a reminder that I'm moving away from that time when we were together. I think sometimes that I am almost unrecognizable to my prewidow self, and in some ways, it feels like a betrayal. I must remain here, as Kevin's widow, to keep his story alive. If not me, who? Who will continue his story so that his life, not his death, is his legacy?

Yet I also know that moving on, raising our children, and making a happy and successful life is also a tribute to Kevin and to his memory. Now that I am no longer in the deepest throes of grief, I find myself considering these new issues. Not just how to go on, but what is the best way? Deep in these thoughts, it occurs to me that honor and betrayal can be two inextricable sides of the same coin. I'm not sure it has ever been that way for Sandy Chapin, though. From the early days after Harry's death, she knew her job would be to carry on his social justice work. She has done this, perhaps at the cost of her own identity, though she has always demurred from taking much of the credit she deserves. Seeing his work go forward, along with raising their children, was always the most important thing.

"There was so much work to be done after Harry's death. He was in the midst of so many projects—he always had multiple projects. I just knew we had to keep things going. I had five children, and the youngest was only seven. I was immediately wrapped up in soccer games and schoolwork and getting the oldest one off to college. I never had time to mourn. I had to keep life going for us. And Harry was so involved in the community. When I think about how my [grief] experience differed from other people's, it's very apparent."

Sandy stops for a moment to reflect.

"There were all these connections with organizations doing tributes and asking me to speak at ceremonies and graduations and music events. And then there were questions; very soon these questions came up. How to keep World Hunger Year going and what to do about the Performing Arts Foundation which he started. We had to get involved quickly to keep things moving along.

"And of course, there was the business. People think that Harry left a lot of money. If you've read about Harry, you know that he gave away half of his money to others. He really did give away pretty much everything. He had a family to support, and a band, and office, and lighting guys, but otherwise, he gave it all away. So, there was all that to deal with. There were lawsuits and people trying to cash in.

"Through it all, there's a feeling of having to keep his music alive. He was so proud of his music and his songs. When I think about how others grieve when they lose someone, when they lose their husband or wife, it seems that there's this slow, sweet, fading away. For me, there's no fading away. I have the voice still in my house, and the photos and videos, of course. But then everyone has stories [about Harry] and the connections that seem to go on and on. Even today, people will stop me to tell me a story about Harry.

"In the months after his death, there were trips to LA to hear people talking about different music projects. And I think about how I had to change. Oh my gosh, before Harry died, if I ever had to speak in public, I would get someone else to do it, and of course, Harry was always out front. We would go to some large dinner function, and I would sit at our table while Harry circulated through the entire hall. We would talk about ideas together and have vigorous discussions, but Harry was the doer; he was out front while I hid in the background. After he died, I had to come to terms with this. I had to be out there; it was either step up or run away. It was terrifying. But there was no alternative. All these things that Harry had going on, I couldn't just let them die with him."

Within a month of his death, there was a memorial concert at the theater where he should have performed on the night of his death, and the theater was renamed the Harry Chapin Lakeside Theater. Six years after his death, Sandy organized an all-star tribute concert during which he was posthumously awarded the Congressional Medal of Freedom.

Legacy indeed.

Sandy was already married when she met Harry, living a comfortable life in a Manhattan brownstone with a reserved and distant husband and three children. It was because of her children that she wanted to learn to play guitar.

"I could play the piano, but I thought that wouldn't be good to sit with my back to my children and play. With the guitar, we could sit in a circle on the floor or even march around the room, which we eventually did. I asked a few friends about guitar teachers, and there weren't any close by. Someone recommended Harry. I called his home, but his mother told me he was working in California on a film. So I dropped the idea and just decided it wasn't going to work out. Then I think it was about a year and a half later I got the call from Harry that he was back in town. His mother saved my number, and I guess she thought with him just back to New York and hanging around without any work, she would give him my number for something to do before he got settled. A year and a half after we were supposed to meet, we finally did."

Their relationship remained professional for the first several months, not only because of Sandy's marriage but also because the lessons were pretty hit or miss.

"Sometimes, he would call and cancel because something came up, and sometimes he just wouldn't show up. Sometimes, I would cancel because I couldn't get anyone to watch the kids. But each time he came over, with each lesson, he would teach me something, and then he would give me a little concert of his own music. That was very sweet."

During this time, Sandy was making the decision to end her marriage and decided to spend the summer in a rented house on Long Island. This would give her time and space to figure out her next steps. She purposely told Harry that she would be out of touch through the summer and would connect with him again in the fall.

"But then he ended up calling me at the beach house. I often asked him about that, and I never got an answer. I was always curious. I asked him, 'How come you called me because I said I wouldn't be around, and I would call you in the fall?' and he would never give me an answer. Every now and then, I think about that. Why did he persist?

"But we were in phone conversations a few times through the summer. In the meantime, I decided to stay in the rental house and leave my marriage, so I stayed on Long Island. I had signed up for six sessions of a poetry reading series at the Y in New York, and I told Harry about it once when he called. He said, 'I'd like to go to that. Sign me up too, and I'll pay you later.' The series was once a week for six weeks, so I guess that was how we started dating. Sometimes, before I moved to Long Island, he would stop by the brownstone and drop off a poem he had been working on. I was also writing poetry, but my husband thought it was frivolous; he discouraged it and didn't want to know about it. I considered myself a closet poet, and it was neat to have someone to share that with. We would exchange poems and edit each other's work and then talk about it later."

Harry would later write the song "I Wanna Learn a Love Song" about his time teaching Sandy to play guitar. The couple dated for a year, then married in 1968.

"Harry was so loquacious; he was a man of words and stories. Our relationship started because of our love of words and writing."

Though their early relationship was one of words, it was not one of music. At the time they met, Harry was getting a few jobs making films and had worked for some time as a film editor, even earning an Academy Award nomination for his documentary film *Legendary Champions*. He occasionally played music with his brothers Tom and Steve. The Chapin Brothers had played music together on and off for several years. Harry would often travel to Cornell, where his brothers were students, to play weekend gigs around Ithaca. Harry had never really settled on a career in music but rather saw his career path going from documentary filmmaking to writing and producing feature films.

"He would go off to northern New York State and play up there. It was really just for money."

In 1971, Steve and Tom Chapin were being managed by Fred Kewley and were looking for a record deal. Kewley decided to rent out the Village Gate, a Greenwich Village folk club, where he would feature the duo every night, hoping for record company executives and music critics to take notice. Harry decided he would be the opening act because he was looking for a music publishing deal that would fund a move to California so he could break into filmmaking. He brought together a small band (Tim Scott, John Wallace, and Ron Palmer, all of whom would end up playing with Harry for several years) and rehearsed for one week before the shows opened.

Rather than get a deal for Harry's older brothers, however, record executives became interested in Harry, with his storytelling style and rapport with the audience. Soon after, Harry was offered deals by both Elektra and Columbia. He signed with Elektra and began making albums. His first, *Heads and Tales*, reached #60 on the Billboard charts in 1972, with the single "Taxi" reaching #24 on the singles charts and introducing Harry's "story-song" style to the world. The album sold over a million copies.

"During the beginning of our marriage, I was working on a PhD at Columbia, and Harry was working on writing screenplays and various other projects. He was basically a freelance writer and would sometimes get film work or write an article and make $100. I was always typing. Sometimes, he would work on an article up until the very last minute, and then I would type through the night so he could make his deadline. I really thought that would be our life. I would finish my PhD and work as a college professor and Harry would be a writer. We would be poor but happy. Evenings in the winter we would sit by the fire and read aloud from Tolstoy and have this great literary romance."

Instead, Harry's music took off, and their lives became very different.

"The moment I always remember, and I actually wrote a poem about it, was when Harry signed the record deal with Elektra, and we were invited to Jac Holzman's [founder of Elektra Records] summer home for a weekend along with Fred Kewley and his wife. No sooner had we arrived than Jac invited Harry into his home studio. I walked in and saw Harry singing and realized very quickly that this was a whole new world that I didn't really feel a part of. I really knew nothing about making music. Harry was in this room with all these buttons and knobs on consoles. That was the first time I realized there was a division coming, because he was in that world, and I wouldn't be. I was very strong visually but not aurally. That weekend was a big awakening for me. That was when I could see that there was another aspect of Harry, almost another person, that I wasn't going to be as connected to.

"I also never realized how much Harry needed an audience; I never really knew Harry the performer. For a while, the kids and I were his audience, and it was all for fun. But the first time I saw him in front of a real audience, well again, I just realized that this was a different part of him that I didn't know."

He released several albums to varying degrees of success, with critics often seeing his songs as superficial. His only #1 chart hit was "Cat's in the Cradle," a song about a father's realization that he had neglected his son. The song was actually cowritten by Sandy, who first wrote the lyrics as a poem. It was not about Harry but rather about her first husband and his relationship with his father. Harry at first dismissed the poem's potential as a song, but later, after their own son Josh was born, he revisited the poem and set it to music, adding the refrain. When I tell others that Harry and Sandy cowrote the song, they are surprised. When I ask Sandy if she feels she received proper credit, she demurs.

"Harry was just so prolific, much more so than I. One of the songs that I was most proud of that I cowrote was 'Tangled-Up Puppet,' but it took me eighteen months of picking it up and revising. Harry could write three songs in a day. We shared the interest, but I could never keep up with him. We worked together on writing songs for [the children's television show] *Make a Wish*. I would write a poem, but it was always a poem. Harry would fix them, make them into song lyrics. He was always teaching me the difference between writing a poem and writing a lyric."

With his popularity hitting a plateau, Harry realized that live performances would be the best way to keep his music growing and help his various causes. He had an unparalleled rapport with audiences and played a continuous circuit of college towns and midsized venues.

That performing schedule took Harry on the road to over two hundred concerts each year. It was difficult for Sandy and put a strain on their marriage. According to Peter Coan's biography, *Taxi*, published after his death, Harry also dabbled in extramarital relationships that caused Sandy to challenge him to be more than a music star. Sandy doesn't want to talk about that and even sued Coan to stop publication of the book, mostly, she says, because Coan hadn't signed the contract, so there was no legally executed arrangement for him to author the book. The contract stipulated that Harry would have final approval of the content, which Coan refused to offer to Sandy after Harry's death. It is known that Sandy questioned Harry about the legacy he wanted to leave and suggested that social and political work could give him an additional purpose. Sandy challenged him, asking, "So what if you're a superstar, what does it really mean?" Shortly after he became an international folk singer, he also cofounded the organization World Hunger Year with Bill Ayers and raised hundreds of thousands of dollars for organizations that addressed poverty, the environment, and the arts.

Harry's work was significant and vast. Between gifts and benefit concerts, he raised over $500,000 for Long Island's Performing Arts Foundation, which was one of more than a dozen organizations that Chapin helped. In addition, he spent considerable time in Washington, D.C., lobbying to create the President's Commission on World Hunger. Harry famously stood on the steps of Congress throughout the day of the commission vote and sang songs for the gathered crowd.

"Harry was never hanging out with other musicians, except to get them to perform benefit concerts," Sandy says. "He was so involved in the life on Long Island, which was really hard work. No one has done so much for life on Long Island before or since, really. But it meant that he was always on the run, always doing things. He would be at a meeting one day, come up with an idea, and the next morning be implementing it. He was getting amazing things accomplished. He had a terrible schedule, and everyone complained about his schedule, especially his managers. He would do a professional gig in Seattle one day, then go to a meeting in Washington, D.C., then go to Maine for a fundraiser, all in the same week. He never really had the celebrity kind of life. And it was nearly impossible for him to say no."

It wasn't unusual, then, that on July 16, 1981, Harry was rushing from a meeting with his agent in New York City to return home and do a benefit concert that night on Long Island. As he drove along the Jericho Turnpike, Harry turned on his emergency lights and slowed the car, but he was struck by a tractor-trailer and killed.

"The accident happened around 3:00 in the afternoon, but I don't think I knew until almost 7:00 that night. I think people were trying to decide who was going to come to the house and tell me. The concert had been planned, and there was a barbeque that was going to happen after. I remember all the kids were out of the house at various events and friends' houses. Often, Harry would invite a large group of people over to the house after a show, and sometimes as many as fifty or sixty people would just show up. We were planning for one of those barbeques that night. I was in touch with the people planning the barbeque and asked if I should come over, and they told me to wait and not come, so I knew something was off. Don Ruthig, Harry's secretary, eventually came and told me. I think his band members were there also and eventually his brothers were there. I remember after a few hours, that the house just seemed full of people. We were serving food and drinks and people were congregating about. No one knew quite what to do."

In the time since Harry's death, Sandy has raised their five children and carried on Harry's work with World Hunger Year and various arts organizations on Long Island, but she has also pursued her own arts interests, including ownership of a Native American gallery and development of an arts education program within Long Island Community Schools.

"I guess, though, I'm proudest of our kids. I'm proud that our kids on their own decided to follow in Harry's footsteps in some way," she says.

"My oldest daughter, Jaime, is very involved with her kids and for many years worked for Common Ground in Manhattan. My second son, Jonathan, is involved in community projects in Vermont and is an organic farmer. Jason works for Westchester County Association as Director of Workforce Development. Jen is a singer-songwriter and very much involved in the world of Harry Chapin fans. She's on the board of World Hunger Year. She was chairman but had to leave that position when she was diagnosed with MS. Our youngest, Josh, is still finding his interests, but he has worked a lot on many of his father's projects. He edited the second book of Harry's poetry and compiled the *Chapin Family Photo Book* with help from Harry's mom. I think he's had the hardest time with Harry's loss. The two were so close; Harry used to take him everywhere."

I ask Sandy if she ever thinks of what might have happened or where she and Harry might be if he had lived.

"There were three scenarios for our life. One was that he would keep on performing. It would be hard for me to imagine him stopping because he loved the attention and the audience. I didn't really see him doing less or being away less. In fact, it may have been more.

"The second was filmmaking. His last album was intended to be a soundtrack for a movie. He still wanted to make a movie. He had scripts and screenplays and an idea for a movie about three revolutionaries called *The Protest Singer*. I didn't want to move to Hollywood. We had lived for short periods in Los Angeles while he was recording, and it wasn't for me.

"At the same time, he was also distributing literature and building a mailing list because he was considering a run for Senate to unseat Alphonse D'Amato. Well, I didn't really want to be a senator's wife, either. I didn't want to be out there stumping and making speeches. I couldn't really picture myself in that role.

"But in the end, I would have done the best I could with whatever Harry wanted to do."

What role do we move into when the one we love most is taken from us? Only-parent and caregiver? Breadwinner? Those are obvious and easily defined, but what about "keeper of the flame?" What is our responsibility to keep and maintain their legacy, and how do we do it? When someone is lost at a young age, especially someone as creative and powerful a force as Harry Chapin, the natural inclination is to keep that life visible in whatever way possible. The risk, of course, is that we lose our own lives, or that our life becomes something else in the process. As I say goodbye to Sandy and wish her well, I realize that her life is now one of travel, appointments, and public-speaking engagements, things she never wanted to do when Harry was alive; things that make her life much like her late husband's. And yet, the alternative is to let his legacy be determined by others (like critics), or to fade away altogether, neither of which is acceptable to those who remain.

"You know," she says as if caught by an afterthought, "I kept going back to school to work on that PhD between babies and Harry's recording. I was always trying to finish before the next baby was born. There was a time when Harry would drive me to Columbia when I was nursing Jen, and he would stay in the car with her while I went to class, then we'd go back home. Yet I still didn't finish. I keep thinking someday I might. I wonder how many ninety-year-old doctoral students there are."

NOTES

Chapter 1 - Gloria Jones

1. Rachel Porter, "My life with Marc Bolan," *Express.co.uk*, September 3, 2007, https://www.express.co.uk/expressyourself/18094/My-life-with-Marc-Bolan.

Chapter 2 - Peggy Sue Honeyman-Scott

1. Rhino Entertainment Company, *This Is Pirate Radio*, by Ben Edmonds. Pirate Radio Box Set booklet, 2006.

Chapter 4 - Nancy Jones

1. https://www.tennessean.com/story/entertainment/2015/04/22/george-jones-nancy-jones-alcoholism/26201255/.

Chapter 6 - Annette Walter-Lax

1. Annette Walter-Lax, *The Last Four Years* (London, self-published, 2019), 44.

Chapter 7 - Gretchen Parsons Carpenter

1. Jim Washburn, "Tales from a Rocky Roadie: Pop Music: Phil Kaufman, the Gram Parsons Cremator and Charles Manson Album Producer, Signs His Raucous Memoirs in Anaheim Today," *Los Angeles Times*, March 6, 2019, https://www.latimes.com/archives/la-xpm -1994-02-19-ca-24775-story.html.

Chapter 9 - Judy Van Zant

1. Jim Jerome, "The Rock Road Claims Another Victim: Ronnie Van Zant of the Lynyrd Skynyrd Band," *People*, November 1977.

Chapter 10 - Jamie Weiland

1. David Ritz and Scott Weiland, *Not Dead and Not for Sale: A Memoir* (New York: Scribner, 2012).
2. Ritz and Weiland, *Not Dead and Not for Sale*.
3. Mary Forsberg, *Rolling Stone*, June 25, 2018, https://www.roll ingstone.com/music/music-news/scott-weilands-family-dont-glorify -this-tragedy-44427/.
4. Forsberg, *Rolling Stone*.

Chapter 11 - Sandy Helm

1. Steven Davis and Levon Helm, *This Wheel's on Fire: Levon Helm and the Story of The Band* (Chicago: Chicago Review Press, 2013).

Chapter 12 - Catherine Mayer

1. Catherine Mayer and Anne Mayer Bird, *Good Grief* (London: Harper Collins, 2020).
2. Mayer, *Good Grief*.

Chapter 13 - Ingrid Croce

1. Bart Mendoza, "A Conversation with Ingrid Croce and Jimmy Rock," *San Diego Troubadour | Alternative Country, Americana, Roots, Folk, Blues, Gospel, Jazz and Bluegrass Music News*, September 2012, https://sandiegotroubadour.com/a-conversation-with-ingrid-croce-and-jimmy-rock/.
2. Ingrid Croce, *I've Got a Name, the Jim Croce Story* (New York: Da Capo Press, 2012).

ACKNOWLEDGMENTS

First and foremost, this book would not have been possible without the support of so many widows of musicians and rock stars. Each woman featured in these pages was generous, welcoming, and forthright. I couldn't ask for better subjects. Several have become friends, and all have enriched my life. I thank the universe for bringing us together.

I must thank Scott Bomar, previously at BMG Books. Thank you for taking the initial chance on this project, for connecting me to so many potential subjects, and for caring enough about it to hand it off to the perfect someone else. Thanks also to Ian Ramage and the UK team for welcoming me to London and assisting with interviews there.

To John Cerullo, Barbara Claire, and the team at Backbeat Books, thank you for taking a chance on a nearly finished project at a time when I thought I might be back at square one. Your belief in seeing this book through and ushering it into the world makes me believe in the beauty of second chances.

There are so many people who have cheered me on from the sidelines as I continued to persevere over seven years to complete this book. My family of brothers and sisters: thank you Tom, Carol, Barb, Dennis, Sandy, and Dennis. And thanks to my Sullivan family: Chris, Kathy, Ron, Maureen, Chuck, Daniel, and Becky (and all of my nieces and nephews, too). To my parents, now gone several years, your early encouragement has never been forgotten.

I have so many friends who have believed in this project and rooted for it. To Jennifer, Mary, Kelly, Sharon, you've been cheering my writing since our high school days. I appreciate and love you. And to so many others that I can't possibly list. You know who you are. If you responded to a social media post, sent a message, told me to keep going, validated the premise of this book, let me leave the office early for an interview, or promised to find a copy in a bookstore, I thank you and offer so much gratitude. I truly would have given up if not for all of you. I am grateful every day for a tremendous circle of friends.

To my Detroit writing group (plus Laura in Canada), you kept me writing through it all. I appreciate the camaraderie and friendship we've built and the trust and feedback you so generously provide. Thank you all for reading chapters and challenging me to improve, I am forever grateful (and a better writer for it).

Continued support came from my Spalding University family, where the idea for this book was born in the Brown Hotel over a few bourbons. Thank you to leaders, mentors, and lifelong writer friends, especially Dania and Kelly. To be introduced in those sessions as a writer meant more to me than I ever realized.

Thanks to Jas Obrecht and my Ann Arbor writing group friends who read the very first chapters of this book and also offered valued feedback and direction. Though I've moved away, your belief at the start was vital, and I miss you.

To Kevin, you are with me all the time, rooting me on. I know it; I feel it. It is not lost on me that this book probably would never have entered my thoughts without having lost you fourteen years ago. So much of my life has changed as a result of our time together and my time alone. Like so many of the women I interviewed, I am grateful for the experience of our marriage, sad that it ended so soon, and fulfilled in the knowledge that I had twenty-six years with an exceptional partner. You were my rockstar. How could I ever ask for anything more?

And yet, there is more. There are two amazing, wonderful adult children that exemplify the very best of their father. I am so thankful for Austin and Shanna, and Madeleine. Thankful that you are happy, healthy adults who know right from wrong and who welcome me into your lives. I wouldn't be writing at all without your support and encouragement, without the knowledge that you appreciate your mom finding life and fun and adventure and coolness outside my role as wife and mother. I wish for you to also have a full, multifaceted life. I love you all, always.

INDEX

SUGGESTED FURTHER READING

This list includes books by or about the musicians included here, as well as other works about favorite musicians and performers who have died that I have found to be particularly insightful.

Galadrielle Allman, *Please Be with Me: A Song for My Father*, Duane Allman
Marley Brant, *Freebirds: The Lynyrd Skynyrd Story*
Sandy Chapin with Elspeth Hart, *Story of a Life, The Harry Chapin Family Album*
Ingrid Croce and Jim Rock, *I Got a Name, The Jim Croce Story*
Tony Fletcher, *Moon: The Life and Death of a Rock Legend*
Ben Fong Torres, *Hickory Wind, The Life and Times of Gram Parsons*
Jan Gaye, *After the Dance: My Life with Marvin Gaye*
Levon Helm with Stephen David, *This Wheel's on Fire: Levon Helm and the Story of The Band*
Janna Lapidus Leblanc, *Four Years in Pictures: Offstage with Stevie Ray Vaughan, 1986–1990*
Dave Marsh, *Before I Get Old: The Story of the Who*
Catherine Mayer and Anne Mayer Bird, *Good Grief, Embracing Life at a Time of Death*
David Meyer, *Twenty Thousand Roads: The Ballad of Gram Parsons and His Cosmic American Music*
Alan Paul and Andy Aledort, *Texas Flood: The Inside Story of Stevie Ray Vaughan*
Mark Paytress, *Bolan: The Rise and Fall of a Twentieth Century Superstar*

Vera Ramone King, *Poisoned Heart: I Married Dee Dee Ramone*

Annette Walter-Lax, *The Last Four Years, A Rock Noir Romance*

Pete Way, *A Fast Ride Out of Here, The Life and Times of Rock's Most Dangerous Man*

Scott Weiland, *Not Dead and Not for Sale: A Memoir*

Crystal Zevon, *I'll Sleep When I'm Dead: The Dirty Life and Times of Warren Zevon*